SHEELA-NA-G.

An air of mystery has surrounded the crude carvings of naked females, called Sheela-na-gigs, since their scholarly discovery some one hundred and sixty years ago. Especially puzzling is the fact that they occur predominantly in medieval religious buildings. High-minded clergymen have since defaced or destroyed many of these carvings, and for a long time archaeologists dismissed them as rude and repulsive.

Only in the less puritanical atmosphere of the past few decades have academics and artists turned their interest to Sheela-na-gigs. Divergent views emerged: some see them as ancient goddesses, some as vestiges of a pagan cult, others as protective talismans or Christian warnings against lust. Here **Barbara Freitag** examines all the literature on the subject, highlighting the inconsistencies of the various interpretations with regard to origin, function and name. By considering the Sheela-na-gigs in their medieval social context, she suggests that they were folk deities with particular responsibility for assistance in childbirth.

This fascinating survey sheds new light on this controversial phenomenon, and also contains a complete catalogue of all known carvings, including hitherto unrecorded or unpublished figures. It is the most comprehensive study of Sheela-na-gigs yet published.

Barbara Freitag is Lecturer in Intercultural Studies at Dublin City University, Ireland.

SHEELA-NA-GIGS

Unravelling an enigma

Barbara Freitag

Routledge
Taylor & Francis Group

LONDON AND NEW YORK

First published 2004
by Routledge
2 Park Square, Milton Park, Abingdon, Oxon, OX14 4RN

Simultaneously published in the USA and Canada
by Routledge
270 Madison Ave, New York, NY 10016

Routledge is an imprint of the Taylor & Francis Group

© 2004 Barbara Freitag

Typeset in 11/12pt Garamond 3 by
Graphicraft Limited, Hong Kong
Printed and bound in Great Britain by
TJ International Ltd, Padstow, Cornwall

British Library Cataloguing in Publication Data
A catalogue record for this book is available from the British Library

Library of Congress Cataloging in Publication Data
A catalog record for this book has been requested

ISBN 0–415–34552–9 (hbk)
0–415–34553–7 (pbk)

CONTENTS

CONTENTS

ACKNOWLEDGEMENTS

Many people have contributed to this book, and I am deeply indebted to them all, but particular recognition must go to Conleth Manning. I have greatly benefited from his professional generosity and his rigorous but always constructive criticism.

I should like to express my gratitude to Eddie Geraghty and Shae Clancy for taking me to unrecorded Sheela sites; to Christian Oeser for giving most generously of his time; to Mary Woodworth for allowing me to use her late husband's notebooks; to Richard Avent, John Billingsley, Anne Coogan, Chris Corlett, John Harding and Siobhan Kavanagh for bringing new discoveries to my attention; to Rachel Milotte for the drawings; and to Gay Cannon, Sandy Firth, Keith Jones and Heather King for supplying me with pictures. I wish to thank the church wardens who opened up churches and often helped me to locate Sheelas, and all the people who gave me permission to inspect carvings in their possession.

I am also grateful to my colleagues in the School of Applied Language and Intercultural Studies, Dublin City University, who provided information, help and support, and in particular I would like to thank Tony Coulson, Maggie Gibbon, Juliette Pechenart, Sylvia Schröder and Maurice Scully. The library staff of Dublin City University must also be thanked for their kind assistance throughout the writing process.

Thanks are due to the following friends and acquaintances who at various times and in various ways have given assistance: Werner Huber, Lilly McKeown, Danae Maguire, Mary Mulvihill, Enda O'Boyle, Helen O'Meara, Iris Taylor and Michael Townson. Finally, it is a pleasure to thank my husband, Rory Meehan, for his loving support and his constant encouragement of my quest for the Sheela-na-gig.

Sections of Chapters 2 and 3 have appeared in an earlier version in: *Éire-Ireland*, vols 33(3/4) and 34(1) (1998 and 1999), 50–69.

ABBREVIATIONS

JCHAS   *Journal of the Cork Historical and Archaeological Society*
JKAS   *Journal of the County Kildare Archaeological Society*
JRSAI   *Journal of the Royal Society of Antiquaries of Ireland*
NMAJ   *North Munster Antiquarian Journal* (Limerick)
PRIA   *Proceedings of the Royal Irish Academy*
RIA   Royal Irish Academy

INTRODUCTION

For centuries Sheela-na-gigs led a quiet existence on churches all over the British Isles. When they were brought to scientific attention in Ireland, some 160 years ago, their discovery, understandably, was not greeted with an unqualified welcome. After all, what were these carvings of naked females doing on medieval churches? And not only naked, but openly displaying their genitalia. Embarrassed clergymen and high-minded churchgoers physically removed and hid or destroyed the offensive figures. Archaeologists tended either to ignore them altogether or to label them as lewd, barbarous or repulsive. Museums kept them locked away safely from public scrutiny. Only in the less puritanical atmosphere of the past few decades did academics as well as artists turn their interest to these carvings. Divergent views emerged as regards the origin and function of the Sheela-na-gigs. Some see them as ancient goddesses, some as vestiges of a pagan cult, others as protective talismans or good luck charms, to name but a few interpretations.

The most favoured critical opinion, however, claims that they are copies of French sculptures put on Romanesque churches as warnings against lust, portraying evil in the battle against moral corruption. Although the reasons advanced for this view are rather unconvincing and, what is more, even contradicted by folk tradition, it has been widely accepted and found its way into dictionaries of art, museum guides and generally into all academic literature on the subject. The definition of the name, Sheela-na-gig, took an equally surprising course. None of the constituents of the name is an unambiguously identifiable word. Yet a Gaelic pedigree was fabricated which, ironically, strangely contradicts the characteristic features of the sculpture. The problem with both interpretations is twofold. First, their justification is primarily based on a fortuitous resemblance: of form, in the case of the carving, of sound, in the case of the name. Second, they are assumptions imposed from the present on to the past, and from a biased academic on to a rural peasant background.

Sheela-na-gigs are not an urban phenomenon. The vast majority of the figures are found in simple country churches, predominantly in remote agricultural areas where, apart from obvious Christian iconography, they often represent the only form of artistic imagery. Judging by their crude realism and poor workmanship they appear to be produced by local amateur carvers rather than by skilled stonemasons. This suggests that the sculptures belong to folk art and a tradition, too important and too intimately bound up with the welfare of the common people to be disregarded by the Christian Church. Incorporated in a Christian context, but divorced from her roots in pre-Christian tradition, the Sheela-na-gig needs to be seen as some powerful manifestation of continuity with the past. The key to an understanding of her real meaning can thus only be found in a sympathetic appreciation of her medieval social context.

More specifically, in the following chapters I shall argue that the Sheela-na-gig belongs to the realm of folk deities and as such is associated with life-giving powers, birth and death and the renewal of life. Folk deities are found in peasant societies where they preside over certain 'departments' of life. Knowledge of the special power they exercise is transmitted orally and forms part of the folk tradition. Central to the survival of any rural society is the biological reproduction of its members, a close relationship with nature and a reverence for traditional custom. Placed in a cyclical agricultural pattern, the Sheela generally, it seems, was regarded as the guarantor of crops, animals and humans. But in particular, she was the divine assistant at child-birth who, at the same time, formed a link with the realm of the dead.

It will emerge from my investigation that the Sheela-na-gig was in great demand in medieval times, and that she had many sisters in other countries, who, while operating under different names and manifesting themselves in numerous other ways, fulfilled the very same role.

1

THE SHEELA-NA-GIG
PHENOMENON

Sheela-na-gigs are stone carvings of naked women exposing their genitals. Although basically representational in character, these carvings have at the same time other-worldly overtones suggestive of a hidden symbolical meaning. This is partly conveyed through the disproportionate portrayal of the body and body postures which are impossible in naturalistic terms, and partly also through certain prevailing gestures and features whose significance to a large extent eludes us today.

Sheelas come in different shapes and sizes, with heights ranging from approximately 9 to 90 cm. The majority of the figures are quite clumsily made, suggesting the efforts of amateur carvers, but there are also some well executed examples whose assured mastery points to the hands of skilled craftsmen. Sheelas may be sculpted in the round or they may be modelled on blocks, slabs, pillars or other artefacts, cut in high, low or false relief. The most basic examples are those carved from natural rounded stones or boulders, and in these cases usually only one side is dressed, leaving the remainder of the stone untouched. What makes these sculptures so puzzling is the fact that they occur predominantly in medieval religious buildings – mainly on parish churches, but also on monastic sites. Furthermore, a sizeable number have been found on castles, and to a lesser extent were discovered overlooking holy wells, inset on bridges or built into town walls, gate pillars or the walls of dwelling places. The provenance of numerous other Sheelas, unattached and absolutely freed from any background, most of which accidentally came to light during grave-digging or clear-up operations, will presumably remain a secret forever.

When placed inside the church, the Sheela is generally set in isolation. However, several of these carvings also form part of a decorative scheme, on arches, capitals etc. In three English churches Sheelas appear among the roof bosses, and what makes one of these specimens, the South Tawton Sheela (146), even more special is the fact that it is made of wood.[1] When placed into the outer walls, irrespective of whether the surrounding is ecclesiastical or secular, Sheelas are usually located in liminal or border-line positions, above doorways, by windows, at the springing of the gables, on corbels or quoins. According to some curious convention, several carvings are employed horizontally, so that the figure despite having been carved as standing is inserted sideways, with the effect that it appears to be lying on its side. Six of these reclining Sheelas are on church buildings – Cashel (22), Kiltinane Church (59), Liathmore (62), Abson (111), Buncton (122) and Etton (131) – and a further four are on the castles of Cloghan (29), Clomantagh (30), Doon (39) and Tullavin (90). And there is one case, in Merlin Park (66), where the Sheela is inserted upside down.

Although existing elsewhere, the majority of Sheelas have been found in the British Isles, with Ireland, where at least 110 figures were found scattered all over the country, boasting the largest concentration. Sixty of these Irish examples are still *in situ*, but not necessarily in their primary settings. A further 25 are in museums, five are in private possession and of the remaining 20 only records (occasionally together with photographs or drawings) survive. A breakdown of their location shows that out of the total number of known sculptures, 39 are associated with castles. Twenty-eight of these castle Sheelas have either survived in their recorded place or are kept safe in museums, while the remaining 11 appear to have been removed and hidden or destroyed. Castle Sheelas seem to be a peculiarly Irish phenomenon because to date only one Sheela has been found in a castle outside Ireland, and this is the Welsh figure from Raglan Castle. If confirmed, a recently discovered specimen will add one English example to the list.[2]

Most of the over 40 known English figures are located in ecclesiastical surroundings. Otherwise the distribution is similar to Ireland where, although there are areas of greater concentration than others, Sheelas are sited all over the country. Only a handful have been discovered in Scotland and Wales, and a similarly small number have been reported from Denmark, Germany and France. Because of evidence that Sheelas were hacked away from church buildings and destroyed, buried or thrown into rivers in post-medieval times, we know that many more once existed.

Special identifying features, distinctive gestures, objects and classification

The common denominator of the Sheela-na-gigs is the frontal representation of a standing, squatting or seated nude female displaying her pudenda. The greatest value was obviously attached to the head and the genital area because these two parts are strongly modelled and represented disproportionally large compared to the rest of the figure. But whereas the vulva looks big and plump, giving the impression of fertility, the head and chest look bony and emaciated, suggesting old age. Many of the figures are quite badly weathered or deliberately defaced to an extent that they can no longer be discerned easily. In other cases positive identification of certain features is onerous because the figures are placed beyond the normal range of vision from the ground or they are obscured by ivy. However, no two Sheelas are exactly alike and variations exist with regard to all the features.

From top to bottom, a Sheela typically consists of a combination of the following characteristics. The head is disproportionately large in relation to the torso. It is bald, triangular in shape, with prominent ears. The most compelling features of the face are the large eyes, a wedge nose – quite often with clearly marked nostrils – and a grimacing mouth. Overall the impression conveyed is that of a skull.

While this description fits many heads, there are variations. The head also comes in round or oblong shapes, sometimes without ears, and in two cases, i.e. Caherelly (20) and Killaloe (53), it was cut off and is missing altogether. And not all Sheelas are bald. Some have hair or a kind of headdress. This is represented as what looks like a tight-fitting cap in the case of five English Sheelas, namely Ampney St Peter (113), Darley Dale (127), Easthorpe (130) and the two Tugford figures (151 and 152), and there are also the two Irish examples from Cloghan (29) and Rahan (69). Short-cropped hair appears to be indicated in Cavan (26) and Rathcline (71). The few strands of hair clearly incised on the forehead of Llandrindod Wells (165) are an unusual example, and hair may possibly also be indicated in Clonbulloge (31). More distinct are the hairdos of Kildare (52), Tullavin (90), Diddlebury 1 (128) and figure 155, and in the case of Kilsarkan (56) a rope-like feature crowns the head of the figure.

Long hair appears to be depicted in Ballinderry (8), Emlaghmore (43) and Rahara (70). Of these, Ballinderry, however, is a little doubtful because the Sheela looks decidedly bald. A plait-like ornament protrudes from behind both sides of the head at a right angle, showing a different pattern on each side. While the one on the right resembles plaited hair, the one on the left forms a guilloche, imitating a looplike ribbon. In Rahara, on the other hand, the depiction is quite definite. Not only are the two plaits braided in the same three-strand interlaced pattern hanging down either side of the head and reaching as far as the elbow, but the same pattern runs across the flat top of her head. Emlaghmore (43) also seems to have two exceedingly long tresses of hair hanging down both sides of the body. The figure is sitting on her rump with the feet folded back underneath, where they seem to be joined to the tresses of hair.

It has also been suggested that the Castle Widenham figure (25) is depicted with some kind of wild hairstyle. Not having seen it and limited to judging from photographs only, I think that both the rectangular shape and the huge size militate against such an interpretation. Further, as in Ballinderry, the head is egg-shaped giving it a bald appearance, and what some interpret as hair is clearly delineated behind the head.

A small number of Sheelas have no ears at all, but generally the ears are conspicuously large and splayed. In Ballynacarriga (11) they are so big as to have tricked Andersen into thinking that they were plaits.[3] Rarely do the two ears of the figure exactly correspond in shape, size and angle. In many cases the difference is so obvious that it looks like an intentional attempt at asymmetry, but sometimes one suspects that it might instead be due to the poor craftsmanship of the carver. Most Sheelas have jug ears. Exceptions to the rule are Kilsarkan (56) and the larger of the two Scregg figures (77), showing elongated, almost cow-like ears. Pennington (141) is also different in that the ears are triangular and pointy, but as the rest of the body is also quite angular the explanation again may very well be that the peculiar form is more attributable to the sculptor's inability to carve curvilinear shapes.

Quite a number of faces show deep, wavy lines – mostly two or three – running across the forehead. They are most pre-eminent in Ballinderry (8), Ballynahinch (12), Cavan (26), Clonbulloge (31), Fethard Abbey (46), Kiltinane Castle (58), Moate (67), Rahan (69), Fiddington (132), Romsey 1 (142) and Llandrindod Wells (165).

Eyebrows are delineated in Ballylarkin (10), Clonbulloge (31), Rosnaree (76), Easthorpe (130) and Kilpeck (136). The eyes are invariably large and clearly demarcated. Occasionally they simply consist of two cavities. In the majority of cases the upper and lower eyelids are joined to form an oval. Many eyes have an owl-like quality, seemingly glaring or staring, and thus creating a strong visual impact which is frequently further enhanced by asymmetry. The carver of Shanrahan (80) highlighted the eyes by giving them a greyish-white colour in contrast to the red sandstone out of which the rest of the figure is made. Two quite dissimilar eyes can be seen in Ballynacarriga (11), where the right eye is circular and much larger than the left, which is oval. The Tullaroan Sheela (89) also has a much larger right eye and the difference between the two eyes is further accentuated in that the left eye is surrounded

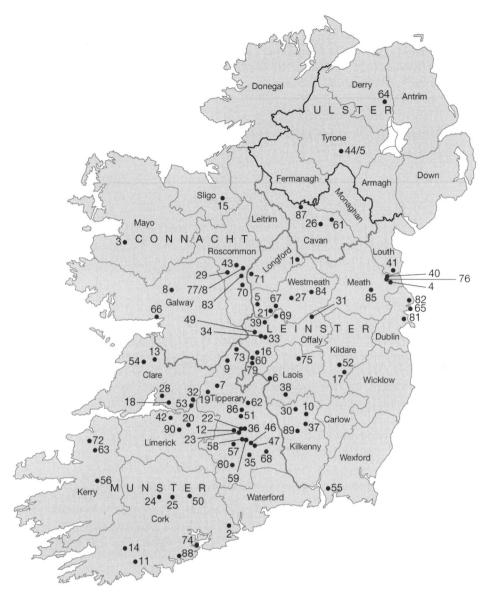

Map 1 Map of Ireland showing distribution of Sheela-na-gigs.

by a circle of tiny incisions, almost looking like a monocle, and by the fact that it has a small punctured hole in the middle. In the case of Newtown Lennan (68) the only difference between the two eyes is size, the right one again being considerably bigger. In Moate (67) the right eye appears to have an eyeball, whereas the left one looks empty.

Mouths are predominantly depicted as grim or ghastly. Sometimes they are a mere slit without lips, sometimes they form round or oval holes, and there are also cases where thin, thick or exaggerated lips are indicated. Generally the mouth is shown

6

Map 2 Map of England, Scotland and Wales showing location of Sheela-na-gigs.

as gaping with the two corners pointing downwards, but the two Sheelas from Clonmacnoise (33) and Kilpeck (136) wear a smirk. A tongue is seen to protrude between the lips of Cavan (26), Cloghan (29), Clonbulloge (31), Rahara (70), Scregg 1 (77), and Tugford 1 (151). Fourteen Sheelas bare their teeth and most of these are gritted. In some cases teeth are indicated as beading or as short vertical lines crossing the lips. The Sheelas with dental display are Ballyportry (13), Bunratty (18), Cavan (26), Chloran (27), Clonmel (35), Fethard Wall (47), Freshford (48), Glanworth (50), Lavey (61), Moate (67), Rahan (69), Taghmon (84), Pennington (141) and Tugford 1 (151).

A very intriguing feature is the striations or tattoo marks found on the faces of several figures. Three, sometimes four or five streaks slanting downwards across both cheeks are marked on the Sheelas in Fethard Abbey (46), Freshford (48), Redwood (73), Seir Kieran (79) and Romsey 1 (142). In Athlone (5) and Clonbulloge (31) they run down the left cheek only. Fethard Wall (47) has a whole pattern of striated triangles on the left cheek. In Rosnaree (76) the striations appear only on the right cheek, but they go beyond the head down the side of the slab.

The neck of the Sheela shows no particular or consistent features: it can be thick or thin, long or short or non-existent. A few necks do, however, show deeply incised vertical grooves looking like folds of skin. Some scholars are inclined to interpret these, along with the wavy lines across the forehead, as striations. They stand out very clearly in Clonulty (36), Fethard Wall (47) and Killinaboy (54) where they further intensify the overall impression of old age and scrawniness. A big hole was cut into the throat of Kilmokea (55) and Seir Kieran (79).

Continuing with the torso, its most striking feature has already been alluded to, namely the curious contrast between barrenness and fertility. The upper part with its signs of emaciation and sterility seems to belong to an old woman, an impression that is further emphasized by the appearance of the head, while the lower part with its emphatic focus on the fertile pudenda seems to be that of a young woman.

The notion of barrenness is first of all suggested by the breasts. These may be disproportionally small, shrunken looking or missing altogether, but generally they are on the slighter, never on the exaggerated, side. In those cases where they are in due proportion their shape is flat and droopy, giving them a post-menopausal look, which in the case of Clonmel (35) and possibly also Glanworth (50) is further accentuated by striations. As with the eyes and ears, the two breasts tend to be unequal with regard to size and shape, and stressing their difference even further the carver of the Kiltinane Church Sheela (59) put two nipples at the end of her left and one on her right breast. Quite often the breasts are located in an unnatural position. They are protruding from under the armpits in Ballinderry (8), Birr (16), Rahara (70), Oaksey (139), Egremont (157) and Llandrindod Wells (165). Others start too high up at the base of the neck and are placed close together along the breastbone in, for instance, Aghadoe (2), Ballylarkin (10), Seir Kieran (79), Taghboy (83) and Tullaroan (89), while at Freshford (48) and Stanton St Quintin (147) they are indicated at shoulder level.

Another sign of sterility is the ribbing, a feature favoured it seems in particular by Irish carvers, because of the 31 figures clearly indicating ribs, only three belong to England, i.e. Ampney St Peter (113), Easthorpe (130) and Oaksey (139), and one to Wales, i.e. Llandrindod Wells (165), while the rest are located in Ireland.[4] Here ribs not only occur far more frequently but are also carved with greater determination. The incisions are more resolute and regular, quite often forming patterns of straight but sloping lines across the whole upper part of the body. In Dunnaman (42), Kiltinane Castle (58) and Tullaroan (89) the ribcage even extends over the abdomen. On the other hand, English Sheelas, broadly speaking, tend to have a longer, slimmer, often rod-like torso contrasting with the squatter body of their Irish counterparts. The actual number of figures with ribbing may of course be higher, what with many Sheelas being weather-worn or not clearly discernible. And there may have been further examples among those figures now lost for which only a record remains with no detailed description.

A surprising detail found on numerous Sheelas is the belly button. Sometimes it is sitting in its proper position and looks about the right size, but there are also some Sheelas with a very pronounced, unusually deep or large navel, such as Ballinderry (8), Ballyportry (13), Caherelly (20), Freshford (48), Kildare (52), Rahara (70), Croft-on-Tees (126) and Fiddington (132).

The vulva is the most emphasized feature of the sculpture. In most cases it is highlighted in three ways, through its magnified size, through its anatomically incorrect location and by gestures of the hands and legs which draw attention to it. Its shape is predominantly oval, and in England where the largest genitals occur, some are so big as to actually touch the ground. A hugely exaggerated oval vulva hanging down between the two open legs can be seen in Buncton (122), Copgrove (125), Easthorpe (130), Kilpeck (136), Oaksey (139) and Studland (149). Similarly shaped, positioned and enlarged, albeit on a somewhat smaller scale, are the Irish specimens from Aghadoe (2), Ballyfinboy (9), Ballinacarriga (11), Blackhall (17), Cashel Palace Hotel (23), Cavan (26), Chloran (27), Clenagh (28), Liathmore (62) and Redwood (73). Tullaroan (89) also belongs in this group, but instead of the oval shape the vulva is depicted as a long straight narrow slit. Genitals of enormous size can also be seen in Buckland (120), where the Sheela has both legs up in the air to expose huge cavernous pudenda.

The most regular pudenda are sagging, but some figures have shapeless genitals which look as if they have been injured, almost torn apart, like Ballyportry (13), Carne (21), Clonmacnoise 2 (34) and Llandrindod Wells (165). Others look swollen, like Rathcline (71) and Scregg 2 (78), and others again just consist of a remarkably deep hole, like Burgesbeg (19) and Tracton (88). In Clomantagh (30) the vulva has the shape of a square cut out of the abdomen. Yet another type is portrayed in Penmon (166), where a balloon-like feature with an oval slit fills the space between the open thighs. In two other cases, Newtown-Lennan (68) and Rosnaree (76), the genitals are portrayed in a more stylized fashion, just appearing as concave indentations. And lastly, there are also some 'decorated' vulvas, including Rahan (69) with its indented lip, Llandrindod Wells (165), which looks as if it is surrounded by a rim of hair, and Glanworth (50), which has a thick rim of flesh around it.

Judging by the various signs of attacks on the figure clearly aimed at defacing or completely destroying it after it had been put in place, it is quite obvious that the conspicuously highlighted genitals caused the most offence. While it is true that weathering may also have had a hand in the disfigurement, overall there is enough evidence left behind by tools to indicate that hacking away the offensive abdomen was foremost in the minds of the attackers. Examples of this mentality are Ballinaclough (7), Birr (16), Clonlara (32), Dowth (40), Fethard Abbey (46), Holycross (51), Maghera (64), Thurles (86), Ampney St Peter (113), Bilton 2 (116) and Fiddington (132).

Quite surprisingly, in the vast majority of figures embedded *in situ* low enough to touch or on display in museums one can discover yet another hole placed underneath the vulva. Judging by photographs only the hole often remains unnoticed, and it is only by running a finger along that area that one becomes aware of it. Thus generally it is not commented on, but some archaeologists who did notice a conspicuous cavity in this position believe that it represents the anus. If their assumption is correct, its location below the vulva, given that it is the frontal representation of a woman, would represent yet another anatomical anomaly.

The limbs are generally under-sized in comparison with the torso, the legs even more so than the arms, and rarely do the two arms or legs correspond in width, length or pose. Their purpose first and foremost is to draw attention to the genital area. To this end the legs are splayed out and the hands are pointing or pulling at the vulva. The figure is shown in a standing, squatting or sitting posture. When standing the legs are widely splayed, slightly apart or straight and parallel, and of these the first mentioned position occurs most frequently, often with one or both legs bent at the knee, and with both feet outward-turned. In the squatting posture the knees are generally spread wide open. This is also the case when the figure is seated, but occasionally thighs and knees are tightly flexed over the abdomen or the legs are raised above the head. No matter which leg position is adopted, the vulva is always exposed.

A common position of the arms is with the hands placed in front, gesturing towards the vulva, touching it or literally tearing it open. However, quite a number of Sheelas are depicted in the most awkward stance to draw attention to the genitals, and sometimes this pose, in naturalistic terms, would be impossible to adopt because either anatomically speaking the arms would not be long enough or the body could not be forced into certain positions without causing it physical damage. Typical examples of this are the Sheelas who reach out from behind the widely splayed legs to clutch the vulva.

But the limbs are also employed to give expression to something more mysterious, some magical significance whose meaning escapes us today. Examining the legs, we find that whereas both feet typically turn outwards, and often very noticeably so, in Ringaskiddy (74) the two legs of the Sheela are turned inwards. In Ardcath (4), Clonmacnoise 2 (34), Doon (39) and possibly also Shanrahan (80), both feet face in the same direction, which happens to be to the right in all cases. A substantial number of figures cock just one leg, and among this group Cooliaghmore (28) and Egremont (157) display the most peculiar stance. In both these cases the foot on the ground, on which the whole figure stands, is inclined inwards, while the other leg bent at the knee seems to be using the heel to indicate the pudenda.

Even more conspicuous may be the gesture of the arms. Two Sheelas have both arms raised. The Castlemagner figure (24) simply extends both hands skywards, while the Kiltinane Castle Sheela (58) is depicted with a slender object in her right and a round object in her left hand. Far more frequently, Sheelas raise just one hand, while the other pulls at the vulva. The elevated hand may touch part of the head, or it may grasp an unidentified object. As it may prove significant whether the gesture involves the left or the right hand, the two sides will be listed separately.

Raising the left arm to touch some part on the left side of their head are Ballynaclogh (7), Kiltinane Church (59), Tullavin (90) and Kirkwall (161). Aghadoe (2) and

Fiddington (132) also lift the left arm, but they grip a slim object in their hand. At least five more figures hold on to an object with their left arm or hand without raising it; of these Lixnaw (63) and Tugford 1 (151) clutch an object under their arm, while Lavey (61) has a circular object depicted on top of it, and Seir Kieran (79) grasps a round object with the hand close to the body in the abdominal area. Romsey 1 (142) uses both hands: while the left holds an object pointing in the direction of the abdomen, the right is grasping a band-like feature which is loosely draped around the whole height of the figure.

The right arm is involved in a similar number of Sheelas. Clomantagh (30) simply raises it, whereas Behy (15), Clonmacnoise 2 (34), Portnahinch (103) and figure 156 use the hand to touch the right hand side of the head, most probably indicating the ear. Croft-on-Tees (126) places the hand on top of her head, and Tugford 2 (152) covers her mouth with it. Copgrove (125) and Egremont (157) hold on to some item with their right hand. In Copgrove it is a circular object held away from the body at the height of the abdominal area. This is also the area where the Egremont figure holds a slender object which is pointing to the vulva.

In an effort to create criteria that would allow researchers to compare these figures on common ground and to establish categories that would determine regional peculiarities or deviations, Edith Guest in the 1930s devised a taxonomy that was based on the different postures. Guest adopted the following division into basically three types:

Type I   Arms (which are usually in front of the thighs but may pass behind them)
           flexed, and hands directed to lower abdomen:
           (a)   Thighs splayed (20)
           (b)   Thighs absent or slightly indicated (7)
           (c)   Legs straight down (3)
Type II   One arm and hand raised to the head: legs as in type I (a) (3)
Type III   Thighs and knees tightly flexed over the abdomen (2)[5]

Applying her taxonomy to Irish carvings only the figures in parentheses represent the actual number of Sheelas she found in each of these categories. The total number of Irish carvings known to her was slightly higher but she desisted from including specimens where she could not be definite about their classification.

Type I obviously takes the lion's share. However, if we make a distributive chart, we somewhat surprisingly find an even spread of Guest's various categories across the whole country, with no pockets or clusters of favourite types emerging anywhere. And when A. L. Hutchinson employed her division on British Sheelas in the late 1960s, he found a very similar distribution. He classified 17 figures out of a total number of 21, and of these he judged 15 to be type I, whereas for type II and III he only found one example each.[6]

James Jerman regarded Guest's typology as 'not a very productive one', criticizing in particular the strong emphasis on the position of thighs and legs. He suggested a reclassification of the Sheelas focusing on the part played by the hands because, he argues that if 'the aim of a sheela is to draw attention to her sexual display then the role of the hands is far more arresting than the position of the legs and thighs'.[7] But before we examine Jerman's suggested taxonomy, his criticism of Guest's typology ought to be qualified because two out of Guest's three main categories are indeed based on the position of the arms, and the different leg positions are only taken into account as subdivisions within the first category.

Not unlike Guest, Jerman bases his type-divisions entirely on the posture of the figure, ignoring all other features. He differentiates between five types depending on the position of arms and hands:

Type I   Sheelas who pass both hands under the thighs in such a way as to draw attention to the pudenda, either by touching or indicating, or by spreading the legs to ensure display. (10) (3)

Type II   Sheelas who pass one hand only under the thighs, while the other hand rests elsewhere. (4) (2)

Type III Sheelas who pass both hands in front of the body to touch or indicate the pudenda. (19) (9)

Type IV   Sheelas who pass one arm only in front of the body to touch or indicate the pudenda, while the other hand rests elsewhere. (12) (6)

Type V   Anomalous sheelas, whose display does not involve the hands. (10) (4)

Again the figures in parentheses indicate the actual number of Sheelas which he thought answered to his description, with the first set referring to Ireland and the second to Britain. Jerman had hoped that by plotting what he saw as these stylistically linked groupings on the map, distinct regional patterns would emerge. Alas, this was not to be.

In England he found that there were too few attested Sheelas 'to permit meaningful analysis of their distribution', and in Ireland where he thought he could trace the outlines of various rough distribution curves, his patterns can no longer stand up to close scrutiny. This is not necessarily his fault, but a combination of factors which will become clear when analysing one or two of his groupings. Taking his first category, for example, Jerman comments that 'Type I sheelas form a rough curve from Cork to Kildare passing through Tipperary, Clare and Offaly.' The subsequent discovery of just two Sheelas falling into this category at Rahara (70) and Tullaroan (89) already stretches his curve in two further directions, north and east, besides adding two other counties to the list, namely Roscommon and Kilkenny. The distributional pattern of his second category is completely invalidated due to a mixture of incorrect classification (according to his own criteria) and the discovery of new Sheelas. Jerman erroneously puts Clomantagh (30) in the second group although this Sheela, holding arm and hand in front of her body, quite clearly belongs in his Type IV group. Errigal Keeroge 1 (44), on the other hand, who by definition belongs to group II,[8] is listed under Type III. Aghadoe (2), Behy (15), Clonoulty (36), Glanworth (50) and Thurles (86) – Sheelas Jerman was not aware of at the time – also fall into this category. Therefore his Type II is scattered all over Ireland, occurring in the north, south, east and west, obviously negating his assumption that this group can only be found in a narrowly defined area in the southern half of the country which he saw held within the two curves of Type I and IV.[9]

An extension of the investigation into Jerman's other group divisions reveals that additions and corrections within each of them render his distribution range untenable. Nobody else appears to have proffered any other classifying criteria since.

The problem of dating

The question of dating the Sheelas has proved to be just as frustrating and elusive as the search for distribution patterns. As stone artefacts cannot be dated by methods currently available to archaeologists, there are no certain clues that could determine the time and place of origin for the significant number of detached Sheelas. But a question mark even hangs over those figures which are placed on churches because their application in datable medieval buildings in itself provides no reliable evidence. Having been built on top of older ones, most churches are composite. Late medieval churches were usually imposed on earlier foundations, preserving wherever possible structural and decorative features of the pre-existing church within its walls. So while the extant building may often date back to ascertainable epochs, the actual history of the church invariably is much older. And going back further in time, it often transpires that the original church foundation was chosen to replace a pagan place of worship which was later converted to the worship of God.

Because they seemed to be so crude in conception and coarse in execution the understandable supposition was, when Sheelas were first discovered, that their origin must be ancient and that the carvings occurring in medieval church buildings were transfers from some earlier foundation or pagan sites. Guest also pioneered the investigation into the dating of the Sheela-na-gig, in that she endeavoured to overcome the inherent difficulties by associating those figures still *in situ* with the architectural setting and ornaments of the building. Again confining herself to Irish examples,[10] she discusses in detail churches and castles where decorative features, building material, architectural style and design appear to harmonize with the Sheela, thus suggesting contemporaneity. The period Guest establishes for these Sheelas spans from the eleventh to the seventeenth centuries, with those found on castles appearing to be generally later in date than the examples from ecclesiastical sites. While a significant number of the latter appear to have been transferred from earlier surroundings, from neighbouring churches according to information gathered from local informants, there are also castle figures which show all the signs of being original carvings in their primary settings.

In those cases where there are obvious indications that the sculpture has been re-set, re-worked or derived from an older building, Guest ruled out any attempts at dating them. However, one of her observations is potentially very telling. She notes that while some of the detached stones are cut in high relief, a feature not belonging to very early sculpture, there are others which have every appearance of antiquity. This suggests a continuum of tradition, and if verified would mean that Sheelas go back a long way. Thus Guest concludes with the observation that her argument for the late date of many church and castle Sheelas 'is not directed against the early origin and practice of the relative cult nor the probability of earlier symbols'.[11]

Jerman looked into the dating of British Sheelas by using a decorative feature, i.e. the beakhead ornament, as dating evidence. This is a Romanesque voussoir decoration which was in vogue in twelfth-century France, from where it was imported into the British Isles.[12] However, tracing the distribution of churches in which Sheelas and this Romanesque sculptural motif co-exist had disappointing results.[13] Out of a total number of 24 figures known to Jerman, he could only find five Sheelas in co-existence with beakhead. According to him four of these belong in a twelfth-century context

13

– Austerfield (114), Bilton (115), Holdgate (135) and Kilpeck (136) – while one, Croft-on-Tees (126), has a thirteenth-century background. With the help of different criteria he establishes a twelfth-century date for a further three Sheelas – Bridlington (118), Church Stretton (123) and Tugford (151/2) – while offering no supposition on the date of the remaining figures.

A close investigation of Jerman's dating reveals a serious problem. Only in Austerfield, Bilton, Bridlington and Kilpeck do the Sheelas form an integral part of the iconographical decoration; the other four examples do not. The latter are on separate slabs or carved in the round, and they are quite crude sculptures differing considerably from the rest of the church's ornamentation. Thus they do not appear to be in their original setting. As a corollary of this Sheelas and beakhead can definitely only be said to occur coevally in three churches, Austerfield, Bilton and Kilpeck, which is of course too slight a basis to propound any general dating theory of Sheelas on.

What Guest's and Jerman's proposals with regard to distribution range and the general dating of Sheela-na-gigs have demonstrated is that none of the criteria collated to date has yielded any definite or significant results. But amidst all the prevailing uncertainty one thing has become clear, namely that focusing on one single feature such as posture or co-existence with specific ornaments is at best insufficient and at worst misleading.

Built on Guest's foundation, I therefore suggest setting up a table that consists of four types of Sheelas:

1   Figures which form part of a larger decorative pattern on corbels, arches, or capitals.
2   Single figures carved on material forming structural parts of the buildings' fabric such as quoins, keystones, lintels, apex stones or roof bosses.
3   Single figures set in isolation.
4   Unattached free-standing and re-used figures.

In the first category it should prove relatively easy to establish the contemporaneous nature with the rest of the decorative scheme. These Sheelas are only found in ecclesiastical buildings, and generally speaking, because no specimens from the early or middle period survive, the main question to be answered would be whether a late medieval or early modern period applies.

Figures of the second category appear on both churches and castles. In order to determine whether they are in their primary location the main thrust of the investigation here would concern the building material, in particular the use of other similar stones, the type of dressing of stone and a close examination of the architectural setting.

The third type embraces all those Sheelas which are separately placed pieces of artistic imagery found in any setting, ecclesiastical or secular, where concomitant carvings, decorative details and style provide some indication that the Sheela was part of the original construction.

Figures of the fourth type are either completely unattached and unconnected with any building, or are clearly transfers, showing signs of having been removed from older sites and re-used in the present context. These are obviously, if not impossible, the most difficult to date, but in these cases a microscopic analysis of the marks left by the carvers' tools may be of help for dating purposes.

Sheelas could then be put into these four categories according to iconographical features, of which the basic posture – standing, squatting or seated – could form a main group, with any of the other special identifying features constituting sub-divisions. Of the latter some appear to be more significant or frequent than others, and understandably opinions would differ as to which of these are more pertinent, or perhaps even important enough to form a sub-group. However, to my mind there is one aspect which must not be excluded under any circumstance and should thus form part of all enquiries, and that is the (raised) hands as well as the objects they hold, because these more than any other feature strongly indicate some form of hidden magic behind the employment of the Sheelas.

Such a table would show the correlation between the total number of Sheelas and individual feature density, and it would allow the illustration of their distribution range. At the same time, while it would not resolve the thorny questions of origin and date, it would nevertheless be apparent from the table whether the features in question generally belong to older traditions or more recent developments.

2

SHEELAS AND ACADEMIC RESEARCH

When Sheela-na-gigs were first brought to scholarly attention, during the first half of the nineteenth century, antiquaries were baffled and embarrassed. No serious attempt was made to make sense of the sculptures, apart from interpretations that were little more than guesswork, until almost a century after their discovery. In order to trace this development here, nineteenth-century reactions to the sculptures are presented in roughly chronological sequence. This chronological sequence also applies to the twentieth century. In the case of the twentieth century, newly proposed theoretical approaches with regard to the origin and function of the sculptures will be discussed briefly in the light of further evidence, additions or corrections and later advancements.

Each interpreter's particular area of research is highlighted. Wherever it seems necessary, brief reference is made to the *zeitgeist*. The arguments explaining why these carvings turn up in Christian churches are also outlined.

Scholarly discovery and early speculations during the nineteenth century

Ireland

In 1791 the English Board of Ordnance established the Ordnance Survey, which was given the task of producing detailed maps of Britain in anticipation of a feared invasion from France. A corollary of this was an Irish commission, set up in the mid-1820s, to map Ireland to new levels of accuracy. This survey was carried out county by county, starting in Derry and completed with Kerry, some 20 years later. Besides cartographic details, it accumulated additional information on, among other things, history, place names, architectural remains and other cultural artefacts. When, in 1830, George Petrie was put in charge of a topographical section, he engaged a team of scholars, writers and painters to assist him, including men like John O'Donovan, Eugene O'Curry, George Du Noyer and, briefly, James Clarence Mangan. Those carrying out field work would supply descriptions of historical monuments, gather local information on these and send back reports and queries to Petrie's headquarters where other helpers, like Samuel Ferguson, would check out documentary evidence to substantiate and complete reported findings. In this way the research team amassed a tremendous amount of authentic information about the Irish physical and cultural landscape.

On 3 October 1840, Thomas O'Conor, involved in field work in Tipperary, recorded the first discovery of a Sheela-na-gig.[1] He had noticed the figure on the old church of

Kiltinane (59). The lengthy letter which he sent to Dublin is a charming testimony to his baffled confusion. O'Conor admits to being completely mystified as to why this 'ill excuted [*sic*] piece of sculpture', rudely done by an unskillful artist, should be placed at a house of public worship when it so blatantly impresses the 'grossest idea of immorality and licentiousness . . . being in its way in direct opposition to the sentiment of . . . people professing the Christian faith'. As it seemed incongruous that the figure had been set up in its present situation for producing any good effect on the minds of a Christian congregation, he could only assume that it was never intended to be placed in the church. He speculated that it must have belonged originally to another building, a castle perhaps, and that it was laid in its present situation 'by some one [*sic*] who delighted in inconsistencies' after the church had been abandoned as a place of worship. If that were not the case, the figure owed its origin 'to the wantonness of some loose mind'.

So there was a good deal of moral indignation, but O'Conor did not leave it at that. He genuinely strove for explanations, and in the end, on the grounds of analogy, he tentatively favoured the idea of a pagan origin. Perhaps pagans had been wronged by Christians, he tolerantly mused. He referred to John Milton's preliminary observations to *Samson Agonistes*, where he says that in physic[2] things of melancholic hue and quality are used against melancholy, sour against sour, salt to remove salt humours. Aristotle and Solon are also cited in support of the argument that the pagans may have put up the lewd Sheela to eradicate lewdness. 'The good effect was perhaps expected . . . by raising a disgust in the mind against all excesses in the indulgence of animal passion'. However, he himself remained sceptical until the end, which is reflected in his concluding remarks: 'But it is much to be feared no such thing is possible. And it is highly discreditable to a Christian congregation to have had before their eyes a representation of the kind'.

O'Donovan, equally perplexed, echoed O'Conor's disapproval when he wrote about the same Sheela two weeks later, agreeing it to be 'very bad taste to exhibit such a figure on a Christian chapel at so late a period'.[3] Despite their moral scruples, both men gathered information about local traditions surrounding the figure. O'Conor's enquiries revealed that the carving represents a woman who was known locally, 'by the name of *Síle Ni Ghig*, a person described as having plunged herself into all kinds of excesses, and having precipitated herself by her follies into the gulph [*sic*] of destruction'. In the language of his informants, this woman was not so much represented as a human being, but rather as 'in all respects a brute'.

O'Donovan reported that the sculpture was said by tradition 'to have been set up to annoy the descendants of *Sheela Ny Gigg*, who was such a character here as Grania Wael (O'Mailey) was in Connaught'.[4] In his view, the figure was no more than 300 years old, but in order to remove every doubt, he asked George Du Noyer to make careful drawings of this as well as of three other similar stone carvings. He would use these for discussions with his colleagues. The other similar figures in question were the Sheelas from Ballyfinboy, Co. Tipperary (9), and from Shane Castle, Co. Laois (106). The former he described as a rudely carved 'representation of a woman in naked majesty', the latter as a 'figure of similar hideous character'.[5]

This kind of Puritanism, which is usually attributed to the Victorian era, had, according to some sources, already been well established by the second half of the eighteenth century.[6] By the mid-nineteenth century several laws had been passed

17

which subjected printed material to censorship, focusing specifically on obscene contents.[7] So when John Prim, in his study of popular sports and amusements in Kilkenny, referred to wake orgies, he spared the feelings of the modest reader by passing over graphic details that were either too 'obscene' or 'strongly indicative of a pagan origin from circumstances too indelicate to be particularised'.[8] A similar coyness or fear of the censor prevented Macculloch in his *Highlands and Western Isles* from describing the Sheela-na-gig on the church of Rodil (162), which, as far as he was concerned, did not bear description.[9] Similarly in Lynch's learned article on the old monastic site at Liathmore a drawing of the Sheela shows the figure minus her prominent pudenda.[10]

Had O'Conor omitted mentioning the Kiltinane Sheela, it is highly unlikely that O'Donovan would have referred to these figures at all. As pointed out earlier, the Ordnance Survey started in the north, taking a southward course. O'Donovan had already seen these Sheelas, but he, like the other members of the Ordnance Survey team, had failed to report them. Some Sheelas might have escaped detection, but others were displayed in such a conspicuous way that it would have been downright impossible *not* to notice them. A good example is the Killinaboy Sheela (54). In 1839, O'Curry described the church and the ornaments therein in great detail. He produced exact measurements and some drawings but omitted any mention of the Sheela which is sitting right over the church entrance door. When O'Donovan referred to the Shane Castle Sheela in the above letter, he had known of its existence for the preceding two years.[11]

The third figure O'Donovan mentions he regarded as in a different league. He saw it in Cashel where it had been dug out of a churchyard. O'Donovan describes it as 'a stone idol of a truly Eastern character'. Uncertain as to whether he was dealing with a genuine ancient sculpture or a hoax, he sought the opinion of George Petrie. If it were genuine, O'Donovan wrote, it would be 'the only thing of the kind . . . ever discovered in Ireland'. Unfortunately there is no record of Petrie's verdict on this particular matter, but during a discussion about Sheela-na-gigs at the RIA, some four years later, it was noted that Petrie had expressed the desire to be given more information on these figures.[12] In the absence of any further minuted contributions on his part during the debate, one has to assume that he himself had no fixed opinions in this regard. He also remained silent on the Sheela-na-gig in his book on the ecclesiastical architecture of Ireland, which rather suggests that he, like O'Donovan, O'Curry and all the other eminent antiquaries of his time, preferred to leave the subject matter alone.[13] A further indication of this is the fact that the Shane Castle Sheela, which took O'Donovan so long to report in his letters, is mentioned in neither Clibborn's list of 'known' Sheelas four years later nor the official catalogue of antiquities published in 1863.[14]

O'Donovan was right of course in putting the Cashel figure into a completely different category: without arms, without genitals and with legs not widely splayed, but tightly entwined, it has none of the hallmarks of a Sheela.[15] Ironically, a 'true' Sheela (22), fulfilling all the requirements, but unnoticed by him, was sitting only a few yards away, on the Hall of Vicar's Choral. It was only discovered over a century later.

While O'Conor's and O'Donovan's letters, to our knowledge, represent the earliest written records applying the term *Síle Ni Ghig/Sheela ny Gigg* to this type of stone carving, the two men were neither the first to draw scholarly attention to Sheelas nor were they the first to use that name. In connection with the Kiltinane Sheela, O'Donovan himself pointed out that E. Clibborn and Sir Gay Ollgohagh were both talking 'so much' of the figure of *Sheela ny Gigg*. Unfortunately, only Clibborn appears to have left his trace in the RIA records. In 1844 he led the above-mentioned debate on Sheela-na-gigs, where he presented his own views on the subject. Before we take a closer look at this debate, Johann Georg Kohl must be mentioned, as his observations predate Clibborn's.

On 22 September 1842, Kohl, an eminent German geographer, historian and author of travel books, sailed from Anglesey to Kingstown for a two months' stay in Ireland.[16] Upon his arrival at Dowth (Co. Meath), he visited the ruins of an old church whose picturesque setting he greatly admired. Having waxed lyrical about tombs rank with ivy, he professed that these were not the actual reason for his visit. He had come for something else, he was in search of what he called a *Shila na Gigh*.[17]

Regrettably, Kohl does not divulge who had sent him there or where he had first read or heard about the figure. He mentions a local informant who knew of at least ten or eleven examples, and who had explained to him that such stone carvings were used as antidotes to the Evil Eye. In ancient times, men afflicted by bad luck would turn to certain women who counteracted evil influences by displaying their genitalia: 'Persuadent nempe mulierem, ut exhibeat iis quod mulieres secretissimum habent', Kohl writes, and it is quite amusing that in a book comprising 870 pages it is only in connection with the Sheela (40) that he has recourse to Latin.

His informant told him that these immodest women used to be and still were called *Shila na Gigh*, and that this name had been transferred to the sculptures. He surmised that the priests tolerated the stone effigies in their churches not only because they were a lesser evil than 'the real thing', but also because displayed as they were, they would presumably cause such superstitious practices to die out. Kohl was struck by the similarity between this Irish custom and ancient oriental practices. Having eventually found the sculpture, he again lapses into a mixture of Latin and English: 'nuda erat, nec non exhibuit, quod juvenes "for good luck's sake" spectare optarent'.[18] Before his mental eye he had visions of women offering themselves in the holy temples of ancient Babylon.

And now to Clibborn who, on 8 April 1844, gave a paper on Sheela-na-gigs after presenting one of these carvings to the RIA. He started off by reading the following abstracts from a letter written by a Dr Charles Halpin.

> About two years ago, as I drove past the old grave-yard of Lavey Church, I discovered this curious figure, laid loosely, in a half reclining position, on the top of a gate pier that had been built recently, to hang a gate upon, at the ancient entrance of the old church-yard. I believe the stones used in building those piers were taken from the ruins of the old church of Lavey (there is scarcely a trace of the old church on the site it occupied); and I think probable, that this figure was found amongst them, and laid in the position in which I found it, by the masons employed at the work. I was not aware of its real value, until apprised of it by my brother, the Rev. N. J. Halpin. He immediately recognized it as a 'Sheela-na-gig', and the most perfect of any he had seen.[19]

Clibborn then revealed his knowledge of ten other similar figures, found in old churches and castles. Beside three figures then in the museum,[20] he had been informed of the existence of many Sheelas in different parts of Ireland, but had received drawings and exact descriptions of five others only.[21] Lest his keen interest and lively correspondence should be misconstrued, Clibborn used the epithet 'hideous' to describe the sculptures.[22]

He declared himself unable to determine their actual antiquity because, as with the Lavey example, there were signs which indicated that they had been reused, originally belonging to older buildings. Judging by the form of the stones on which several of the Sheelas were carved, he surmised that some of them had been used as grave-stones.[23] All in all he detected a great similitude to figures which the natives of the east coast of Africa used as good luck charms or to ward off the Evil Eye. This, Clibborn felt inclined to believe, was also the intended function of the Sheela-na-gigs, namely to act as charms to avert the Evil Eye or its influence; consequently, they were placed over windows or doors of churches and castles. In graveyards they protected the sleep of the dead, making sure that they rested in peace, by neutralizing the disturb-ing influence of the Evil Eye principle.[24]

Clibborn went to great lengths to elucidate a possible early Christian origin of the Sheela-na-gigs by linking them to the round towers of Ireland. Such a connection had already been made by Ian Webber-Smith, in 1838, albeit not within a Christian context and without any reference to the name Sheela. Webber-Smith had claimed that the round towers in Ireland were emblematic of the same phallic power represented by the obelisks of Syria and Babylon, Egypt and India. Those who doubted or rejected his theory he advised, 'to examine the female figures carved on some of the old Irish churches, which . . . strengthen most remarkably my ideas relative to the round towers'.[25]

During the eighteenth and nineteenth centuries, the round towers had been the focus of much scholarly speculation, which may be divided, for the sake of the present argument, into two categories, the more sober, positivistic ones and the more eccen-tric, romantic ones. According to the former, to which Petrie subscribed, they were ecclesiastical buildings, in all probability bell towers associated with monasteries, and therefore necessarily posterior to the introduction of Christianity. According to the latter, to which Webber-Smith and Henry O'Brien subscribed, they had an exotic Eastern (Phoenician) origin, they were introduced by Buddhist émigrés from India and they were relics of a phallic religion, monuments to Priapus, temples designed for Sun worship or intended for celestial observations, but in any case dating back to pre-Christian times. O'Brien was awarded £20 for his contribution to the debate by the RIA, paid, one commentator suspects, as an attempt to keep him quiet.[26]

Drawing on O'Brien's eccentric Eastern model concerning the round towers,[27] but avoiding any overt reference to their alleged sexual symbolism, Clibborn bridged the gap between the two schools of thought. Like many scholars of his time, he deemed it likely that early Irish Christianity had its roots in Africa and the Near East. Coming from the north-eastern regions of Africa, the first Christians in Ireland might have brought with them more or less of Gnosticism, and with it syncretistic notions and practices observed by the ascetics of Egypt and the East. One of these would have been a belief in 'malevolent genii', said to possess the Evil Eye. Upon their arrival in Ireland, these rigorously abstinent Eastern ascetics may have constructed the round towers as their residence, regarding them as 'masculine', 'positive' and representing spirituality. The earth, grave, crypt or church near it, in which were deposited the bodies of the deceased, would have been considered to be the 'feminine', 'negative' material principle.[28] Clibborn connected the two principles and interpreted the Sheela-na-gigs as the female counterparts to the masculine towers, with their almost skeleton appearance possibly reflecting the Gnostics' insistence on fasting and the rule of abstinence. He was by no means dogmatic about this, readily admitting that it was premature to formulate definite opinions about this 'new' subject. But he was not alone in thinking along these lines. Apparently his colleague R. P. Colles drew the same connection.[29]

The archaeologist R. Hitchcock, in 1853, generally seems to have approved of Clibborn's ideas because he recommended his 'interesting communication' in the Academy's *Proceedings*. But Hitchcock was more inclined to see Sheelas as remnants of pagan times. Their placement in old churches did not invalidate this conjecture, he argued: 'on the contrary, it rather strengthens it: for we know that undoubted Pagan monuments have been found in close connexion with many of our ancient churches'.[30]

Roughly at the same time, the topographer John Windele noted the discovery of a stone female figure at Barnahealy, or Castle Warren, Co. Cork (92), described by him as one of these old fetishes often found in Ireland on the fronts of churches as well as castles. According to him the people who called them 'Hags of the Castle' were claiming that they possessed 'a tutelary or protective power, so that the enemy passing by would be disarmed of evil intent against the building on seeing it'.[31] This belief was actually widespread. What is more, it was thought that persons unknown to themselves might possess the Evil Eye, so that by simply admiring or looking at a beast, crop or building, they would unintentionally cause it to sicken or decay by its evil influence. To prevent this, it was thought that Sheelas and other grotesquely cut carvings were built into castles near the entrance in order to attract the Evil Eye, and so prevent its bad effects. Apparently it was the *first* glance that did the damage, and if that first glance could be arrested by any object, the building was safe. What better way of attracting people's attention than by using indecent objects?

There is an obvious qualitative difference between this more 'modern' guardian role attributed to the Sheela figure, centring on the protection of buildings from human harm, and the more archaic sexual character hinted at by Kohl, Clibborn and later Thomas Wright.[32]

Neither name nor function is suggested for the Dunnaman Sheela (42) in Caroline and Edwin Dunraven's report on the castle, dated 1865. They point to other similar 'strange' and 'extraordinary' sculptured stones representing the female figure 'in the most repulsive way', for which no plausible explanation has been given.[33]

George Du Noyer, on the other hand, like Clibborn, deemed an early Christian origin of the Sheelas possible, but having been part of Petrie's more factually oriented Ordnance Survey team, he refrained from coupling Sheelas with round towers. Although he had produced several drawings of Sheela-na-gigs, it was not before 1860 that he made his own views known. In his discussion of three stone effigies on the old church on White Island, he directed attention to their ancient costumes and tonsure which, according to him, portrayed the style of dress and shaven head worn by Irish ecclesiastics, male and female alike, until the close of the seventh century, when it was condemned.[34] To him these three sculptures represented early Irish ecclesiastics, but only one of these, i.e. the entirely nude figure, he classified as a Sheela. Out of disrespect for the early Irish fashion, he thought they were later mutilated and applied to the degraded but useful purpose of mere building materials when the church was rebuilt in the eighth or ninth century.

The official RIA catalogue of Irish antiquities, published in 1863, shied away from using the name Sheela-na-gigs, instead calling them 'grotesque female figures' or 'curious relics'.[35] No ideas were advanced with regard to their function or origin. It was only pointed out that they were deemed to be of great antiquity, frequently found in old churches, sometimes behind Ogham stones and, occasionally, in old castles. Readers are referred to Clibborn's account in the Academy's *Proceedings*.

However, Thomas Wright, in 1866, firmly adduced Sheelas as survivals of a pre-Christian fertility worship. He appears to be the first scholar who actually referred to the hitherto unmentionable 'female organ' and who provided several illustrations of Sheelas. According to him, the worship of both the male and female reproductive organs duly solemnized the fertilizing and saving powers of nature. Thus Phallus and Yoni conferred fertility and prosperity as well as protection. Wright saw in Sheelas sexual symbols placed upon churches as protectors against enchantments, and especially against that great object of popular terror, the Evil Eye.[36] Hence he judged the belief in the salutary power of this image to be of great antiquity, and certainly not confined to Ireland, but universal. Small figures of nude females exposing themselves in exactly the same manner 'are found not only among Roman, Greek, and Egyptian antiquities, but among every people who had any knowledge of art',[37] with statuettes from many parts of the world cited as proof. Some of the engraved examples indeed have an amazing similarity to Sheelas, so much so that one cannot but agree with him that these figurines represent an exact counterpart.[38]

However, Wright, along with O'Brien and Webber-Smith, found himself in a minority camp, with his books scoffed at and greeted with derision.[39] They remained silent in public, and exchanged their ideas privately. Copies of Wright's illustrations complete with comments on various fertility figures, including the seven Irish Sheelas[40] he portrayed, are found in two private manuscripts preserved in the British Museum in London.[41]

Richard Rolt Brash seems to be the last scholar of the century who professed himself a follower of the Eastern pagan-fertility-worship idea. Witness his careful wording when referring to those 'indecent' representations known as Sheela-na-gigs:

> The subject ... points unmistakably to a pagan cultus, a reverence of the powers of nature which at one period was prevalent over the eastern world, and still exists both in the Hindoo and Buddhist systems. That the worship of the reciprocal principles once prevailed in Ireland there can be no doubt. How its relics came to be identified with Christianity is one of those puzzling problems that seems peculiar to Ireland.[42]

In an article in the *JRSAI*, published in the early 1880s, W. F. Wakeman, while fully understanding the reasons for it, deplores the complete silence of all leading archaeologists concerning the *Sheelanagigg* [sic].

> The subject is ... not an agreeable topic to touch with pencil or with pen; yet, nevertheless, it is to be hoped that some antiquary, skilled in the idiosyncrasy of our mediaeval architects ... will present the archaeological world with a publication bearing at length upon the purport of these very often repulsive, and at present unintelligible, carvings.[43]

These comments were made in connection with the effigies occupying the walls of the old church of White Island, the very ones Du Noyer thought represented female ecclesiastics. Wakeman could not attach any value to that interpretation. In an attempt to 'explain the present mystery' of these figures, he presented archaeologists with a new idea.

He referred to suggestions concerning medieval symbolism and allegory advanced by a Mr Phillips, a leading architect of his time. This gentleman had interpreted the ubiquitous chimerical monsters crouching on every Gothic edifice, as personifications of human vices and evil passions. The more hideous ones which were placed outside the building were probably meant to be a caustic hint to churchgoers to leave their sinful thoughts outside the church. Might this not also have been the intended purpose of the Sheela-na-gig, Wakeman wondered.[44] Having turned from female ecclesiastic into reminder of immoral thoughts, this particular figure would, some 50 years later, 'unmistakably' personify *Luxuria*, what with its ugliness being such that it served as a compendium of all Seven Deadly Sins.[45]

Wakeman's suggestion that a moral purpose may have been intended with the insertion of Sheelas in church buildings echoes the very first scholarly speculation made by Thomas O'Conor: only that the latter had held the pagans responsible for this. While Wakeman does not seem to have made an immediate impact with his conjectures, the idea that Sheelas were images of Lust would overwhelmingly dominate the scholarly debate 100 years later. There are no further records of debates on the subject during the nineteenth century, but several scattered papers contained in archaeological journals reported new discoveries of Sheela-na-gigs throughout Ireland. Information culled from these, plus communication obtained from 'private sources', formed the basis of a first list aiming at completeness which appeared in 1894 under the title *Figures known as Hags of the Castle, Sheelas, or Sheela na gigs*.[46] The same list, with minor changes, was reprinted in 1905.[47] It comprised 36 figures in Ireland, three in England, two in Wales, five in Scotland and one each in France and Italy.[48] No views are advanced to explain these 'remarkable figures'; in fact the compiler deliberately eschewed entering into any discussion on matters of such a controversial nature.

Although claiming a neutral stance, the list rejects the idea that the figures may represent pagan deities, on the grounds of lack of evidence. Furthermore, it was observed that most figures originally seem to have been attached to ecclesiastical edifices, with a possible few exceptions, 'limited to districts held by Anglo-Norman invaders', or they were placed near the churches for some special decorative purpose. When the earlier stone churches had fallen into decay about the fourteenth or fifteenth centuries,

> the figures were appropriated by the builders of stone castles erected about that time, and transferred to their walls either for ornament, or under the idea of their possessing some occult and sacred influence, such as conferring good fortune or additional safety on the owner.[49]

By the close of the nineteenth century, then, 60 years after coming to scholarly attention, Sheela-na-gigs were still a mystery. Leading scholars preferred to leave the subject alone, partly or, more likely, mainly because of the delicate subject matter. The prevalent taboo against mentioning genitalia in public resulted in the description of Sheelas as hideous, ugly or repulsive without any reference to the offensive object.

There was a general consensus among those who did voice an opinion that the figures were undatable since they had been removed from their original context. Most antiquaries associated the Sheela with a belief in the Evil Eye, but some suggested a didactic purpose, claiming it portrayed immoral behaviour as repulsive. These two views were put forward within both a Christian and a pagan context. In the discussions on date and provenance the focus gradually shifted from an exotic oriental heritage to a more mundane factualism concentrating on comparisons with similar figures in other, mostly Southern European, countries. With that the idea of a connection with the round towers was dropped. But whereas over time the round towers, alongside the harp and the shamrock, became part of Irish iconography, the Sheela-na-gigs were secretly hacked away, mutilated, unceremoniously dumped into rivers or hidden away in the basements of museums.

England, Scotland and Wales

Scholars of the neighbouring island were hampered by similar puritanical reservations. When R. Payne Knight published *A Discourse on the Worship of Priapus*, in 1786, the sensibilities of the higher classes of English society were so completely shocked that the work had to be withdrawn.[50] And Boswell, encountering what appears to be a Sheela-na-gig in a Swiss chapel in 1764, would not even entrust a frank description to his own diary when he wrote,

> Above the door was a niche in which was formerly placed a statue of the Virgin, and under this niche, by way of ornament, was carved a woman's thighs wide open and all her nakedness fully displayed. It has appeared so indecent that they have effaced it a little, yet still the *ipsa res* appears.[51]

Unfortunately, the Ordnance Survey organization in Britain operated within its narrowly defined military remit producing detailed maps of the country and disregarding the kind of information that led to the antiquarian discovery of the Sheela-na-gigs in Ireland. As a rule nineteenth-century accounts of the architecture, churches or history of Christianity in Britain do not mention, and drawings of churches do not depict, Sheela-na-gigs. But there are a few exceptions.

First of all there is one example of a purged Sheela. Instead of holding open her huge vulva with both hands, the Kilpeck figure (136), in G. R. Lewis's illustration of 1842, turns her hands outwards, away from her body. With the legs omitted, the oval slit is explained as a cut in the chest, denoting an open heart.[52] Then there is mention of the Binstead carving (117) on the Isle of Wight, of which it was said that 'the inhabitants give it the name of the idol' and which was referred to in books about the island as early as 1781, and again in 1795.[53] Without specifically referring to any particular figure, the reviewer of a new publication on the Evil Eye, in 1895, was wondering whether the indecent female figures 'known in Ireland as Sheela-na-gigs' belonged in the same category as the gross subjects sculpted on Norman corbel tables and the later Gothic gargoyles whose purpose was, he assumed, to attract the Evil Eye and absorb its influence.[54]

Another example is the Sheela found in Egremont Church (157). This figure was publicly discussed in a paper on early sculptured stones in 1901. The speaker, C. Parker, did not mention a name for the figure, and did not know what to make of the find, but he provided a photograph, a good description and food for thought. The quality of the workmanship was judged to be so poor that Parker thought the figure must have been carved by an amateur, 'evidently never taught in any school of figure drawing'.[55] Yet it seemed vigorous for a first attempt, and there was also the question of what this nude female was holding in her right hand. It could be an infant, but it could also be a pair of shears. 'What was passing in the Egremont workman's mind', Parker pondered, 'is difficult to say. Something has evidently been intended, but what? A maniac? – a martyr? – a woman and new-born child? – a sort of crazy representation of a Madonna?'[56] Parker could not decide which, but if it had not been for his curiosity, we would probably not even know it existed because, like other Sheelas, it has disappeared since.

Twentieth-century theories

In the twentieth century, English women added a strong voice to the academic enquiry into the Sheela phenomenon, thus giving the research a new impetus. This resulted in many different theories being proposed before the end of the century. Before this revival of archaeological interest, which started in the 1930s, there were only scattered references to these sculptures, usually confined to reports of new discoveries with summary descriptions in local or regional papers.

A Norse fertility goddess

Contrary to their Irish counterparts who had mostly been searching for answers in Southern regions – the Near East, Africa or Southern Europe – antiquaries in England and Scotland thought that for explanations one needed to turn to Northern Europe. The general assumption was that Sheela-na-gigs were of a pre-Christian origin and related to pagan beliefs. Some archaeologists, like James Richardson, Inspector of Ancient Monuments for Scotland, suspected that there was some connection with Norse mythology.[57] While goddess Freya's (or Freyja's) name specifically appears in a number of articles, generally the view prevailed that Sheelas were most likely representations of some Northern European fertility cult.

Of course the idea of a northern connection has its roots in the history of the early colonization of the country. The ancient Britons, themselves thought to be descendants of peoples from north-west Europe, were later joined by groups of peoples who, crossing the North Sea as settlers or marauders, appear to have come from the very same areas: the Angles, Saxons and Jutes, Danes, Norwegians and Swedes, Celts and Normans.[58] For many generations these early settlers would have kept alive the memory and traditions of their ancestors. Proof of this can be seen in their earliest epics, in which they sing the praise of heroes like Beowulf, Hrothgar, Finn and others whose homes and exploits were on the continent.[59] Many places are named after pagan German and Scandinavian deities. So are feast days: the festival of Easter, for example, was named for Eostre, the Germanic goddess of spring and the dawn. And the days of the week: Wednesday takes its name from the god Woden, Thursday from Thunor, Friday from Frigg and so on.

Fortunately, we have two very revealing and interesting newspaper reports on the discovery of a Sheela (141) from north-west England, dating back to the 1920s.

During the reconstruction of the local church, a quoin was found to bear on its inner surface the carving of 'a nude manakin [*sic*] figure of extraordinary design', Canon Kenworthy reported in the *Pennington Parish Magazine* for December 1925. The canon was sufficiently intrigued by this find to submit a photograph of it to some of the chief archaeological experts in the British Isles, requesting their opinion. Among these were Professor Baldwin Brown, of Edinburgh University, Professor Macalister, of the National University, Dublin, Mr Louis Clark, Curator of the Museum of Archaeology and Ethnology, Cambridge University, and the Society of Antiquaries, London.

The following sums up the result of his inquiries:

> The carving is attributed to the Bronze Age, and the figure is connected with pagan worship. Similar stones are known to exist at about four other places in England (many more have doubtless been destroyed), and half a dozen in Scotland. In Ireland they are fairly numerous . . . Professor Baldwin Brown has supplied us with a picture of a bronze image of the Goddess of Fertility, of similar character to the Pennington stone, which was discovered in a field near Helsingberg, Finland, in 1920. The date of this bronze image, judging from its appearance and workmanship, is given as the last period of the Bronze Age, about the Eighth Century before Christ. . . . An interesting thing connected with the stone just discovered and the bronze image found in Finland is the fact that Pennington has a number of names associated with the old Norsemen.[60]

Four years later in 1929 *The Barrow News*[61] carried a full account of the discovery of the Pennington Sheela and of the discussions of the Cumberland and Westmorland Antiquarian and Archaeological Society, who visited Pennington during a field trip. According to this article, again supplied by Canon Kenworthy, the old church was pulled to the ground in 1826 and rebuilt. One of the many parts reused for the new church was the quoin with the Sheela-na-gig, but it was reversed, with the figure facing inwards. A century later when the corner needed repair the quoin was taken out and the Sheela came to light again. While the workmen were so shocked and embarrassed at the sight of it that they nearly destroyed it but for the intervention of a foreman, the canon refers to the carving as 'thrilling in its interest'.

At this stage, however, he had changed his mind regarding the dating of the stone. He no longer concurred with the idea that it belonged to the Bronze Age. He now believed that it was the work of the heathen Northmen, who after the Anglo-Saxons had become Christianized, settled in this part of the country, bringing with them their pagan creed.

In the meantime he had communicated at length with a number of scholars and he quotes from some of his correspondence. From Professor Macalister, 'the greatest living authority upon all Irish antiquities', he had learned that in Ireland two different views on the matter were being debated, neither of which Macalister subscribed to. The first of these saw the Sheela as an expression of a debased imagination on the part of the engraver. Macalister dismissed this because of the generally uniform character of the figure over the whole country. The second view, that they were intended to avert the Evil Eye, though not entirely without merit, was also rejected. Macalister himself was inclined to a third interpretation, which saw in the Sheelas relics of an otherwise forgotten phase of Celtic paganism after the introduction of Christianity. Lately some altars had come to light in which certain Gaulish deities, notably the god Cernunnos, were represented, whose cross-legged posture, he thought, was reminiscent of that of the Sheela-na-gigs.[62]

Professor G. Baldwin-Brown of Edinburgh University, an authority on Anglo-Saxon art and architecture, now also dismissed a Bronze Age origin. He supplied the canon with an article on the Sheela-na-gig from the church at Oaksey (139).[63] Writing about the same church elsewhere, Baldwin-Brown expressed the opinion that the Sheela might well be of Saxon origin.[64] However, upon reading Macalister's *Archaeology of Ireland*,[65] he not only agreed with the idea of a 'pagan recrudescence' in Christian times, but he gladly accepted that for the Sheelas the 'Romanesque period seems about the right one to take', asserting, somewhat relieved, that one would look for them 'rather in the Celtic than the Teutonic parts' of the British Isles.[66] After due consideration of all the different views, Canon Kenworthy concluded that Sheelas had been carved by marauding pagan Danes to desecrate churches and insult Christian beliefs.[67]

There are a number of interesting observations to be made in connection with this find. Apart from the Sheela, the church's original tympanum with a Runic inscription in Scandinavian characters was found in a farmhouse nearby. The inscription reads something like, 'Gamel built this church, Hubert the Mason carved . . .' According to local history, this records the foundation of the church, in all likelihood in place of an ancient church, by Gamel de Pennington in the mid-twelfth century.[68] As has been pointed out by others, it is quite intriguing to find that a century after the Norman conquest, the inhabitants of this part of north-west England still used Norse, and runes, even for ecclesiastical inscriptions. Anyway, the tympanum was restored to the church, but not the Sheela. She was bundled off to Kendal Museum, allegedly because the Pennington parson felt that, as a pagan image, she might put a curse on people.

The object file in the museum provides some information on the area by the curator, Lynn Fade. From this we learn that although eventually converting to Christianity, the Norse and Germanic settlers, it seems, clung to their old ways, and their pagan beliefs died hard. An indication of this was seen in the fact that they inserted the nude figure of the Norse goddess Freya into the wall beside the altar, thus propitiating both new and old gods. Another leaflet in the file contains a personal account of one Andy Roberts, who travelled in the area in the late 1920s and who was told by an old Pennington villager that the sculpture had always been called Freya by the local people. Over 50 years later, the academic Richard Bailey searched in vain for information on the figure in the official inventory of Westmorland antiquities. To his surprise he discovered that the Cumberland and Westmorland Antiquarian and Archaeological Society had failed to mention a single word about the Sheela in their account of the visit to Pennington printed in their journal. For the record, Bailey confirmed that one of the residents identified the figure to him as Freya.[69]

The British archaeologist Brian Branston was also of the opinion that Sheela-na-gigs were representations of the goddess Freya, whom he calls the Great Earth Mother, but he believed that her cult was brought to the British Isles by an earlier influx of Northmen. On the continent she was venerated as Nerthus. He felt that there was ample evidence to prove that the Old English knew of a cult of Mother Earth together with the god Frey and his sister Freya. 'There can be little doubt', he claimed, 'that we have in the sheela the actual representation of the Great Goddess Earth Mother on English soil'.[70] Sheelas represent the Earth Mother waiting to be fertilized by the Sky Father, and that is why, he thought, the vulva is so invitingly being held open.[71]

A divine patron of women

In an effort to overcome the haphazard approach and scant attention to the Sheela-na-gig in England and Scotland, Margaret Murray attempted to present a more systematic view of the figure. In the early 1930s, she confidently stated that the sculpture generally belonged in the category of mother-goddesses. Already in her report on the Oaksey Sheela, in 1923,[72] she had expressed the idea that Sheelas might be the remains of an old fertility cult, a view which was shared by Dina Dobson as far as the function was concerned, but with regard to origin Dobson tended to agree with Baldwin-Brown, who at that stage considered them to be Saxon.[73]

Margaret Murray was an Egyptologist, indeed the first woman to make a mark in this discipline. She published over 80 books and articles on the ancient Near East alone, but she also took a lively interest in medieval religious cults in Western Europe.[74] Having studied mother-goddess figures from various parts of the world, she identified three recurrent types, all of which she considered as divine, but having derived from different religio-psychological needs.

The first of these, *the Universal Mother*, the true 'mother'-goddess, or Isis type, constant throughout the world, and well known in ancient times, is represented with full breasts, pregnant or with a child in her arms. The child, actual or implied, is an essential part of this type. The earliest examples quoted are the Palaeolithic figures at Laussel and the polymastic Diana of Ephesus. 'At all times and in all religions the Mother-goddess was equally worshipped by men, women, and children, for the relation of mother and child is universal'.[75]

The second category, *the Divine Woman*, or Ishtar type, the virgin or young, attractive woman, sometimes nude and sometimes veiled, but in any case without any emphasis laid on the sexual parts of the body, appeals to the male imagination and is therefore a goddess worshipped only by men.

The figures of the third class, on the other hand, in which the Sheela-na-gig belongs, hold a special appeal for women, and thus are goddesses of women only. Murray calls them *the Personified Yoni*, or *Baubo* type, in which the genitalia form the essential part. These goddesses are connected with childbirth and the promotion of fertility. 'In this type beauty of form or features is disregarded, the secondary sexual characters, such as the breasts, are minimized; the whole emphasis is laid on the pudenda'.[76] One example mentioned is the Roman Bona Dea, goddess of fruitfulness, both in the earth and in women, whose temple was worshipped by women only. Another example is the Egyptian *Baubo*, of which a huge number of statuettes survive. Though these are of the Roman period, the figures represent an ancient goddess in a new form. Her precursors are those stiff nude female figures with expressionless faces and a strongly marked sexual triangle, which stretches across the body from one hip to the other. Whether this is marked with dots or lines, or painted in solid black, it is always so emphasized as to attract immediate attention. Later, with the advent of the naturalistic Greek and Roman art, the sexual nature of the figure was indicated in a more realistic attitude rather than with incised lines or colour. Because of the difficulty of representing the female genitalia, the front view would always be portrayed, with the legs spread out so as to display the vulva, whose size is exaggerated and position distorted.

Where the finding of such figurines was recorded, it invariably showed that the figures had been kept in the inner part of the houses, i.e. the women's quarters, or they had been buried in women's graves. This would indicate that they were for the use of women, employed in rites from which men were excluded.

But to what end, and for what reason, display the vulva in this way? There are two possible answers, in Murray's view. The first is concerned with religion. The *Baubo* legend[77] suggested to her that some form of homosexuality, connected with pleasure and laughter, might have been practised by women as a religious rite.[78]

An alternative explanation could be that the figures were used to rouse the desire of women to have sexual intercourse with men. Murray had read a local newspaper report on the removal of a Sheela from the tower of St Michael's Church at Oxford (140). According to this article, brides were made to look at the figure on their way to church for the wedding. Murray interprets this as an invitation to women to identify themselves with the figure because she holds that women's sexual desire is more easily stimulated by representations of their own genitalia than by those of the opposite sex. So the Sheela figure represents the woman ready to welcome her mate.

What her explanations have in common is the claim that these figures appeal to women's nature, and that this is the reason for their original use and long survival. Murray asserts that their 'importance in the life of women is seen in the fact that the Christian Church was forced to allow them to be placed in conspicuous positions in and on the sacred edifices'.[79]

However, it stretches credulity to accept that the male-dominated medieval church with its express antagonism to sex – its idealization of celibacy in men and virginity in women – would have given in to women's pressure to have Sheela-na-gigs put up to prepare brides for their marital bed by offering them sexual stimulation. And then the question would have to be asked why the women would want this figure publicly displayed when beforehand it appears to have been used secretly or at least privately, and moreover exclusively by women.

A pagan symbol of fertility

Edith Guest was another researcher unhappy with the unsystematic approach to the Sheela investigation, but, as outlined in the first chapter, her efforts to rectify the situation took a completely different course: she produced a proper archaeological survey. Because of the greater concentration of Sheelas in Ireland she focused on Irish examples using as the starting point the list which had appeared in the *JRSAI* in 1894.[80] Guest retained its items and numeration, but she altered and added comments in accordance with more recent information, and she supplemented the list with further discoveries. She accumulated as much information as she could on all recorded figures, including folkloric evidence, and wherever possible she carefully examined, measured, described and photographed the sculptures. Her proposals with regard to a categorization have already been referred to, as well as her attempts at dating the figures, which had heretofore been a well-spring of wild speculation. All this informa-tion was fed into an Irish Sheela-na-gig corpus, which over the years has been, and in fact is still being, augmented by a steady trickle of new discoveries and by ongoing research into already recorded figures. Guest's work forms the basis of all subsequent academic research.

Although Guest did not enter the discussion of theories, her comments are based on the assumption that the Sheela 'is a symbol of a fertility cult',[81] whose presence in churches defies interpretation. She abstains from comparing the carving with similar ones elsewhere, and from speculating about its origin. Yet her research was clearly influenced by Margaret Murray's article, referred to in her very first sentence. More importantly, Guest had obviously investigated a possible link between Sheelas and specifically female aspects of their location. For instance, she pointed out that their association with wells might date back to a time when water was venerated for its fertilizing rather than its curative qualities. She also commented that Sheelas occur in a number of ecclesiastical foundations pertaining especially to women.[82] Not unlike Murray, who had claimed that the Egyptian Baubo statuettes were a 'modern' representation of a much older goddess, Guest stressed that the relatively late date which she had established for many church and castle Sheelas did not argue against the probability of earlier symbols.

The local information she gathered further reinforced the supposition that women used Sheela-na-gigs for specific cult purposes. All these practices were connected with womanhood, and some of them were still pursued in the 1930s. Therefore Guest argued 'that pagan ideas and practices were associated with these figures in comparatively recent times and [that they] are so even to-day can hardly be doubted'.[83]

A Celtic goddess

Given that the Sheela-na-gig first came to light in Ireland – then considered to be the bastion of all things Celtic – and furthermore, that she occurs most frequently in the British Isles, a reading of her as a Celtic divinity seems inevitable.

The vague notion that she may somehow form part of a Celtic tradition had sporadically been mooted in the nineteenth century by antiquaries, who, to the dismay of Thomas Westropp, 'sat and created, without study, visions of Phoenician, Cuthite, Indian, serpent-, cow-, and even pig-gods worshipped in Ireland'.[84] One such member of the RIA and adherent of the Oriental theory of Irish origins, Marcus Keane, based his opinion mainly on etymological conjectures. For instance, he held that place names beginning with *Clon-* (the customary spelling for Irish *cluain*, meaning meadow) had been derived from *Clo(ch)ain*, the stone of Ana, the Mother of the Celtic *Tuatha Dé Danann* (Tribes of the goddess Dana). As many towns and villages in Ireland indeed begin with *Clon-*, Ana worship was supposedly widespread. Ana or Aine also meant the moon, so she was probably also a moon goddess, and the moon's manifest connection with the tides may have resulted in the goddess also being assigned as the divinity of rivers, thus ultimately representing female nature *per se*. Material evidence, like pillar stones used in ancient worship to Ana, would have been removed or effaced by early Christians, Keane argued, but he thought that some had escaped destruction. One such example sacred to the goddess Ana, he believed, was the pillar stone on the Hill of Tara with the Sheela-na-gig (85) carved upon it.[85]

An echo of this dubious conjecture can be found in an encyclopaedia of religions published in 1906, where one finds under 'Síla-na-gig. Sheela-na-gig' the ill-defined entry: 'A Keltik lunar and phallic charm. . . . It is a female figure, and considered to avert the evil eye'.[86]

When the liberal-minded Canon J. F. M. Ffrench refers to Sheelas as being Celtic, he really only uses the term to denote their autochthonic origin. He briefly comments on these sculptures in connection with the example on the Nuns' Chapel at Clonmacnoise (33). To him these 'weird and hideous' little sculptures were an indication of 'how the conservative Celt still clung to old pagan customs long after their meaning was forgotten'.[87] He thought he had observed another remnant of this old religion within the cemetery of Clonmacnoise, when he noticed little groups of pins and small objects left behind by worshippers. Sheelas and pins, just like rags still hung on thorns at holy wells, he interpreted as telltale signs of the long-forgotten worship of a far-distant past.

For Macalister the term Celtic has an ethnological and linguistic significance, denoting a people with a recognizable archaeological and distinct linguistic track record. He, too, contemplated on the Sheela at Tara. Though not assigning her specifically to the goddess Ana, as Keane had done, Macalister did believe that the monument represented some pagan divinity, repeating his hunch earlier referred to, that there might be some link between these 'strange fertility- and luck-bringing figure(s)' and the male Celtic god Cernunnos.[88] However, beyond an accidental analogy between their cross-legged posture, he could produce no other proof of a possible connection.[89]

Macalister's opinion *vis-à-vis* a Celtic origin of the Sheela-na-gig was by no means definite, and it seems to have vacillated over the years. But Ana had certainly crossed his mind, too. He thought it likely that the Sheela figure was modelled on a pagan deity, with Aphrodite, the Greek goddess of sexual love and beauty, being 'surely' in her direct line of ancestry.[90] Iconographically, he saw a connection with the Eastern Mediterranean goddess Anath, the *magna mater* of the Canaanites whose worship had been denounced by the prophet Jeremiah. He suggested that Anath, 'in the thin disguise of the *Mór-rígu*, "the great queen", otherwise suggestively named *Ana*, and termed . . . *mater deorum Hibernensium*, entered Ireland in the train of the Beaker people, as one of the triplicity of war-goddesses who came in the same company'.[91]

To Macalister, then, Sheelas were relatively late adaptations of a pagan divinity, most probably Celtic. But nothing could be said with any degree of certainty, other than that 'they speak to us of a pre-druidic past – in a language which we cannot understand'.[92] Unsolved too, of course, was the other mystery as to why these figures were put up on Christian churches. As a vague possibility, Macalister called to mind the rude medieval sense of humour, characterized by an indefinite line of demarcation between the horrible, the grotesque and the ludicrous. Originally it might have been the didactic intention of the church to convey the sin of lust as an ugly woman. Carvers might have used a pagan goddess for its symbolical personification, quite deliberately turning her into a frivolous figure of fun.[93]

Unlike Macalister, who asserted that no ancient literature, Celtic or otherwise, threw the smallest spark of light on these figures,[94] Vivian Mercier, some 30 years later, thought he had found traces of Sheela footprints in early Irish literature. Mercier had set out to prove an unbroken continuity of the comic spirit from early Gaelic customs to contemporary Anglo-Irish literature.[95] He found that the Irish have a highly developed appetite for the macabre and the grotesque, and argued that the impulses underlying macabre and grotesque humour are the fear of death and reproduction

– forces man cannot control.[96] To represent these forces in exaggerated, absurd or ugly form evokes laughter, thus releasing the dread of dying, and sexual repression.

Irish wake amusements are one example of this propensity for macabre and grotesque humour. Mercier sees in these playful survivals of early fertility rituals where death offered an incitement to reproduction. Besides elaborate horse-play, convivial drinking and dancing in the presence of the corpse, bawdy games, euphemistically referred to as 'mock marriages', were played at wakes in Ireland until very recent times.[97] The Sheela-na-gig is a further instance of this amalgam of the macabre and grotesque. The figure reveals symbolically, according to Mercier, 'a universal truth of which the Irish, as perhaps the most archaic and conservative people in Western Europe, have never lost sight. Sex implies death, for if there were no death there would be no need for reproduction'.[98]

Like Macalister, Mercier saw the carving essentially as a representation of the goddess of creation and destruction, 'known by many different names in Celtic mythology'.[99] Her myth found its way into print only in fragmentary or disguised form, but Mercier, who based his literary evidence on Marie-Louise Sjoestedt's work,[100] thought he could glimpse the original Sheela.

Sjoestedt introduces us to Celtic mother goddesses, territorial goddesses, seasonal goddesses, goddesses of fertility, of feasts and of war, but she points out that, in the Irish tradition, no clear dividing line can be drawn between any of these various aspects. The somewhat contradictory characteristics of maternity, war, season and sovereignty are all closely aligned and more often than not represented in one and the same deity. Sometimes goddesses appear in single form, but frequently we are to imagine them as a triad, i.e. an individual goddess in her three different manifestations. There is, for example, the group of triadic mother goddesses concerned with the prosperity of the land, childbirth and war. The trio of tutelary goddesses Ériu, Banbha and Fódla are almost identical eponymous personifications of Ireland. Then there is the triplicate war goddess, the Morrigán, Badb and Macha, and so on.

Typically, then, the Irish goddess embraces at once bellicose and benign attributes as powers of destruction and fertility merge in her character – a duality that is also reflected in her appearance. The war goddess might appear in anthropomorphic shape or change into zoomorphic guise. She might be a young maiden of startling beauty or an old hag of revolting ugliness. As Mac Cana has highlighted,[101] in the case of the goddess of sovereignty, the transformation from decrepit old crone to stately young beauty is of highly symbolical importance. The goddess personified the land and was linked with the sovereignty and fertility of that land. Only through ritual union with her, by the rite of the sacred marriage, could the mortal king ensure his legal title to kingship. The goddess would, however, only enter this union if the prospective king were suitable. In order to test his suitability, she would appear in her loathsome hag guise and invite him to have sexual intercourse with her. Only if he lay with her would he pass the test, and she would immediately turn into a beautiful young girl. Health, abundance of crops and livestock, good weather and peace, a state of harmony in nature and society would follow.

Thus the prospective king depended on her, but she was equally dependent on him.[102] Without being espoused to the rightful king, the *puella senilis* would seek a fitting partner, roaming the country as an ugly old hag, lost and sometimes deranged, only to be restored to youth and beauty through union with the worthy king. Curiously, the sexual element that features so prominently in the accession tales is also common in the death tales.[103] Only in these narratives, the role of the goddess is reversed, for she provokes the downfall and death of the unjust king whose reign has ceased to be productive.[104]

Sjoestedt renders, as an example of the goddess in her monstrous form, the two ugly hags King Conaire encounters in *The Destruction of Da Derga's Hostel*. One of these, Sjoestedt writes, has a huge mouth and pudenda hanging down to her knees. The other, similarly hideous, when asked her name, recites a litany of over 30 names, including Badb and Macha.[105] For Mercier this seemed to be a description not just of the triplicate war goddess, but surely also of the Sheela-na-gig.[106] He checked this passage in the most recent edition of the tale to discover that instead of 'pudenda' the translator, Eleanor Knott, spoke of the first hag's 'lower lip' reaching her knees. Of the second it was said that 'her lower beard was reaching as far as the knee'. Both these, what Mercier termed bowdlerized, descriptions of the most prominent feature of the stone carvings reinforced his belief 'that those Sheela-na-gigs whose skeletal upper halves contrast so sharply with their sexual lower halves are indeed representations of a goddess or goddesses who can both destroy and create'.[107]

The question as to why the Sheelas found their way into churches Mercier answers by following Macalister's tentative suggestion that initially the pagan goddess was perhaps incorporated into churches as a representation of the deadly sin of *luxuria* or lust. In time, the strictly homilist Sheela would have been represented as grinning, and now with much of her primary significance forgotten, she can be called an unmistakably comic figure.[108]

As the two hags in *The Destruction of Da Derga's Hostel* are the prime examples invariably referred to by adherents of the Celtic goddess theory, it is both pertinent and insightful to take a closer look at the original Irish text, preserved in the *Book of the Dun Cow*.[109] The story tells of King Conaire's untimely death. Like many other characters in Irish tales, this youthful king is subject to absolute prohibitions (*gessa*) whose violation ends in certain disaster. The fairy folk cause him to break his taboos, and this of course has predictable, tragic consequences.

On his way to Da Derga's Hostel, the doomed king is overtaken by a repulsively ugly man, with black-cropped hair, one-eyed, one-legged, one-handed. 'Though his snout were flung on a branch they would remain together. Long and thick as an outer yoke was each of his two shins'.[110] On his back he carries a singed swine, squealing continually. Behind him is a big-mouthed woman, huge, dark, ugly and hideous. 'Though her snout were flung on a branch, the branch would support it. Her lower lip would reach her knee'.[111]

The frightful looking churl calls himself Fer Caille ('forest man'), and when the king enquires about his wife's name, he refers to her as Cichuil. Despite its enormous size, Cichuil never opens her mouth. The king cannot persuade this ugly pair with their squealing pig not to go towards the hostel, and thus breaks one of his taboos.

Another of King Conaire's taboos was that he should not admit a woman on her own after sunset. Alas, when he has settled down in the hostel, a lone woman arrives after sunset, and seeks to be let in. She is a soothsayer, and asked what her name is, answers Cailb (Cía do chomainmsiu or se a banscál. Cailb or sisi), but, standing on one foot and holding up one hand, she rattles off over 30 other names. Her features are similar to those of Fer Caille and Cichuil. 'As long as a weaver's beam was each of her two shins, and they were as dark as the back of a stag-beetle. . . . Her lower hair reached as far as her knee. Her lips were on one side of her head'.[112] Despite her wearing a dark woolly mantle (brat ríabach rolómar impi) her pubic hair is visible as it reaches down to her knees. Asked what it was she desired, she enigmatically answers the king, 'That which thou, too, desirest'.[113] Against his better judgement, the king lets her in and thus goes to his fate.

A few points should be raised here. With regard to the first hag, Cross and Slover translate *ben* (and *mná*) as 'wife', which could also be translated as 'woman'. However, the use of the possessive pronoun, 'What is *your* woman's/wife's name' (Cia ainm *do* mná), and 'He went . . . with *his* big-mouthed wife behind him' (Téit . . . ocus *a* ben bélmar már ina díaid),[114] justifies the translation. In any case we are obviously dealing with a look-alike couple. Of the two, the husband is clearly the more important. He is the one the king addresses. Later in the story, it is he who so ably prophesies the destruction of the king at the hands of his foster brothers.[115] The couple are residing in a cubicle which is named after him (*Imda Fir Chaille*), and there we find his still-squealing pig over a fire, and his big-lipped but quiet wife still in his company (ocus ben bélmar már inna fharrad).[116] That is all we hear about her – not the stuff fierce battle-furies are made of. Moreover, war goddesses are not in the habit of appearing side by side with their spouses.

Cailb, Cichuil and Fer Caille, frightful as they may strike us, are in fact stock characters of many Irish tales, and in this particular story they are surrounded, if not outdone in ghastly appearance, by dozens of similarly weird creatures. Cailb's thick shins resemble not only those of Fer Caille, but those of many other male characters in the story. The same can be said of the enormously big mouths capable of being flung on a branch. Other characters in the story can put a whole ox plus a pig into their mouths, and that ration 'is visible till it comes down past their navels'.[117] To single out the two hags and identify them as goddesses on account of their looks cannot be considered as overwhelming evidence, particularly when they are in the company of so many characters with similar features.

One of the scribes of *The Book of the Dun Cow* obviously did not think so either because he interpolated 14 short episodes in the tale. Among these insertions we find the trio of war goddesses, the three Badb. So while Cichuil is sitting quietly in her husband's room, the three naked Badb are dangling from the roof with bloody ropes tied around their necks.[118]

Having said that, an analysis of Cailb's possible metaphorical significance in the story might have resulted in more fruitful comments. If Mercier, or for that matter anybody else, had considered the death tales, many key elements in this story would have merited a close reading. A doomed king is sought out by a hag who brings about his downfall. She is looking for a bed and hints at the king's desires, persuading him to make her his ultimate bride.[119]

There remains the other claim that the hags in the tale literally look like Sheela-na-gigs. In the absence of any mention of baldness, shrunken breasts, skeletal ribs, splayed legs or nakedness, it is difficult to detect any of the special identifying Sheela features. In fact in Cailb's case we can be certain that she is not naked because we have a description of her cloak. On the other hand, the few details we do learn about the hags' appearance do not figure prominently in the stone carvings. Sheelas have no thick black legs, huge mouths or lips on the side of their heads.

Mercier understood the 'lower lip' and the 'lower hair' to be an expurgated description of the pudenda. That may very well be the case, but in the original text it actually says in connection with Cailb: 'Taicmainged a *fés* íchtarach co rrici a glún'. In early Irish the word *fés* is used as a collective word for hair, especially coarse hair growing on the lower part of the body. In late middle Irish it was used for any coarse fibrous hair.[120] In our story, the colour, shape, length or even absence of hair of almost every character is described. Noble kings, queens, princes and other elevated members of the royal household tend to be goldilocks, while the rest of the characters have either dark, cropped hair or manes reaching down to their heels. There are, for example, three mighty and manly heroes, whose tresses of equine manes are spread out down their sides. 'Dark equine back-manes on them, which reach to their two heels'.[121] In the light of this, the equation of 'lower hair' with pudenda is at least questionable.

Although Mercier himself makes no mention of it, most followers of his Celtic goddess theory usually quote as a further example the divine hag in *The Adventure of the Sons of Eochaid*, generally without taking the trouble to give a full description of her. It runs like this:

> every joint and limb of her, from the top of her head to the earth, was as black as coal. Like the tail of a wild horse was the gray bristly mane that came through the upper part of her head-crown. The green branch of an oak in bearing would be severed by the sickle of green teeth that lay in her head and reached to her ears. Dark smoky eyes she had: a nose crooked and hollow. She had a middle fibrous, spotted with pustules, diseased, and shins distorted and awry. Her ankles were thick, her shoulder-blades were broad, her knees were big, and her nails were green. Loathsome in sooth was the hag's appearance.[122]

Loathsome indeed, but there is no trace of a Sheela-na-gig. Small wonder, then, that this hag is denied the kiss she demands in return for water from the well which she is guarding. Only Niall of the Nine Hostages consents to kiss her and to lie with her, whereupon she is transformed into a beautiful young maiden who identifies herself as the sovereignty of Ireland. She prophesies Niall's descendants will rule the land.

Anne Ross, an acknowledged Celtic authority, further explored the idea of a Celtic origin by drawing on early Irish myths and sagas. Initially she did not make this connection. She had different ideas about Sheelas, which, regrettably, she did not pursue further. Her later position convinced many scholars, so much so that to this day adherents of the Celtic goddess theory expatiate on her arguments, producing further corroborative material, as they see it, to strengthen her position.

The purpose of her earlier study *Pagan Celtic Britain*[123] was to analyse various sources of evidence for a pagan Celtic religion in the British Isles. Ross found that being a restless, mobile people, and demonstrating little concern for permanent settlements or for religious monuments on a grand scale, the Celts built no temples. Instead they met their gods in architecturally unadorned sacred places, in groves, at springs, wells or rivers. So while the material evidence turned out to be disappointingly slight, Ross felt that this was amply compensated for by the wealth of the vernacular literatures from Wales and Ireland. These she considered to be rich repositories of ancient traditions from which valuable insights could be culled, not only into the social structures, but more importantly into the religious cults of the Celtic peoples. Of the two, early Irish literature was preferable because it was older, more copious and uncontaminated by Roman domination. It seemed to contain genuine memories of ancient deities who, after the introduction of Christianity, became embedded in the folk memory and perpetuated in the tales and topographical legends of the country.[124]

In early Irish literature we are presented with a plethora of powerful women, noted for their immense sexual capacity and adeptness in the arts of witchcraft. This suggested to Ross that the belief in the power of the goddess was very pronounced in Celtic traditions.[125] Alas, despite the dominant role allocated to goddesses in the Irish literary tradition, there were no iconographic representations to be found in Ireland. In Britain, on the other hand, goddesses do appear in Romano-British epigraphy and iconography, with trios of mother goddesses appearing throughout the entire area under Roman influence, clearly, she argued, imported *representationally* into the British Isles in Roman times.[126]

Apart from the divine mothers, Ross noted another type of female portrayal from Roman Britain: the enigmatic face-pots, which appear to have been associated with fertility–funerary rites. Without epigraphic clues, or any literary tradition attached to them, these sculptures, culturally and socially, seemed to her to belong to a different class altogether. Given the crude execution and the lewd manner in which many of the women are represented on these, Ross surmised that they were some religious expression of the more humble members of Romano-British society. Intriguingly, she hinted that there might be a connection between these pots and the Sheela-na-gigs, in that the same type of belief had probably underlain both groups of sculptures, with their obvious fertility and presumably apotropaic significance.[127]

> The widespread face-pot . . . seems to link up with fertility–funerary cults, and may reveal some concept similar to that which . . . stimulated the fashioning of the strange Irish figures known as *sheelagh-na-gigs*, whose origin and precise significance have so far eluded scholars.[128]

However, six years later Ross elevated the Sheela from a lowly peasant background into the realm of Celtic goddesses, thus giving further investigations into similarities with the face-pots a miss.[129] At this stage, Ross deemed it to be 'a reasonable explanation for the so-called Sheelagh figures that they are, in fact, portrayals of the ancient goddess, war or territorial, long-remembered in the traditions and festivals of the people'.[130] The strongly sexual characteristics of the war goddesses had Sheela-like attributes, and the territorial goddess, ritually mating with the king-elect, was 'an almost exact parallel to the imagery of these enigmatic Sheelagh figures'.[131]

Although allegedly a 'typical description', the evidence presented is that of the two hags from *The Destruction of Da Derga's Hostel* which Mercier had already used in support of his argument.[132] The other example cited is the above-mentioned pustulous crone in *The Adventure of the Sons of Eochaid*. The same hags figure again in her article on *The Divine Hag of the Pagan Celts*,[133] where she repeats her suggestion that, in their earliest iconographic form, Sheelas 'do in fact portray the territorial or war-goddess in her hag-like aspect'.[134]

However, to explain how they came to be built into Christian churches, Ross furthermore assigns an evil-averting significance to them, based on the general and widespread belief that the exposure of the genitalia acts as a powerful apotropaic gesture. As early churches were often built on pagan shrines, Ross deemed it logical that the evil-averting powers believed to be inherent in the Sheelas were tapped by the Church and used to keep evil influences away from places of Christian worship.[135] Just as the Romans had not interfered with the veneration of native deities in the Empire, so the Christian Church allowed pagan practices to continue wherever these could be given a Christian veneer. This meant that 'any latent paganism in the area would find a *double* satisfaction both in the continuing homage offered to this once-powerful deity and in her inclusion in the wider Christian pantheon as a still-vital protectress of the ground over which she was once sovereign'.[136]

John Sharkey simply predicates that the Sheela-na-gig is a graphic representation of the Celtic goddess of creation and destruction. To prove his point, he too makes use of the Da Derga's Hostel story, embellishing it with particulars of his own imagination.[137] He furthermore completely misrepresents contextual details and the whole train of events. In Sharkey's version, the 'forest man' Fer Caille is lumped together with Cichuil and Cailb as the triple goddess. He tells us that,

> After sunset, three monsters – the triple goddess in her Kali or devouring-mother aspect – arrive at one of the seven doors and demand to be admitted. On the night of the year, Samhain (or Hallowe'en), between midnight and dawn – the time between times – they cannot be refused. The face of one hag is described as being so ugly that if 'her snout were flung up on a branch and stuck there . . . her lower lip would reach her knees'. The second has 'lips on the side of her head . . . and her lower beard hanging as far as her knees'. The triad is made up by a hideous one-eyed and one-legged black creature carrying a pig under his one arm.[138]

We need not concern ourselves any further with Sharkey's interpretation of the story because he clearly had not read it.

For Barry Cunliffe it is also a foregone conclusion that the Sheela-na-gig represents the *Irish* goddess of creation.[139] To account for the Kilpeck Sheela in England, we are informed that the belief in a goddess of creation and destruction was not confined to Ireland. It was a deep-rooted belief which, in spite of a veneer of Christianity, can be traced throughout medieval Europe.[140] It is not made clear what veneer he is referring to, but presumably he follows Ross's suggestion that the church drew upon the sculpture's alleged evil-averting powers.

Whereas Sharkey and Cunliffe only touch upon the Sheela phenomenon, it takes centre stage in James Dunn's article called *Síle-na-Gcíoch*.[141] Dunn gives the erroneous impression that Douglas Fraser associated the Sheela-na-gig with the Mórrígna,[142] when in fact Fraser was only referring to Mercier's view expressed on the matter.[143] Moreover, in his brief overview of the discovery and discussion of the figure, though alluding to Mercier, Ross and Sharkey, Dunn omits to mention that they had already resorted to early Irish tales as literary evidence. So when he produces his literary proof he, somewhat disingenuously, treats the story of Da Derga's Hostel as a new discovery. What is worse, he relies on Sharkey's garbled version, and Cailb and Cichuil merge into one and the same hag.[144] And lest the reader has any doubts about the hag's identity, Dunn even asserts that she identifies herself by name 'as the Mórrígan',[145] which is not the case. Although she calls herself over 30 names, the Mórrígan is not among them.

Dunn concludes with the familiar contention, espousing Ross's line of reasoning that, in time, Sheelas became apotropaic devices. As the once powerful goddess who degenerated to bestial hag, the Sheela-na-gig, he claims, still guards the land.

Another adherent of the Celtic goddess theory is Patrick Ford,[146] who basically reiterates the position of those before him. He too takes recourse to the same story, but at least he renders a faithful account of *The Destruction of Da Derga's Hostel*. Ford emphasizes the idea that the fiercely protective role which the war goddesses played – and the Sheelas inherited – would have appealed to the Christian monks who were eager to have this powerful force on their side.[147]

Frank Battaglia fully subscribes to Anne Ross's ideas on the matter,[148] accepting her literary example of the 'fertility goddess in her threatening aspect' (in the Da Derga's Hostel story) as clear evidence of an early Irish origin. In fact he argues that this particular tale conclusively refutes a proposed twelfth-century French origin for Sheelas.

Finally, there is the work of Jack Roberts, who, in collaboration with Joanne McMahon, has produced two very useful illustrated guides of the Sheela-na-gigs of Ireland and Britain.[149] The subtitle of their most recent publication, *The Divine Hag of the Christian Celts*, is an indication of both their indebtedness to and deviation from Anne Ross's theory. Roberts and McMahon agree with Ross in that they too see the figure as a representation of a Celtic goddess and they support their arguments by reference to the very same two tales. Like others before them, they 'improve' the original text a little to accentuate their reasoning. So we learn here that the hag in Da Derga's Hostel – Cailb is alluded to – appears 'naked with a beard to her knees', when in fact it says in the original text that she was wearing a dark woolly mantle.

Furthermore, we are told that the hag in many old Irish tales has all the hallmarks of a Sheela: 'Typically she is described as an old woman with a bald head, cadaverous ribs, sagging abdomen and small flat breasts'.[150] Unfortunately, however, it remains a secret where this typical hag can be found, and one can only wonder why Cailb takes centre stage in their discussion when she clearly does not share these regular features. Anyhow, Roberts and McMahon are convinced that the corresponding looks to the literary hag go a long way to explain Sheela's fierce countenance, her nakedness and her otherworldly looks.[151]

They differ from Ross in that they, like Macalister at the outset, interpret the incorporation of Sheelas in churches as part of a Celtic resurgence during the late Early Christian period.[152] During this time (fifth to eleventh or twelfth centuries), Roberts claims, the British Isles were in the process of being taken over by the Normans, the 'Lords' of Normandy, who, as mercenaries of the church of Rome, ousted the old Gaelic/Celtic church and instituted a new order. This in turn brought about a Celtic revivalism.[153] Whereas in the early Christian era, goddess imagery in the shape of Sheelas had only been used sparingly, they suddenly occur everywhere and always in a religious context in defiance of the new regime. They appear as an emblem of the once powerful position of women in the older Gaelic system.

In Ireland, as a result of the Anglo-Norman invasion of 1169, a second resurgence of the image took place during the fourteenth to sixteenth centuries, together with an expansion of its use to castles and other secular structures.[154] This time it was the invaders themselves, the Normans, who, having rapidly merged into the Irish culture and become more Irish than the Irish themselves, induced this Gaelic revival. As patrons of the arts and other native Irish traditions, they put up Sheelas on their castles for the very same reason they had been incorporated in churches, namely as sacred religious symbols.[155] However, this argument ignores the fact that most of the castles with Sheela-na-gigs were in areas of Gaelic and not Anglo-Norman lordship.

It has to be said that Roberts and McMahon put forward these arguments in a non-dogmatic fashion. They are meant more as a suggestion for further research and express their hope that in future Sheelas will be accepted as valid and valuable artefacts, rather than treated as curious oddities.[156]

In the end, proponents of the Celtic goddess theory who base their arguments on literary evidence have not progressed since the middle of the twentieth century when the stories of Da Derga's Hostel and Níall of the Nine Hostages were first examined as potential sources of Sheela portrayals. The same two stories were used over and over again without new insights, or advancement of arguments, or indeed further research. The only developments are the wilful embellishments of the stories which sprang from wishful thinking on the part of its interpreters.

However, it is not only the accuracy of contextual detail that is under dispute. The very use of such stories as evidence of a mythic past and of actual historical practice must also be called into question. Ross assumed, and many writers still subscribe to this idea, that the early Irish tales are essentially an expression of pagan ideas and a reflection of ancient traditions. But more recent scholarship has increasingly cast doubts on this notion.

These tales do not present contemporary literary testimony. They were only committed to writing in medieval times – centuries after the country's conversion to Christianity – and, moreover, have all come down to us from Christian hands. The earliest extant versions, kept safe in monasteries, are from the beginning of the twelfth century AD.[157] It is generally argued that they had had a long life in oral tradition before they were written down. But this of course begs the question as to why the monasteries would have preserved records of alien religious practices at a time when the Christian church was still struggling against a pagan environment and fulminating as well as legislating against pagan survivals. This conundrum has never been resolved satisfactorily. It is, however, usually pointed out that the Christian redactors did not preserve an accurate account, that, for instance, they omitted reference to a cohesive religious system and to explicit ritual worship, and that they euhemerized the Celtic gods; that is, reduced them to a semi-humanized, mortal shape.

While it stands to reason to assume that the stories were not simply the brainchild of monastic literati, but rather that they were rooted, at least partially, in an oral tradition going back to the pre-Christian past, it still has to be said that this assumption is unprovable because we have no direct knowledge of such an oral tradition.[158] In other words, we do not know what and how much the monastic scribes left out, but neither do we know what and how much they put in. As far back as 1955, the Celtic scholar James Carney already rejected the notion that the medieval manuscripts could possibly be in any way close to the form in which they would have been told on a purely oral level; that is, in so far as they actually did exist.[159] He maintains that the scribes would have been anxious to preserve the material at hand as 'proper' literature and that they would have presented it with a degree of sophistication which reflected the very fact of having become literate. This is indeed borne out by his linguistic and stylistic analysis, with which he demonstrates that some Irish sagas had been composed in early Christian Ireland.[160] Later studies would prove Carney right by revealing, for instance, that the heroes in these 'ancient' tales fight with swords, which belong to the Viking age, and ride chariots, which are not attested in pre-Christian times.[161]

When it comes to stories dealing with the legendary invasions of Ireland, these can relatively safely be traced to their monastic origin. History, as we understand it, was not cultivated in the early schools of the *fili*, the Celtic poets and professional storytellers.[162] Pride in their own country, according to MacNeill, prompted the Irish monastic literati to draw up a historical fabric based on the Chronicle of Eusebius. This pseudo-history, nowadays generally referred to as 'synthetic history', or '*Geschichtsklitterung*',[163] as Thurneysen calls it, was partly concocted and partly made up of mythology, legend and epic narrative, arranged under an arbitrary chronology.[164]

Kim McCone goes one step further, in that he interprets the very creative role of the medieval scribe as going far beyond a mere stylistic make-over or vain harmonizing of various sources. The close connection between royal families and Irish monasteries, he argues, led to the merging, nay, co-identity, of secular and ecclesiastical interests. So when the 'monastic moulders' created an early Irish literature, it was to suit both them and the aristocracy to which they were tied by birth and/or patronage. Transferring myths from sacred time into history not only meant filling up voids of blank time, but naming families and traditions of the race, thus ensuring that their own and their patrons' places were asserted in a unique cultural continuum stretching back to the creation of man. Intimately familiar with the Bible and other Latin literary models, the monastic redactors fabricated a coherent native mytho-history forged with the help of key features culled from the great biblical narrative.[165] They equated early Irish history with that of biblical Israel by creating suggestive parallels, on occasion even contacts between the two, thus implying that God had selected Ireland as a promised land for her Gaelic conquerors.[166]

While the era prior to Patrick's arrival in Ireland (conventionally dated to AD 432) was presented as a kind of 'Old Testament' of the Irish race, replete with murder, mayhem and other unsavoury activities, Patrick's mission marked the turning point, presented as a partial re-enactment of Christ's mission to Israel.[167] McCone points out that when we enter the epoch after conversion to the new faith, the kings are referred to as believers, and the first name in this list of kings is that of Lóegaire. This first 'Christian' king is no other than the son of Níall of the Nine Hostages who had to kiss the pustulous hag in *The Adventure of the Sons of Eochaid* in order to acquire the seal of legitimacy, and whose descendants, it was prophesied, would rule the land.

Máire Herbert's study of what she terms sovereignty-ideology not only corroborates, but also ineluctably substantiates, McCone's point.[168] Herbert distinguishes between the literary representation of the idea of sacred marriage on the one hand, and evidence for its existence as a historical practice on the other. As a literary *topos*, the *puella senilis* took a persistent hold on the imagination of poets, playwrights and writers alike, running as a continuous motif through Irish literature from the twelfth to the twentieth centuries.[169] Thus the poetic image of the woman who represents Ireland and is waiting for the rightful king to wed her has been perpetuated as an obviously potent cultural myth into modern time long after the traditional institution of kingship had been attenuated.

What of the actual practice of sovereignty in early Ireland? As with the mythic tradition, we have no direct access to the social reality of pre-Christian Irish society.

The earliest contemporary historical records date from the late sixth century AD. From the seventh century onward, Herbert found evidence of the increasing power of major royal dynasties, of the growth of territorially based kingdoms, of claims with regard to the title of 'king of all Ireland' and of busy contact with the outside world.[170] All of this suggested to her that in the practice of Irish sovereignty rulers actively seized power and shaped their own destiny rather than functioning as sacral figures in a cultural backwater.

Herbert paid particular attention to different text versions of Níall's accession tale.[171] She examined king-lists and historical records, she identified scribes and compilers and tracked down their allegiances, and she cross-checked related events. In the end she exposed the sacred marriage myth as propaganda. It had been co-opted to serve the purpose of projecting the Uí Néill dynasty's claim to the sovereignty of Ireland back to primordial time.[172] Uí Néill literally means 'the descendants of Níall', and their right to kingship is reasserted by demonstrating that their eponymous ancestor and divine founder father had acquired this right in an era reaching back before Christianity. Sacred time is linked with historical time, *quasi* according it legitimating status. Herbert concludes that in the historical era representations of the sacred marriage have to be viewed not as functional myth, but as metamyth.[173]

Miranda Green arrived at a very similar conclusion when she investigated whether there was any historical basis for the concept of a sacred marriage in the insular tradition, and found none. She ascertained that in early historical Ireland, kings ruled independently. Kings who, according to early Irish tales, were espoused to sovereignty goddesses were not historically authenticated. Therefore she consigns the idea of sacral kingship to literary fiction. Summing up her evidence she remarks:

> Thus, the notion of sacral kingship, validated by a goddess of the land, belongs entirely to myth. Historical and mythical traditions became intertwined because storytellers deliberately transferred the mythic idea of the sanctified king to a historical context, so that genuine rulers received a spurious sacred legitimacy.[174]

Generally, then, all statements with regard to the pagan traditions of Ireland culled from literary sources have to be treated with extreme caution because they are not supported by any reliable evidence. But, in particular, the notion of the divine hag being a portrayal of the Ur-Sheela has to be firmly dismissed as wayward conjecture. As regards material evidence, in the form of images, which might prove a Celtic origin for the Sheela, it has already been pointed out by Ross that there is disappointingly little to go on. The insular Celts appear not to have needed monumental shrines or temples because they worshipped in natural sites. They may have had wooden structures, of course, but none of these has survived. On the other hand single, triple and multiple goddesses were found in Gaul and Britain. These are, however, typically fully clothed, and portrayed as seated, with symbols of abundance – babies, animals, fruit, bread or cornucopias[175] – thus displaying none of the Sheela features. Sculptures of a horned god whose squatting position reminds some of the Sheela-na-gig, and whose ancestry seems to derive from the Celtic god Cernunnos, are widely distributed, including in Ireland, but these are representations of a male. Gaulish iconography is rich in paired deities, divine couples whose sacred marriage/partnership seems designed to enhance fertility and the earth's abundance, whose very existence, however, would point to equality of status between the divine female and male partners in the Gaulish system.[176]

Etienne Rynne thought he might have a solution to the problem. He suggested that sculptures of pagan deities which have certain affinities with, and could therefore be seen as prototypes for, the medieval Sheela-na-gigs existed from the Celtic Iron Age. Some of these iconographic forebears seem to have been associated with a fertility cult. At some stage in the past these idols became somehow fused with Cernunnos, thus accounting not only for the squatting position of the Sheela, but also for the absence of distinctive breasts.[177] 'The Celtic love of ambiguity, and a fascination for duality of meaning', he argues, 'surely allows one to speculate that it would take little imagination on the part of the pagan Celt to confuse and merge these two already superficially related cult-figures'.[178] While the Romans eradicated pagan practices elsewhere, their non-arrival in Ireland meant that here pagan beliefs flourished well into Christian times. And the early Irish Church, rather than banish or reject these idols, made them acceptable by 'Christianizing' them. Consequently we find in an Irish context 'the presence of apparent descendants of the pagan Celtic cult-figures'.[179]

But the 'true' Sheela along with Romanesque art and architecture reached Ireland from the continent in the twelfth century. Presumably Rynne has the depiction of the vulva in mind when he talks about this 'new, true Sheela-na-Gig element', or the 'true Sheela concept'.[180] Anyway, when this image arrived, it was readily embraced, because the Irish 'merely adapted their pagan-derived cross-legged figure to the newly-introduced Sheela motif and then forged ahead with renewed enthusiasm and gusto, producing more and better Sheela-na-Gigs than anyone else'.[181]

According to Rynne's quite extraordinary conjecture, then, the Sheela-na-gig suffered various metamorphoses: two Celtic gods with a tenuous fertility aspect were confounded by the Celts and merged into one. This compound deity then underwent a sex-change from male to female, in the process of which it, naturally, lost its horns. After having undergone a de-paganization process it was accepted into the Christian Church, appearing on crosses and on church walls, only yet to undergo a further transformation: with the additional vulva, it turned into a grotesque female exhibitionist, portraying the sins of the flesh.

Even if one were inclined to give credence to this speculation, the question would still remain as to why the Sheelas in Britain – despite Roman rule and without the benefit of an allegedly tolerant embrace by the Irish Church – are basically the same as their Irish counterparts. It also has to be pointed out that Rynne's argument is based entirely on what he sees as correspondences of iconographic representation. The peculiar position of the legs is referred to as the special identifying feature. Rynne thought the squatting position of the Sheela-na-gig was likely to have derived from the Buddha-like posture with which Cernunnos was often presented.[182] Macalister, too, as previously mentioned, was intrigued by this apparent analogy of posture, and so was David Wilson, an English archaeologist. The latter examined what he considered to be an eighth-century Irish mounting in the National Museum, Copenhagen. The artefact in question is decorated with four little cross-legged men. This motif, Wilson argued, which has a long history and may ultimately be traced to the Greek Iron Age, would have pleased the mind of the Celtic workman. 'There is an interesting possibility that it has survived in the folk art of Ireland in the shape of the well-known Sheela-na-gigs'.[183]

But even this single morphological feature on which the whole analogy argument is based – and for which the examples quoted are the Cernunnos-like figures on the Gundestrupp Cauldron (Copenhagen), the Oseberg Bucket (Oslo), the White Island statues and one figure on the North Cross, Clonmacnoise – is anything but obvious. In fact it requires some stretch of the imagination to see how any one of the three positions of the Sheela legs – predominantly widely splayed, sometimes tightly flexed and in exceptional cases stiff – could have been modelled on the folded or entwined legs of the divine Celtic predecessor.

A Christian warning of sin

Contrary to Rynne's position, Jørgen Andersen sees the Sheela-motif develop in the reverse direction. In his view the prototype originated in France, whence it travelled to England, and from there it was subsequently imported into Ireland. In Ireland it was then given the 'true' Sheela characteristics as we understand them now.

Andersen produced the first full-length study of the Sheela-na-gig. This was originally submitted as a doctoral thesis on the subject of medieval art history at the University of Copenhagen.[184] The book provides a comprehensive corpus of Sheelas then known in the British Isles. It also contains plenty of information as well as accurate observation on many of these carvings, folkloric evidence, a history of their discovery and commentary on other scholars' theories with regard to origin and function. Andersen's own theory evolved herein has become the most favoured critical opinion on the subject. It has been widely accepted and found its way into dictionaries of art, museum guides and generally into most of the academic literature on the topic.

According to Andersen the Sheela-na-gig originated in medieval western France as a Norman corbel motif, alongside other playful, rude or menacing figures in the sub-world of Romanesque art. The term 'Romanesque' is applied to a pan-European tradition of religious art and architecture which emerged on the continent during the eleventh century. It is an eclectic style which, although taking Roman models as its basis, also drew on traditional indigenous sources, thus fusing Southern and Northern European modes of expression. It reached Ireland at the start of the twelfth century.

The corbel figures Andersen alternatively refers to as exhibitionists, after René Crozet, or as acrobats, after Jan Svanberg,[185] include, among others, musicians, jugglers, barrel-lifters, misers, tongue-protruders, thorn-pullers, beard-pullers, mermaids, anus-showers, penis-swallowers, exhibiting men, women and devils, megaphallic animals, *femme aux serpens*, men and women combating ghoulish creatures, man-eating monsters, grotesquely copulating couples, as well as almost any combination of the foregoing.

When the medieval carver was called upon to manufacture corbel tables he was apparently afforded great freedom. As corbels were the least important of all church decorations, he was at liberty to portray the holy as well as the unholy forces at work in much his own way. So, mixed in with the moral purpose, the warning of the pitfalls of sin, a humorous element or an erotic colouring crept in. Pondering on the function of such church art, Andersen proposes that these figures were meant to entertain medieval folk, but perhaps also to ridicule their weaknesses, or to secure their awe.[186]

Among the vast array of corbel figures in north-western France, he noticed a leg motif on which he thought the Sheela was modelled. It shows a man lying on his back with his feet pressing against, as if holding it up, the upper part of the corbel, while his head is looking out between his legs. Some of these acrobats appear to be nude or semi-nude. Among these, Andersen thought he could detect some female figures clutching their legs, and in one or two cases exposing a slit of genitalia.[187] From the rudimentary gestures of these sexual exhibitionists, he surmised that the more drastic display of the vulva-tearing Sheela emerged after it had acquired 'a meaning beyond the mere entertainment value'. But he cannot say where and when this occurred, or what the nature is of this added significance.

Whereas in France a huge range of these sculptures is usually clustered together to form large compositions, one of these figures, namely the female exhibitionist, gained independence in England and became a solitary sculpture. The exhibitionist motif may have reached England as a result of pilgrimages. Pilgrims with the necessary funds to travel to the popular destinations in Spain and Italy may have noticed them along the pilgrim routes in France. Fascinated by these, they may have instructed their own masons to carve similar figures. Travelling masons would have taken their inspirations for ornamenting directly from the French sources. Another more obvious explanation would lie in the Norman Conquest and the ensuing union of large parts of western France with England.[188]

Freed from the other composite constituents and from their more decorative service function on corbels, the figures began to appear as a powerful motif on their own. This then won special favour in Ireland, their next country of adoption, in the period following the Norman invasion. And here even the builders of castles felt inclined to adopt the figure.[189] Andersen speaks of a fully developed Sheela motif from about the middle of the twelfth century.[190]

This development towards an increasingly aggressive expression of nudity is interpreted as a reflection of two things: first, a growing emphasis on the denunciation of carnal instincts; second, the belief in the apotropaic power of the nude.

A number of reasons are proffered as to why the Sheela figure should have met with such immense popularity in Ireland. The Irish were generally prone to superstitious beliefs, Andersen argues, and, relying on the observations of Giraldus Cambrensis, he points out that powerful superstitions surrounded particularly holy places.[191]

Another key to the favourable acceptance may be found in the often cited Gaelic recrudescence which Andersen sees as beginning towards the end of the thirteenth century. The recovery of Gaelic lordship on the one hand, coupled with the Gaelicization of the Norman conquerors on the other, resulted in an intermingling of the two cultures. The Romanesque exhibitionist was thus imbued with specifically Gaelic elements of superstition and magic, and was 'somehow found to be related to the crafty hags and wily women of the stories still told about ancient Ireland . . . the war-loving queen, or the gloomy hag who was the queen of the battlefield in disguise'.[192] Furthermore, the sovereignty tales and even the story of Da Derga's Hostel are referred to as indicative of the medieval Irish way of thinking and as providing the imaginative background against which the Sheela came to figure. 'From those native Irish sources was drawn that additional repertoire of lean ribs, tattoed breasts and cheeks, . . . the agonized looks and other elaborations upon the basic posture of display'.[193]

Besides taking their inspiration from figures like the ones featured in Celtic literature, Andersen deems it likely that the medieval Irish carvers, with their backward-looking tendencies, would have also been indebted to an earlier phase of primitive

Irish art. An awareness of carvings like the Boa Island effigies and other dark images associated with heathendom would have fired their imagination and prompted them to give the imported Norman motif a distinctive Irish colouring.[194] Instead of striking down the past with its ominous idols and unwholesome beliefs, the native carvers reinterpreted ancient images and simply carried on shapes and postures derived from paganism.[195] Indeed, in a few exceptional cases the pagan element seems to dominate to such an extent that one cannot simply talk of a background colouring. Faced with figures like the Seir Kieran Sheela (79), Andersen acknowledges:

> Even the sceptic . . . will have to admit that a number of sheelas have been grafted on to a kind of menhir tradition in . . . Ireland, and that, of course, is a remarkable enough expression of a medieval approach, relying for effect on associations with pagan tradition.[196]

So overall, according to Andersen, it was most probably this amalgamation of Norman Christian, Celtic and barbaric pagan traditions which led to the shaping of the Sheela. While there is nothing mysterious about her origin, he insists, the baffling aspect about the figure is what became of it in the course of time. What was once a decorative motif among dozens of merry acrobats developed into a solitary gruesome figure of repellent ugliness. Hand in hand with the changing of shape and expression went its employment, from erotic entertainer to apotropaic device.

As no significant morphological differences between church and castle sheelas were found, and as their employment above doors, by windows or on quoins was consistent too, Andersen assumes that the figures also served the same function, irrespective of whether the building was ecclesiastical or secular. Their main purpose appears to have been to safeguard the structure and to avert evil. Evil forces could be both spiritual, in the shape of the devil and his nefarious cohorts, and mortal, by way of an attack by an enemy army. However, he remarks that there are no reports from France that these newly acquired functions occurred there too.

Andersen, with reference to some literary sources[197] and to superstitious folk traditions, holds that in the popular mind the female genitals were associated with the power to avert the forces of evil. 'It is the . . . for the medieval mind frightening display of the nude, which is the basis for the further development of the image into a . . . demonic figure yielding protection against demons.'[198] For Andersen, such power of display is, for instance, demonstrated in a Charles Eisen illustration for La Fontaine. It depicts a young woman who lifts her skirt in order to ward off the devil. The palpable horror on the face of the latter seems to confirm such an apotropaic effect: beaten by the sight of the bared pudenda, the devil withdraws.[199]

The belief in powerful female protectors warding off evil is not unrelated to that of promoting fertility, Andersen argues.[200] As there were reports of folk practices involving Sheelas to secure pregnancy, he suggests that occasionally the magical use of the figures was extended to this area too.

Although rejected by adherents of the various goddess theories as unexciting and lacking in inspiration, Andersen's conclusion that the Sheela-na-gig has a medieval Christian French origin has generally been accepted as the most likely explanation. However, there are art historians who disagree with him, and of these Frans Carlsson is the most concise.[201] His criticism focuses on Andersen's central argument regarding the leg position, which is based on the assumption that the *ur*-models for the Sheela posture are those acrobats with their feet up against the corbel ceiling. Carlsson identifies these alleged precursors as atlantes. In classical architecture these appear as male (Atlas) figures carved in stone and used as columns to support the entablature of buildings. While these would carry the burden on their heads, shoulders or arms, the Romanesque figures use their legs. They are dressed in the minimal loincloth typical for construction workers of that period, epitomizing manly strength. So where Andersen perceives the 'very characteristic gesture of the Sheelas, with arms passed beneath the legs and the hands joined in a gesture around the genitalia',[202] Carlsson notices atlantes who place their hands on their thighs for support. And where Andersen spots female genitals, Carlsson sees manly muscles.[203]

Medieval people were very much aware of such iconographic motifs, argues Carlsson, to whom it seems incongruous that this well established and widespread motif, by way of an added new meaning, could have developed into a completely different motif signifying the sins of the flesh.[204] Carlsson is dismissive not only of the ideas proffered for the origin, but also of those concerning the function of the Sheelas. Andersen does not provide ample or credible proof that vulva display was thought to have driven evil forces away, nor does he discuss apotropaic iconology to prove his point. Therefore the notion that, within a Christian context, Sheelas had an evil-averting function remains unsubstantiated as far as he is concerned.[205]

Even without the illuminating insights of an art historical study of apotropaic figures, surely Andersen's argument is on very weak grounds. It defies all logic that the devil, who in European literature since medieval times has consistently been associated with lechery and fornication and who stood accused of such in every medieval witch hunt trial, should have been considered shocked at the sight of a naked female figure. This seems all the more incredible considering that this figure was allegedly created in his image, as representing the sins of the flesh.[206]

Equally inconceivable is the suggestion that an enemy army ready to charge should be stopped in its tracks at the sight of a Sheela-na-gig. Andersen even went as far as to explain the horizontal position of some Sheelas as a deliberate ploy to delay the shock effect:

> Enemies could approach a reclining sheela without seeing much of her, up to a certain distance, when the nature of the image would dawn on them, and the delayed effect of her display be far more effective and beat them back in a more efficient manner than could have been the case, if they had spotted her from a distance.[207]

The same criticism directed against Rynne's convoluted explanation applies here. In addition to the iconographical and morphological transformations, one would have to accept that the expression conveyed in the figure changed, that its significance and function shifted and that superstitious beliefs with regard to an evil-averting and a fertility function became attached to it, which completely contravened its original purpose, namely to entertain and/or to warn against the sins of the flesh.

In fairness to Andersen, he does waver in his final judgement. Apart from some question marks raised in connection with pagan aspects redolent of ancient rituals, and his admission that some Sheelas 'defy immediate interpretation', there are phrases like 'one cannot help feeling', 'it is possible that', and plenty of 'mays' and 'maybes', indicating that he himself harboured doubts, and that he did not close his mind to divergent interpretations.

It is precisely this room for opposite views that the two art historians, Anthony Weir and James Jerman,[208] who set out to expand on Andersen's theory by examining the huge corpus of Romanesque art on continental churches, disapprove of. While supporting his thesis and commending Andersen for his work as a whole, Weir and Jerman find fault with his prevaricating. Jerman complains that 'his reluctance . . . to commit himself to the view that France is indubitably the source of sheelas conveys to us in an indefinable way a lack of real conviction'.[209] Also admonished is Andersen's ambivalence with regard to the original meaning and the purpose of the carvings. He had failed to recognize that their function was to vilify Woman. In an era of 'unbelievable misogyny' when Woman was thought to be unclean, and when to touch her meant to be defiled, when the 'Supreme Temptress of the Garden of Eden' was seen as the cause of the Fall of Man, it should have been obvious to him that the monastic fulminations against Eve were at the very centre of Sheela-na-gig invention. More firmly than Andersen, and without any hesitation, then, they declare, 'We believe that her provenance is to be sought in the anti-feminism of the twelfth-century Church'.[210]

Weir and Jerman, confident that Sheelas started off on churches in western France (and northern Spain), see these sculptures as a morality lesson in stone, intended to teach the illiterate villagers Christian virtues. As part of an iconography aimed at castigating the sins of the flesh, the figures portrayed evil in the battle against evil. In fact their horrible appearance is literally meant to be as ugly as sin. So any spiritual dimension is denied, and any notion of a pre-Christian or an autochthonous origin is firmly rejected, as is any consideration of populist Christian subculture. 'The real riddle of the exhibitionist is in France – and there the solution is ultimately to be found, probably in Paitou', writes Weir in 1977,[211] and some years later he and Jerman expanded the area of origin to include the northern provinces of Spain.

From these continental areas the carvings reached the British Isles via the pilgrim route.[212] Like Andersen, they maintain that while the overall architecture of ecclesiastical buildings, including the main decorations, was subject to other decisions, considerations with regard to minor details such as corbel motifs and other iconographical components took place at a local level. Wealthy patrons, the clergy and the masons decided on matters of such decorations, and local artisans carved them according to their instructions.[213] So favourable, striking or pleasing motifs were copied, similar ideas were transmitted and eagerly seized upon by enthusiastic masons and pilgrims.[214]

In their determination to put Sheela-na-gigs firmly in the context of middle age iconography, Weir and Jerman's study of the assumed French and Spanish iconographic forebears takes into account not only the sexual exhibitionists, but also the acrobats, musicians, beard-pullers and related figures because, the two authors argue, a sexual theme connected them all.[215] Even if not displaying their genitalia, they are still considered to be sexual carvings because the very fact that the latter are sitting side by side with sexually explicit exhibitionists makes it probable that they were taken by medieval man to have some sort of sexual connotation.[216] Hence the title of their book, *Images of Lust*. So all these diverse motifs, including male and female figures, are seen as sharing 'the doubtful honour of having created this motif'.[217]

Within these broad bounds of enquiry Weir and Jerman found hundreds of what they deemed prototypes on churches along the well marked pilgrim routes. A closer look at these, however, reveals that the sexual exhibitionists form only a small minority within this wide ambit. Even in the very heartland of exhibitionist sculpture, specimens are in evidence on only 10 per cent of the churches,[218] and of these the majority of figures are male.[219] Often they are not directly on the main roads, but are found 'within easy distance' of the pilgrim roads,[220] usually not more than 8–16 km away from such routes, but 'strangely, though, they are only on rural churches'.[221] In fact sexual exhibitionists feature on the smaller establishments in isolated rural areas, usually in remote hamlets off the beaten track.[222]

Furthermore, the figures were of small size and more often than not put up at such a great height that it would have been quite difficult to spot them. Some were completely out of sight.[223] Even Weir, pondering the logic of this, admits that 'many exhibitionists are so high up as to be of no use in admonition of immoral practices'.[224] A further difficulty would have been to disentangle the exhibitionists from scores of other figures because, as pointed out, they did not occur separately, but formed part of groups. Again, Weir concedes that 'in France and Spain exhibitionists are often hard to find among a riot of exuberant carvings'.[225]

In spite of all these obscuring factors and difficulties, this theory suggests that pilgrims from the British Isles – from the Orkney Islands of Scotland to the Isle of Wight in southern England, from the west coast of Wales to the east coast of England, and from every province of Ireland – uniformly managed to single out one and the same motif which on continental churches played only a minor role. And upon their return, they instructed their local artisans to make a copy of it, albeit, inexplicably, with significantly different features which, according to Weir, were 'quite obviously miscopied' from the French or Spanish models.[226] In contrast with the putative original, they had Sheelas set in isolation, changed the posture and added a menacing expression not shared by the continental carving. And after having taken all this trouble, these wealthy pilgrims then consented to accept a sculpture from their local masons which, more often than not, was so coarse and primitive in its technical execution that later archaeologists would refuse to acknowledge these carvings as the work of craftsmen. But seemingly no such doubts hampered the gratitude of the benefactors. Brushing aside the poor quality of these 'copies', they gave them a prominent position in the churches and castles of Britain and Ireland.

Naturally, Weir and Jerman do not put it quite like that, but it is the assumption underlying their line of reasoning. One might argue that, on their way to the holy shrines in France and Spain, Scottish, Welsh and Irish pilgrims travelled via England, where they came face to face with the already established motif of the Sheela. This is, however, extremely unlikely. Apart from the fact that Irish pilgrims could and did avail themselves of direct sea links with France and Spain, they most certainly would not have encountered an English Sheela if they had chosen to go through England, because here, as indeed everywhere else, Sheelas are tucked away in rural areas, usually in far-away villages which are not places one would pass *en route* to the continent. In conclusion, then, the specific Sheela characteristics are far too definite, distinct and ubiquitous to consider the figure a mere imitation of some Romanesque exhibitionist which passing pilgrims picked from the scores of human, half-human, beastly, divine and diabolic images, only to miscopy it when they returned to their homeland.

To return to the function. The continental Sheela figure, Weir and Jerman argued, was designed to deliver a Christian message: the condemnation of lust. The two mortal sins prominent in the thoughts of the medieval clergy were greed and lust, the two authors reiterate in their book time and again. But despite this intended major communication, in some insular cases Sheelas later acquired an apotropaic function, on account of the forcefulness of their imagery.[227] As in the case of Andersen, this claim, however, remains unsubstantiated. It is based on the assumption that among the common people there may have lingered an ancient belief in the magical power of the genitals. This would imply that, while the clergy thought they were sending out a strong negative message, the ordinary people, unbeknown to them, either misunderstood or deliberately reinterpreted that message and gave the figure a positive meaning. Some post-Romanesque Sheelas may even have been carved expressly with this notion in mind, the authors say.[228] In whose mind, one wonders. Anyway, this is a considerable deviation from Weir's earlier conviction when he held that 'There is no evidence to show that "sheela-na-gigs" [sic] had *any other than* an evil-averting purpose'.[229] And he goes on to state, in order to prove this point, that the distribution of Sheelas is almost wholly in areas of great distress and confrontation caused by civil strife, wars and the plague.

To sum up, Weir and Jerman's categorical mind-set does not make a lot of sense. Apart from the implausibility of the line of arguments, it has to be said that their empirically derived interpretation – confined within the limits of art history and devoid of any spiritual dimension or recourse to other disciplines – fails to open new avenues for further exploration. By lumping Sheelas along with all the grotesque Romanesque corbel figures regardless of sex, human or animal nature, these authors further blur the distinction between the Sheela figure and many other motifs, instead of bringing it more sharply into focus.

A Mater Ecclesia

In complete opposition to the interpretation that views the Sheela as a personification of sin and evil, Erling Rump sees the figure as an *Ecclesia* giving birth. As a medical doctor and obstetrician, he spurns an exclusively erotic interpretation of the female genitalia that ignores its fertility and life-giving function.[230] Rump agrees with Andersen, Jerman and Weir to the extent that he, too, believes that the medieval Church used the Sheelas to convey a message to the illiterate laity – except that he views the message as encouraging. Like bakers or cobblers who advertised their wares and services outside their shop by putting up a sign with a pretzel or a boot, the Church, he contends, placed a Sheela over the entrance inviting Christians to enter. The message would have been clearly understood thus: This is the way of life we all have to pass through, both coming into this world and leaving it.[231] In support of his reading of the figure, Rump quotes various passages from the New Testament;[232] and he also cites the Bible to account for the unattractiveness of the figure. In the Middle Ages, he notes, women were considered unclean after having given birth and thus were not allowed to enter the church or have intercourse before undergoing a special church ceremony,[233] a custom which, incidentally, was kept up in Ireland well into the second half of the twentieth century.

Unlike Weir and Jerman, who criticized Andersen for cataloguing only eleven figures in France when he could have included hundreds more,[234] Rump finds fault with his overenthusiasm, which led him to include far too many figures. Carvings which happened to have anything remotely looking like a vulva were listed as Sheelas. Given Rump's emphasis on the life-giving aspect within a Christian context, he prefers to eliminate from Andersen's corpus of Sheela-na-gigs all those sculptures that appear erotic or obscene, restricting the term to those figures that clearly depict a woman giving birth.[235] If there are no definite medical signs of pregnancy or birth, the figure belongs in a different category.

Rump examines Sheelas through the eyes of an obstetrician, and as such he has some very intriguing comments to make. He believes that the squatting position, the open vulva, even the expression on the face indicate that the Sheela-na-gig was meant to be a realistic representation of a woman in childbirth. From the shape and size of the vulva, he claims he can determine the stage of labour depicted: before, during or after parturition.[236]

Andersen is mildly rebuked for writing that the Sheela at Oaksey (139) has the biggest genitals of all known figures. Not so, says Rump, a vulva would never be illustrated like a pear-shaped bag hanging down to the ground. This Sheela appears to be a representation of a rare birth called *caput galeatum*, where the amniotic sac does not rupture. If the sac remains intact, or if it covers the head of the baby, known as a caul, this is from times immemorial considered to be lucky.[237] A further instance of this he sees in the Bunratty Sheela (8), which, judging by the soft balloon-shaped amniotic sac, has just given birth to a child in *caput galeatum*.[238] Even the Clonmacnoise 1 Sheela (33), which, because of her feet-behind-ears position, Andersen saw more in line with the French acrobats, to Rump is a typical example of a woman giving birth. Women would quite naturally pull up their legs like that in an endeavour to push the baby forward.

It comes as no surprise, then, to find that Rump interprets the Eisen illustration which Andersen mentioned (see p. 45) as fully congruent with the church's teaching. After all, it demonstrates that the devil himself shrinks back terrified at the sight of the young woman who bravely exposes her vulva – the way of life, the holy place. Showing him a cross would have had a similar effect. Rump does not stand alone with this interpretation. Georges Colonna Ceccaldi expressed a similar idea as early as 1877. In his brief reference to the Sheela-na-gigs in Ireland, he states that their presence and their unusual aspects were due to the belief that the Devil is more afraid of the female organ than of the Cross, because the former was the entry point of his greatest enemy, the Son of God, into the world. Ceccaldi further argues that the elongated oval shape of the vulva, what he termed 'losange cyclique', for the very same reason is often used on the seals of abbeys.[239]

In Scandinavia, where a few Sheela-na-gigs have also been discovered, Rump's theory met with approval.[240] But although providing reasonable explanations for some problems – for example, the placement of the figures in graveyards – his interpretation also begs some questions. Why, for example, were some Sheelas placed high up on roofs, hidden from view? Or why did this figure become so unacceptable to the Church in later centuries? Further, given that many carvers were unable to get the basic proportions of the human body right – after all, Rump thought they were realistic representations of women giving birth – it seems unlikely that they should have been able to give expression to various, including rare, types of birth-giving positions and differentiate between pre- and post-parturition.

The Romanesque theory, like all the other theories that archaeologists and art historians evolved during the twentieth century, fails to give a convincing explanation of the Sheela-na-gig phenomenon. Overall, compared with the nineteenth-century discussions, more serious academic criteria were applied and more vigorous surveys carried out during the twentieth century. Bourgeois prurience no longer played a part in the investigations. Understandably, the starting point of all the scholars' enquiries lay within their own subject area. So while serious efforts were made to come to a better understanding of the sculpture, the research has often been hampered by a certain amount of 'tunnel vision'. The Celticists looked for evidence in their own discipline, as did the Anglo-Saxon experts or Scandinavian authorities or indeed the art historians. While supplying important insights and information, none of these modern specialists makes complete sense. The problem is that the underlying presuppositions of the various theories are imposed from the present on to the past, and from a biased academic to a rural peasant background. In other words, we are faced with academic pollution, while the vantage-point of the ordinary people has largely been left out of the equation.

Finally, while many archaeologists and art historians had problems with the figure and were struggling to develop theories, the Sheela-na-gig had a creative influence on poets, painters, artists and musicians, many of whom were inspired by her to produce significant works of art. The most distinguished Irish poets, Seamus Heaney, Michael Longley, John Montague and others, have written poems on her.[241] Sheelas feature in the novels of Austin Clarke and Lindsey Clarke.[242] They were also recreated by painters, sculptors and jewellers.[243]

3

THE PROBLEM OF
THE NAME

Sheela-na-gig: the sculpture

The commonly accepted spelling in English, Sheela-na-gig, or sometimes just Sheela, has become applied as a type-name by archaeologists and art historians, despite the fact that nobody knows what the word actually denotes. Its linguistic origin and meaning are obscure. Most researchers agree with Eamonn P. Kelly that the name derives from the Irish language,[1] but its components have yet to be identified.

Several suggestions have been advanced since the 1840s. The most widely accepted explanation is that the term is derived from the Irish *Síle na gCíoch*, literally meaning 'Sheela of the breasts'.[2] But, as has been pointed out by others, the fact that breasts are seldom prominent, and frequently absent, would militate against such an interpretation. There are some scholars who ignore this and further expand on the idea. Inferring from the premise that *gig* denotes breasts, they deduce that *Síle* must mean something pouring out from these. Hence they consider concoctions like 'Sileadh na gCíoch' meaning 'The shedding (of liquid) from the breast',[3] or they plead for someone to confirm that 'anglice Sheila' really has a Gaelic or Sanskrit root suggestive of 'streaming or trickling'. Collum proposes that Sheila may be cognate with the Breton verb *silein*, 'to flow'. He argues that when Sheila is used in conjunction with *ciche*, 'paps', it indicates the idea of fecundation by water (source of rain) and a nourishment from paps where a liquid flows by pressure, as in the Asiatic figurines of the Mother Goddess pressing her breasts.[4]

A suggested alternative favoured by a smaller number of scholars is *Síle-ina-Giob*, meaning 'Sheela on her hunkers', a term which reflects the crouching position of some of the figures. Then there are those who believe it is not a proper word at all, insisting that the term has no etymological meaning whatsoever and is downright 'silly'.[5] Lawlor calls it 'an absurd name',[6] Branston 'an unsolved puzzle',[7] 'perhaps in the first place a joke',[8] Lynch 'a name for which there is no authority', which has passed into the books without question,[9] and Macalister refers to it as a 'verbal teratology'.[10]

Clibborn stated in 1844 that the name *Shela-na-gig* was used 'in some places'.[11] The first time he heard the name being used was in connection with the Rochestown carving (105) in County Tipperary. It was recorded by R. P. Colles, the librarian of the RIA, who upon discovering the figure had made enquiries about its name. Clibborn assumed that this figure supplied its name to all the others.[12] But while he accepted it as a proper name used by 'the people',[13] it was later made out that it was a tongue-in-cheek concoction by a cunning country man. This notion goes back to an article

52

published in 1894 (see page 23) where the anonymous author somewhat contemptu-
ously states that the name by which these figures are designated

> is attributable to a trifling and accidental circumstance originating in the
> reply of an *uninformed* man to Mr R. P. Colles, who, when visiting the image
> . . . and asking whether it bore a special name, was told it was a 'Sheela na
> gig.' Without any attempt at corroborating the statement, or further investig-
> ation, the term was adopted, and indiscriminately employed for all objects of
> similar nature.[14]

The exact same comments were repeated by James Grove White in 1905, and from
this and the remainder of the article it would appear that he had also authored the first
mentioned essay.[15]

Andersen claims that there is no evidence to prove that Sheela-na-gig was ever a
widespread, popular name for the sculpture. Accepting Kohl's informant's assertion
that the term originally denoted an immodest woman, Andersen voices the opinion
that the aforementioned 'uninformed man' simply applied that name to the sculpture,
and that as a result much learned speculation has been wasted because the term had
nothing to do with the sculpture.[16] As will soon become evident, however, it is not the
Rochestown man to whom ignorance has to be attributed.

Usually, one can read that the earliest written version of the name appeared in John
O'Donovan's *Ordnance Survey Letters* of 1840, and that, unfortunately, O'Donovan spelt
the name in three different ways.[17] But both statements are incorrect. As already
mentioned (see pp. 16ff), the first written use of the term Sheela-na-gig in connection
with these figures occurs with Thomas O'Conor's report from Tipperary (dated 3
October 1840) on the church of Kiltinane. Some two weeks later, in his letters from
Nenagh (18, 19 October 1840), John O'Donovan refers to the Sheelas in Kiltinane
and Finnoe by the same name. Both men relied on local oral tradition, but as pointed
out earlier, O'Donovan was already familiar with the term. He had heard it used by
Clibborn and others in the RIA. The German traveller Johann Kohl, who visited
Ireland in 1842, refers to the Sheela in Dowth, County Meath, by that name – one
learned from his informant who was 'ein sehr guter Kenner der irischen Sitten und
Alterthümer in seiner Nachbarschaft'[18] (a man intimately acquainted with the local
Irish custom). During the debate in the RIA in April 1844, Clibborn read out the
letter from Charles Halpin, who, two years earlier, had discovered this 'curious figure'
in the old church in Lavey, County Cavan, which his brother, the Rev. N. J. Halpin,
'immediately recognized as a Sheela-na-gig, and the most perfect of any he had seen'.[19]

A close examination of the actual spelling used in these early documents, as well as
the stories surrounding the figures, provides us with intriguing clues.

John O'Donovan consistently used the spelling *Sheela Ny Gigg*.[20] The confusion
about his alleged use of three different versions is due to the fact that the letter of 3
October 1840, usually attributed to O'Donovan, stems from the hand of and is signed
by his colleague Thomas O'Conor. O'Donovan, who had reservations about reporting
the sculpture in the first place, was obviously also sceptical about its name. He based
his spelling on the information that it was the proper name of a woman who had lived
in that area. If he had accepted this as genuine he would have used 'i' instead of 'y',
and he would certainly have lenited the 'G'.[21] In fact this more 'correct' spelling was

adopted by his fellow-researcher Thomas O'Conor when writing about the same figure. O'Conor used two versions: the Irishized rendering of *Síle Ní Ghig* as well as the Anglicized rendering of *Sheela ni Ghig*.

In the *PRIA* (of 1840 to 1844) the word is not treated as a personal name. The 'ní', meaning 'daughter of'[22] is changed to 'na', the genitive of the definite article 'an'. Occasionally it is written as one word but predominantly it is hyphenated, thus now appearing as *She(e)la-na-gig*.[23] Most archaeologists have conformed with this spelling ever since. Only Du Noyer, who had been part of O'Donovan's team, still used 'ni' when writing about the White Island effigies in Northern Ireland some 20 years later. He stated that these sculptures were known 'amongst the peasantry of the southern counties' by the name of *Sheela-ni-giggs*.[24]

Johann Kohl used the spelling *Shila na Gigh*. He understood this to translate as 'Cicily of the brench' – obviously meaning 'Cecily of the branch'[25] – or 'with the branch', and that this term applied to females with an immodest reputation. Regrettably, his otherwise knowledgeable informant was unable to provide him with an exact etymology of the term. Common to Kohl's, O'Donovan's and O'Conor's reading of the name is the understanding that we are dealing not with a specific term for a carving, but with one used for human beings, more specifically with a name one would call a woman of morally dubious character, and that this term had later been transferred to the sculptures. The only difference is that the latter had learned that it was the name of a *specific* woman of the area (O'Conor: 'in all respects a brute'), whereas Kohl was assured that it was a term *generally* used for hussies.

The preceding information makes it clear that we must reject the oft-repeated claim that the term Sheela-na-gig is the result of chance invention, attributable to *one* uninformed country man. In the space of two years, between 1840 and 1842, variations of the name Sheela-na-gig were recorded from several small rural places spread over three different counties (Cavan, Meath and Tipperary) in Ireland. Although the same name was used for the figures in various parts of the country, different interpretations and stories were attached to it. But in each case it was the curious antiquarian who had to solicit the name from the 'common people', as he himself was unfamiliar with both the figure and the name. Again, one can only regret that the Ordnance Survey teams in the United Kingdom neither took artefacts into account nor endeavoured to establish local traditions or names for these from the people.

Several sources reinforce Kohl's information about the name denoting wanton women. In George Witt's scrapbook, under a drawing of the Ballynahinch figure (12), there is the following entry: 'The Irish Shela-na-Gig[26] ... a name given to a [*sic*] unsteady woman'. In brackets after it appears the name of one Anthony O'Neill, whom I take to be the provider of this information, and the date, 11 February 1864. On the other hand, Witt may have obtained this communication from Thomas Wright who in 1866 confirmed that the 'people' had named the sculpture *Shelah-na-gig*, which 'is simply a term for an immodest woman'.[27] Both Witt and Wright state that the name means 'Julia(n) the Giddy', a name which the French archaeologist Witkowski later also uses when he refers to the sculptures as the 'Julie-la-Giddy d'Angleterre'.[28]

Edith Guest obtained some indirect corroboration of the general innuendo when she interviewed a farmer's wife in County Cork about Sheela-na-gigs. While she had the sculptures in mind, the farmer's wife 'derived some puzzled amusement' from the query, wondering why the academic should desire to seek out old women of this particular type. Politely, and for the sake of brevity, Guest describes this type as 'hags'.[29] From earliest childhood her middle-aged informant had been 'familiar with the word as a common one used with this connotation', the connotation being: old woman, some kind of magical practice and female genitals. In 1935 Mary Banks confirms that the word Sheela-na-gig has been in common use both in Irish and in Scottish Gaelic 'from early times till now and is very well known'.[30]

No radically different interpretations of the name or clues with regard to its linguistic constituents have ever been advanced. There are, however, some variations, and of these the most promising one is the '*jig*' ending. William Simpson's scrapbook contains a caption to an illustration simply reading: 'Sheela-na-jig or Sheela-na-gig'.[31] Simpson, a copier and collector of material, must have found this version in some other publication. It also crops up in a French journal in 1877 where Colonna-Ceccaldi states, 'Ce personage s'appelle Sheela-na-jig ou gig, en hibernien'.[32]

Yet another variant of this can be found in the works of the Scottish scholar Robert Craig MacLagan. In his discussion of the Rodil figure (162) he writes that its equivalent in Ireland is called a 'Seela of the jig'.[33] 'Seela' may simply be a misprint because MacLagan puts in brackets after it, 'Julia? Cicely?' Curiously enough, Canon Kenworthy, who had made such enormous efforts to find out as much as he possibly could to throw some light on the Pennington Sheela (see pp. 25ff), also drops the 'h', and he maintains that the Irish name for the figure (which he gives as 'Sheela na gich') is a corruption of the term 'Sela na geich', which translates into English as 'of the Breasts'.[34] The second part of MacLagan's term, 'of the jig', is clearly explained by his description of the figure which he thought was 'that of a dancing female'. It may very well be that Simpson and Colonna-Ceccaldi also had the dance – a jig – in mind.

T. C. Lethbridge suggests a different linguistic root for the 'gig'. He sees the word as most probably connected with Gog, the King of Evil in the Bible who is said to manifest himself immediately before the end of the world. What could be more natural, Lethbridge wonders, than to apply the word to effigies which were clearly non-Christian.[35]

Another singular interpretation comes from William Borlase, who touches upon the subject in his book on Irish dolmens in 1897. He proposes two alternatives, 'Sheelanagyg' and 'Sheela na Gyg', but in either case the last three letters are the name in Norse for a female Iötun or giantess. Borlase considered this to be the same word as 'Gig', and therefore he interprets the name as 'Image of the Giantess'.[36] Lest this interpretation be dismissed too rashly, attention should be drawn to an Irish legend about a giantess called Sheela. Robert Hunt heard it in County Cork. Curious to find out why the name 'The Hag's Bed' was given to a cromlech, Hunt was told the story about a giant called Shara and his wife Sheela. These two had a marital row which ended in Sheela seizing her bed and flinging it at her husband. The devil changed the bed into stone in mid-air, so when it fell on Shara it crushed him to death, and to this day he rests beneath the Hag's bed.[37] Of interest here, too, is of course the connection between 'hag' and 'Sheela'.

More recently, William Battersby offered a new reading of the first two components of *Síle-na-gig*. He points out that in the Irish language the letters l and n are interchangeable. So if one were to take the first two words as one this would result in 'Sinena'. 'Si' (or sídhe, pronounced shee), which refers to the other world in Irish mythology, is popularly used as part of any supernatural manifestation such as a 'banshee'. At some stage in the past 'Si' and 'Sen' became interconnected and both were commonly used as a prefix for the name of a river goddess, after whom many rivers, including the Seine, are named. In Ireland variations of this can be found in the rivers Skane, Shannon (from: Sinann) and Blackwater, which was formerly known as Sele from an original Sane.[38]

The name Sheela-na-gig was not recorded for every sculpture of this type. Many figures remained nameless, while others which were thought to represent special personages bore individual names, like 'Síle Ní Guire' ('Ní Dhuibhir') or 'Sheela ni Gara' (Síle ní Ghadhra) on Cullahill Castle, or Cathleen Owen on Moycarky Castle. While no names whatsoever are on record in France (or Spain), a few were reported from Britain. As stated earlier, 'Frey(j)a' was one of them, and the Binstead Sheela (117) was called 'The Idol'. In Ireland, the Lusk Sheela, Co. Dublin, was also known as 'The Idol', and other names recorded are 'The Witch' (Cloghan Castle, Co. Offaly), 'The Evil Eye Stone' (Carrick Castle, Co. Kildare), 'Cathleen Owen' (Moycarky Castle, Co. Tipperary), 'St Inghean Bhaoith'[39] (Killinaboy, Co. Clare) and 'St Shanahan' (Dowth, Co. Meath). But none of these names makes much sense. If the figures were known to be blatantly pagan, it is hardly likely that the clergy, or the nobility for that matter, would have given them such a prominent position in their buildings. And if the figures were supposed to represent saints, it is unthinkable that the church would have allowed these to be represented bald, stark naked and with hands gripping the vulva.

Windele reported that the figures went under the name of 'Hags of the Castle'.[40] However it seems unlikely that this term would have also applied to Sheelas on churches, unless one accepts MacLagan's conjecture that the 'castle' must be euphemistic for the 'protuberant labia majora' represented.[41]

Before we continue with our enquiry into the term Sheela-na-gig we have to digress briefly because there is one Sheela which comes with a name written beside it. The Easthorpe Sheela (130) bears an inscription which is carved vertically down the left side of the figure and reads 'ELUI'. So far no explanations as to what the name might stand for have been forthcoming. Andersen tentatively suggests St Eloi, patron saint of goldsmiths, but finds it hard himself to see a connection between the two. Another unlikely interpretation would be to connect the inscription with the *Homilies* of St Eloi of Limoges (born *c.*588), who warned women not to have recourse to charms and other forms of magic.[42]

However, there are a few indications which point to a Christian background. We find a similar name in a birth charm which medieval German women were advised to carry with them at all times. It runs as follows:

+ el + eloy + eloe
+ anexi + andriary
+ N. von + compunctary
+ ammenn[43]

Different versions of the words in the first line are also found on dozens of birth girdles in France. Aymar mentions the following variations: hel + heloe + heloi + heloy; and also eloy + ely + elion + Eloym + Elyon + Eloy Jhesus.[44] But none of these occur in isolation, they always form part of a string of words or invocations, some of which are unintelligible, while others have an obvious Christian content.

Then there is the account of an English traveller who visited the Western Isles of Scotland twice in the early eighteenth century and was shocked to find that the women of St Kilda had been duped by an illiterate Irishman called Roderick. This impostor taught the women a devout hymn, 'which he called the Virgin Mary's, as sent from her', and which was never delivered in public but always in a private house, or some remote place where no eye could see them.

> But that which seems to be most surprising, in his obscure Prayers, was his mentioning ELI, with the Character of our Preserver. . . . He persuaded the Innocent Women that it was of such Merit and Efficacy that any one who was able to repeat it by heart would not Die in Childbearing.[45]

From all this we may infer that when ELI or any of the other variations thereof is referred to, God is meant. This is the name Jesus uses on the cross when he cries his famous last words: 'ELOI, ELOI, la-ma sa-bach-tha-ni? Which is, being interpreted, My God, my God, why hast thou forsaken me?'[46]

In the next chapter it will become obvious that all three examples are linked together by common elements, one of which is the mixing and mingling of folk beliefs and Christian religion.

Sheela na gigg: the dance

While scholars were unfamiliar with the term, with some even suspecting it was made up, country folk were dancing *Sheela na giggs*. Fifteen years before the word was ever discussed in connection with the sculptures, Michael Banim had used it with regard to music. In his novel *Crohoore of the Billhook*, published in 1825, a musician is asked to play a dance tune: 'Come, Murthock, cried Doran . . . strike up Andrew Carey, or Sheelin-a-gig, or something that's hearty.'[47]

I found three different sources which confirm the existence of the dances. In the National Library, Dublin, there is a small incomplete and partly handwritten booklet bearing the title *Scotch and Irish Dances*. It lists both 'Sheela na Gigg' and 'Andrew Carey' as Irish dances.[48] Then there is a Scottish book of various airs, published in six volumes between 1782 and 1801 in which 'Sheela na Gigg' is also entered as an Irish dance tune.[49] And, fortunately, one publication using the same spelling as the other two books preserves not only both tunes, again labelled 'Irish', but also 'proper figures for dancing'. The publication in question was printed by Hime's Musical Circulating Library.[50] Morris Hime was operating from College Green, Dublin, in the 1790s and again at Eustace's Street, Dublin, *circa* 1820. The book itself shows no date but as it states College Green it must have been published in around 1790.[51] The dance instructions are as follows:

> 1st man dances behind 2nd man; 1st woman the same behind 2nd woman; peeping 4 times at each other, then set & baulk with 2nd couple: cross over & right and left.

All the *Sheela na giggs* are in 9/8 time, which means that they were danced as 'slip jigs'. Slip jigs belong to the category of lively folk dances, performed with rapid footwork.

Apparently the jig dances appeared first in Scotland and northern England in the late sixteenth century. From there they spread to France and Germany in the seventeenth century, where they became very popular in the modified form known as the 'gigue'. They are related to the Italian 'giga', a vivacious couple dance still alive in the folk tradition.[52] These dances do not seem to have reached Ireland before the eighteenth century; in fact all the evidence points to the fact that they are comparatively modern. In its earliest form the jig in Ireland was a round or long dance, 'a *Hey de Gigue* in fact', as it is termed in literature.[53]

Whereas the jig dance itself seems to be a late arrival in Ireland, there is plenty of evidence that the jig tunes are much older, and have in fact been played for centuries. Regrettably, we have no idea whether the *Sheela na gigg* was already a tune before it became a dance.

Michael Banim's familiarity with the customs of the Irish peasantry is well known, and this is also borne out in his choice of 'hearty' dance tunes. It remains a puzzle why he used the deviant spelling of 'Sheelin-a-gig' when the other three documents, written by all accounts some 30–40 years earlier, all agree on a different spelling. There is the possibility of course that the latter are all copies from one and the same original, albeit with some slight variations in the musical notation. On the other hand, Banim often resorted to a kind of phonetic transcription when he wrote about Irish expressions or customs so that his English readership had an idea of what the words sounded like, and he may very well have done the same thing here. Another possibility would be that he, unlike the musicians, had never seen the name of the tune on paper, but was quoting the title from memory. Whatever the explanation, all of this is further proof that our scholars from the RIA were certainly not in tune with the common folk in Ireland.

Quite intriguingly, then, the *Sheela na gigg* is a jig. In the previous chapter it was pointed out that in the late nineteenth and early twentieth centuries some scholars had referred to the figure as Sheela-na-gig or *-jig* or *-of the jig*. Nowadays in Britain, and even more so in Ireland, a music session at which traditional, folk or dance music is played is colloquially called a 'gig'. It is also used as a verb meaning 'to perform a gig'. The origin of the word is unknown, but there may very well be a connection between the sculpture, the dance and the music.

Sheelanagig: the ship

There is further evidence which proves that the term Sheela-na-gig was already in existence before it was recorded for the carvings or for the dance. It was the name of a British Navy vessel which participated in the West Indian fleet in Carlisle Bay, during the American War of Independence.

Attention was first drawn to this ship in a letter to the *Irish Times* by Nóra Ní Shúilliobháin in 1977.[54] This lady had stumbled on the information when browsing the *Dictionary of National Biography*, which says that early on in his career, Home Popham, later Rear-Admiral Sir Home Riggs Popham, had been transferred to the *Sheilanagig* in 1781. And the name is explained here as: 'Sile na Guig = Irish female sprite'.

Since then Popham's biography has been published, from which further details about the vessel emerge.[55] The ship with Popham on board was sent to join forces with

Admiral Rodney, who was in command of the main West Indian fleet. The ship is described as

> a sloop with the curious name of *Shelanagig*. . . . The *Sheilanagig*, to give her her more usual spelling, was a small ship of 14 guns, with a compliment of 40, one of the quick-sailing vessels employed for shadowing, . . . carrying despatches and other similar duties.[56]

The phrase 'to give her her more *usual* spelling' sounded very promising, suggesting that the ship's name was widely used and known. The burning questions were: After whom or what was the ship named? Where and when was it launched? Why did the British Navy pick a name like that for a vessel?

Apart from official listings in connection with its Royal Navy status,[57] the ship is mentioned in various documents contained in the Public Record Office at Kew (England). From these it transpires that the *Shelanagig* had not been commissioned by the Royal Navy. Originally it had served as an inter-island trading vessel in the West Indies, and was purchased locally by the Navy at an indeterminate date, most probably in early 1781. It retained the name given to it by its previous or first owner.

Having received news that a French squadron had laid siege to the island of Tobago, Rodney aboard the *Sandwich* despatched the *Shelanagig* together with two other small ships – the cutter *Fly* and the schooner *Munster Lass* – to Martinique in order to gather intelligence. Each of the three vessels was sent to a different bay, which turned out to be a wise precaution, for on 28 May 1781[58] the *Shelanagig* was overhauled by one of the French squadrons under the command of Comte De Grasse, boarded and captured. The ship and its crew were taken to Martinique as prize and prisoners. On 4 June the *Fly* fared likewise and only the *Munster Lass* escaped the same fate and managed to rejoin the British fleet.

The Captain of the *Shelanagig*, Lieutenant Keith Shepherd, and the ship's master, Mr Edward Parke, were subsequently exchanged as prisoners of war and returned to England, where they had to face a court martial for the loss of their ship. It took place in Portsmouth on 23 January 1782, but was little more than a formality, concluding with the acquittal of both men.

The earliest mention of the vessel appears in the log of a ship called *Hyaena*, and is dated 23 April 1781. It records that a supply of 'gunner's stores' had been sent off on board the *Shelanagig*.[59] Next in time to this document is a 16-page letter by Admiral Rodney to Philip Stephens, dated 22/29 June 1781, in which he explains the problems he had encountered with the French fleet. Rodney was obviously baffled by the name of one of the ships he had lost. In the first rough draft, dated 22 June 1781, he wrote 'Shell-in-a-gig',[60] which he subsequently changed to 'Shell,in,a-gig' in what appears to be a later or final version of the letter. Extracts hereof were published in the *Hibernian Chronicle* in August of that year.[61] The mission of the three ships is carefully reprinted, but now only the *Fly* and the *Munster Lass* are referred to by name. Of the third vessel only its captain is mentioned. Whether Rodney himself hesitated passing on the name, which he quite obviously was not sure of, or whether the editor of the newspaper decided against printing it is impossible to decide.

Other records preserved in Kew which mention the vessel consist of documents pertaining to Shepherd's and Parke's court martial,[62] letters Shepherd himself wrote in connection with this,[63] as well as some certificates and letters, including an enquiry into the missing pay of a man who had been working on board the ship.[64] In the majority of cases the name is spelt as one word: *Shelanagig*. More importantly, this version is used by all the men who had actually worked on board the ship. Leaving aside Admiral Rodney's struggle with the name, there are some other variations of it, all of which occur once only. We find 'Shilahnegig', 'Shilinagig', 'Shelahnagig', 'Shelin a gig' and 'Shelin-a-gig'. Interestingly, nowhere is the name broken up into 'na' or 'ni', a form that might indicate an Irish root, but when it is given as separate words, it is more in line with Banim's spelling. None of these documents backs up Popham's biographer's assertion that the 'more usual' spelling was 'Sheilanagig'.[65]

The more important questions – after whom or what the ship was named, and when and where it was built – remain unanswered. But there are some clues suggestive of a definite line of inquiry which, if followed up, might provide all the answers. There are, for instance, the two other vessels which accompanied the *Shelanagig* on its last British mission. Although no record exists of their purchase, they too were almost certainly acquired in the West Indies where they had been in use as merchant ships.

Two of the three vessels, *Shelanagig* and *Munster Lass*, convey the suggestion of Irish ownership, with the latter pointing to the southern Irish province which at that time boasted three busy harbours, namely Cork, Waterford and Limerick. Of these Cork was the largest; in fact it was reckoned to be the second port in Ireland after Dublin. According to Kerby A. Miller, since the early seventeenth century ships had been sailing regularly from southern Irish ports such as Cork, laden with 'provisions, textiles, and Irish servants to exchange for West Indian sugar and Chesapeake tobacco'.[66]

If one browses through the 'Port-News', a section of the *Hibernian Chronicle*, which kept a watchful eye on all the ships that passed through Cork harbour, one finds that the *Fly* was a familiar visitor there between the early 1770s and 1781, usually loaded with goods for the West Indies. On 10 January 1780, one also hears of Admiral Rodney aboard the *Sandwich* leaving Cove (Cork harbour) for the West Indies, con-voyed by a number of ships among which one recognizes the *Hyaena*, but none of the three ill-fated vessels that Rodney would dispatch to Martinique the following year.

That Cork did not provide maritime services only, but also seized enterprising business opportunities when they presented themselves, is made clear in an article dated 8 January 1781, which says: 'The spirit of privateering prevails so great here, that 3 ships are now getting ready with all possible dispatch . . . to cruise against the Dutch and other enemies. . . . Another privateer is fitting out at Castletownsend in this county, called the *Carberry Lass*, and to be commanded by Captain John Rodney.'[67] There are not many references to shipbuilding and repair work in eighteenth-century Cork, activities which seem to have been confined to small craft like cutters or traders. But there is one record which provides the information that in 1784 a Denis Shine launched the trader *Kerry Lass* from his dockyard in Cork.[68] It seems reasonable to assume that the *Kerry Lass*, the *Carberry Lass* and the *Munster Lass* all belonged to the same proprietor because ship owners tended to use strings of names or sequences which were recognized like trade marks. The owner of these ships may have lived in the province of Munster, but as our three Royal Navy ships were in all likelihood bought in the West Indies the odds are that he was an international trader of Irish extraction who lived over there.

The West Indies were full of Irishmen at that time. After the first influx of indentured servants in the early seventeenth century, there followed a steady trickle of voluntary immigrants from Ireland who worked as servants, planters, farmers or traders. Many of these came from Munster. In the late seventeenth century, poor harvests and livestock disease were so widespread in that region that several heretofore well-to-do families shipped themselves for servants to the West Indies, to make a living.[69] By 1666 the white population of Barbados, the most important Irish settlement out there, was about one-fifth Irish. On Montserrat, known as the Emerald Isle of the Caribbean, there were six Irish to every one English colonist.[70] Here many of the place names are Irish, as are the dominant surnames of its mainly black residents. Apparently their musical instruments and their folk dances bear a remarkable resemblance to the Irish folk tradition, and St Patrick's Day is celebrated with exuberant festivities. Asked what their nationality is, Monserrations are likely to say, 'Mon, I'm Irish!'[71]

If the local island newspapers paid as much attention to shipping news, ship launches, naming ceremonies etc. as the *Hibernian Chronicle* did in Ireland, then there would be a chance of finding not only the owner of the *Shelanagig* but also perhaps an explanation of what the name of the ship meant to him.[72]

Finally, attention must be drawn to the fact that the word 'gig' also denotes a boat. It is an elongated slender boat whose form is quite definitely reminiscent of the vulva. So when Rodney, being a maritime man, put down his two versions – 'Shell-in-a-gig' and 'Shell,in,a,gig' – these were obviously informed by his knowledge of ships. It may also be worth noting in this connection that a stone fertility figure on the small Irish island of Inniskea was called *Neevougee* or *Neevoge*, which also means a small boat.[73] Boats and fertility figures seem to have been closely connected all over Europe, and there are numerous indications that boats were a symbol of the womb. So, for instance, Venus-figures were being drawn in wheeled boats through the streets of medieval Central and Northern European villages and towns, accompanied by dancers whose behaviour, churchmen said, was 'scandalously bacchanalian'.[74] Similarly, Jacob Grimm found traces of spring festivals involving wheeled ships, wild dancing and singing around fertility figures aboard the vessel in different Western European countries, including England.[75] And to stay with the boat metaphor, the fertility goddess Frey(j)a, whose name also gave rise to 'frigging' and to 'frigate', figures in the ship-shaped burial mounds in the same areas. Finally, a twelfth-century chronicler wrote about singing, dancing processions that followed sacred ships mounted on wheels, containing, as he put it, 'I know not what evil genius'.[76]

A new look at the name

The foregoing information demonstrates that the term Sheela-na-gig had a much wider use than previously known. Furthermore, since all the variations share the 'gig' ending, it is extremely unlikely that the term is derived from either of the two most widely accepted explanations, namely that it goes back to the Irish 'Síle na gCíoch' or 'Síle-ina-Giob'. These two unconvincing etymologies were devised at a time when the name was known to exist only for the stone carving of which they were clearly trying to make sense.

Perhaps contrary to all assumptions the term is not rooted in the Irish language. After all, Irish scholars so far have failed to recognize it. Following from this the question arises if the whole term or parts thereof, namely 'Sheela' or 'gig', can be traced in compilations of rural traditions, or in dictionaries of slang, obsolete or provincial English. This exercise yields some astonishing results.

'Sheelagh (i.e. Ireland)'

As pointed out earlier, *Síle* (Sheela) is not an old Irish name, but the medieval Gaelic version of the (Norman) French *Cecilia*. It was and still is a popular woman's name in Ireland, which means that on its own it cannot have had a pejorative meaning such as wanton woman or prostitute. After all, what mother would give her daughter a name with such a connotation?

It is also unthinkable for another reason. In the patriotic tradition from the seventeenth century onwards, *Síle* or Sheela(g)h was one of a variety of female names which stood for Ireland. In the ballad tradition this female personification of the nation is usually given a full name. Thus we hear of *Síle ní Chorbáin, Síle ní Shléibhín, Síle ní Ghadhra*[77] and *Shiela ni Connolan*.[78] All these would-be sovereignty goddesses lament their woeful state: they are wasting away without a royal suitor. One, presumably fortuitous, connection between one of these ladies and the Sheela-na-gig has to be pointed out. The Cullahill figure (38), as we have seen (p. 56) was known as 'Sheela ni Gara', which is the Anglicized version of *Síle ní Ghadhra*.

The same allegorical implications are also contained in political pamphlets denouncing British rule in Ireland. These were circulated in the early nineteenth century, but here the lady is simply referred to as 'Sheelagh (i.e. Ireland)'.[79] One such tract, called 'Sheelah's pulse, by Doctor Faustus',[80] hints at this when Sheelagh complains: 'For six hundred years I have tasted nor peace nor happiness from the solicitations, the treachery and the violence of Mr. Bull. (Signed: by your forsaken and afflicted friend Sheelagh)'. She is indeed in very bad shape because Doctor Faustus writes: 'my wretched Patient, whom I found in as miserable a state of emaciation as can well be described. Her whole form worn to a skeleton; her countenance dejected; her visage at one time wan, at another moment red and suffused'. Why Sheelagh personifies Ireland is not revealed. It may just be a convention.

Sheila: Saint Patrick's stormy wife

That is not all there is to the name. During the past two centuries Irish emigrants introduced this female Christian name to many countries, among others to Newfoundland and Australia, where it is still much in favour.

In Newfoundland the Irish immigrants used to celebrate Sheila's Day in honour of a Saint Sheila. Most people considered her to be the wife of Saint Patrick, while some thought she was his mother. Her feast took place on 18 March, the day after his. However, no calendar of the saints endorses the existence of a St Sheila, a fact which in the 1970s excited the curiosity of Herbert Halpert, then Professor of Folklore at the Memorial University of Newfoundland. Halpert unearthed a number of publications which refer to this particular feast. His oldest document, *A History of the Island of Newfoundland*, dates back to 1819, and here we find the Rev. Lewis Amadeus Anspach complain that the sons of Erin tend to get gloriously drunk, 'on the whole of the 17th of March, as well as the next day in honour of Sheelagh, Saint Patrick's wife'.[81]

Another slightly patronizing account is that of John McGregor, whose *British America* was published in 1832: 'St Patrick's day, and Sheelagh's day (the saint's wife) the day following, are occasions on which the mass of Newfoundland Irish revel in the full glory of feasting and drinking.'[82]

Beside one or two other local sources Halpert also makes reference to two British documents. One is William Hone's *The Every-Day Book* (1827), where he found the following description of how the Irish celebrated Sheila's Day in Great Britain.

> The day after St Patrick's Day is 'Sheelah's Day', or the festival in honour of Sheelah. Its observers are not so anxious to determine who 'Sheelah' was, as they are earnest in her celebration. Some say she was 'Patrick's wife', others that she was 'Patrick's mother', while all agree that her 'immortal memory' is to be maintained by potations of whiskey. The shamrock worn on St Patrick's day should be worn also on Sheelah's day, and, on the latter night, be drowned in the last glass.[83]

The other document is a minor query in the mid-1850s, in that huge miscellany *Notes and Queries*. Under the heading 'Wife of St Patrick', the somewhat piqued enquirer asks:

> Will some one of your Irish contributors inform me when the 18th of March began to be celebrated in honour of St Sheelagh, and the ground on which it is asserted that she was the wife of St Patrick? I cannot find that St Patrick was married.[84]

The tenor of all the articles is condescending, with the underlying suggestion that the Irish invented a matrimonial connection between Patrick and Sheila in order to indulge in two days of drinking. Halpert notes that with one possible exception, none of the accounts is by an Irishman. 'They were apparently written by individuals who took a supercilious, middle-class view of the quaint beliefs and drinking practices of the Irish rabble.'[85]

Nevertheless, most intriguingly in the first half of the nineteenth century, non-Irishmen, both in England and in Newfoundland, commented on an Irish Sheila who was connected with St Patrick and whose feast was celebrated by the Irish in the same way as the saint's. But while Halpert's published sources consist of a handful of records only, his enquiry into Newfoundland's oral tradition bore very exciting results.

A hundred or so reports, with a wide but thin distribution over the whole country, show that in the Irish community Patrick's Sheila and her day are associated with stormy bad weather in general and with snow storms in particular. The most common name for bad weather during March, April or early May is 'Sheila's Brush', but also reported are 'Sheila's Blush' – probably a mishearing of 'brush' – 'Sheila's Breeze', 'Sheila's Batch' and 'Sheila's Gown'.[86] Although Sheila's Brush has called forth numerous folk etymologies, the term 'brush' for weather is an unusual one and not 'officially' recorded. Halpert could not find it in *The Oxford English Dictionary* or in an English dialect dictionary. Of the many tales he collected, at the centre of which there is usually some antagonism or row between Sheila and Patrick, there are two versions which are of particular interest here. One of Halpert's informants wrote: 'I have often heard of "Sheila's Brush". . . . Sheila was St Patrick's wife. If a snow storm came on the day before St Patrick's Day, it meant that Sheila was using her brush, which was a bough from a tree, to brush the snow our way'.[87] In the Irish language a bough or branch is called a *géag*. When Kohl (see p. 54) made enquiries about the etymology of the term Sheela-na-gig his Irish informant assured him that this translated as 'Sheela of or with the branch'. So 'Sheila's Brush' may very well be the same as Sheela-na-gig. A further fascinating facet of this scenario is that in Dinneen's Irish dictionary *géag* is recorded as the name for 'an image of a girl made on Patron day (Aug. 10) and the May festival'.[88]

In a number of stories which Halpert collected, Sheila appears as a wicked old woman. One female informant thought that St Patrick and Sheila had been a happily married couple, but that Sheila, who had started as a good woman, ended her life as a spiteful crone, putting a spell on the country because the people 'went against her'. Each year 'we get a storm called "Sheila's Brush", for Sheila is seeking revenge on the people'.[89] A far cry from a saintly image, the Sheila presented here is an old hag skilled in magic and able to raise a storm.

Halpert also came across many earthy *dites* in connection with bad weather which express the folk view of the antagonism between 'Paddy and Sheila' ('Paddy pissing on Sheila' or 'Sheila shitting on Paddy'). With so much evidence of a stormy Patrick–Sheila relationship accumulated, Halpert's disappointment bordered on disbelief when he received the information from Irish academics that there is no folk tradition in Ireland linking a woman named Sheila with St Patrick. He was also assured that the term 'Sheila's Brush' was unheard of.[90] One can imagine the joy he must have felt when after a lecture at the University of St John's during which he related the disappointing outcome of his enquiries in Ireland, he received a letter from one of his listeners who informed him that while he had never heard the weather idiom used by Newfoundlanders, he had heard it from his Irish-born parents at home:

> The expression 'Sheila's Brush' was used to describe a light snow fall in late winter or early spring. . . . My father learned this expression from my mother who was born in County Clare, Ireland. He says that another person he knows who was born in Ireland was also familiar with the expression.[91]

And there was more joy in store for Halpert. During a discussion of his paper one participant remembered an Irish printed source which brings Patrick and Sheila together. The book in question was found to be by Matthew Archdeacon, called *Legends of Connaught, Irish Stories, etc.* (Dublin: John Cumming, 1839; first published in 1829). One of the stories therein tells of an incident where soldiers of the English dragoons, dressed up in rough clothes as Patrick and Sheelah, paraded the streets of Castlebar in the late eighteenth century:

> Two of them representing Patrick and Sheelah, were escorted through the town by some of their comrades. The male was tricked out with *caubeen*, brogues and *treheens*,[92] and tied with *suggawns* (straw ropes) in derisions of the saint. The female was mantled in a barrack blanket; and the worthy pair were preceded by a third dragoon provided with a mop and bucket of impure water, which he scattered indiscriminately on all he met, male and female.[93]

Judging by the ludicrous description of the pair and their offensive behaviour the author was inclined to interpret the charade as an insulting mockery, an English parody on some Catholic Irish church ritual, all the more regrettable as it was carried out on St Patrick's Day, 'when the spirits of Irishmen are generally so much more inflammable than on any other'.[94] Incredibly, however, no harm came to the performers, who were permitted to pass unmolested. What ritual could have been the target of the English mockery? Or perhaps it was not mockery at all. We may compare this incident with one described by the Rev. John Kenny, Catholic Dean of Killaloe, who in 1856 happily reported that undesirable funeral practices – in his own area in County Clare thanks to his own initiative – had been stamped out. Fifty years earlier country people still clung to wake rituals which he, relying on reports, describes as follows:

> During this mock ceremony several young men and women were married by a mock priest. . . . He was usually dressed in robes made of straw; his stole was a huge *sugaun* made of oaten straw, and his vestments were mats of the same material. He usually carried a huge Paidrín, or beads, made of potatoes of different sizes, on a string, sumounted [*sic*] by a huge frog for a cross. He commenced the profane ceremony by blessing himself with his left hand, and then repeated in Latin, 'Ego jungo vos in matrimonium', &. After each couple was married, he put them to bed in a corner of the room, sprinkling them with water. . . . His drollery was exhaustless, but generally gross, and always in bad taste.[95]

So whether the English dragoons simply carried out a ritual they had watched the Irish themselves perform or whether it was intended as a mockery is not clear, but what Archdeacon's story proves is that the Patrick–Sheela connection was known in Ireland, at least in County Mayo, in the eighteenth century.

I was thrilled to stumble across an even older piece of literary evidence. It is contained in John Carr's book entitled *The Stranger in Ireland*, which was published in 1806. Carr, a keen English observer of Irish customs, had travelled through southern and western parts of Ireland the previous year. He concludes his description of the Irish peasantry's St Patrick's Day celebrations by noting that, 'from a spirit of gallantry, these merry devotees continue drunk the greater part of the next day, viz. the 18th of March, all in honour of Sheelagh, St Patrick's wife'.[96]

Apart from these two sources referring to Ireland there is also a huge study of Irish-Canadian history, called *The Irishman in Canada*, which was published in 1877.[97] Its author, Nicholas Flood Davin, was a native of County Limerick, Ireland, who had moved to Canada at the age of 29. He confirms that Irish immigrants in Newfoundland kept up many old country merry-making customs, such as the wren boy tradition on St Stephen's Day and the St Patrick's Day celebrations. And then he states: 'They also kept up the Sheelagh's Day. This is the day for getting sober.'[98] Davin had only been living in Canada for five years when he published his history of the Canadian Irish. If he had never heard of a Patrick–Sheila connection in Ireland, he would most certainly have expressed surprise at this. The use of the phrase 'kept up the . . . Day' and his interpretation of the event also suggest familiarity with the custom.

A faint echo of this can also be found in a song called 'Sheelah's Wedding, or St Patricks [*sic*] day'.[99]

> Och I sing of a wedding and that of Dunleary,
> and a wedding's no time to be moping and dreary.
> So a wedding took place between Pat and his deary,
> who long had at Cupid been frowning.
> But at length d'ye see they resolv'd to be tied,
> Paddy Shannon the Bridegroom, and Sheelah the Bride,
> For d'ye mind after that whispers Sheela to Pat,
> 'Arrah dear how I blush? But I may have a baby, and then love'
> says she, och how happy we'll be
> on St Patrick's day in the morning.

There are two further stanzas of similar content, both ending with 'on St Patrick's day in the morning'.

Whatever the hidden agenda of this song may be, it is further proof that Patrick's Sheila, to stay with the Newfoundland spelling, contrary to the academic folklorists' assertions, had been part of Irish traditional lore. And given the fact that the majority of Irish settlers in Newfoundland came from counties Waterford and Wexford (that is, from the south-east of Ireland) and that the other two sources are from the south-west (Carr) and the north-west of the country (Archdeacon), it would seem that the distribution in Ireland is also wide but thin. Unfortunately, we have no idea what Sheila's Day meant to the people, whether Sheila was regarded as a patron saint and if so, whom she protected, why there was this antagonism between her and St Patrick, and what her function was in relation to the weather.

Many popular religious festivals began to be eradicated in the late eighteenth century. John O'Donovan repeatedly remarks in his *Ordnance Survey Letters* that popular holidays, festivities, amusements and games were fast disappearing in Ireland because the Catholic clergy had begun to suppress these systematically from the 1790s. In Tom Inglis's view this was due to the changing position of the Catholic Church.[100] After one century of penal laws had failed to eradicate Catholicism, the Protestant Ascendancy realized that it might be more beneficial to have the higher Catholic clergy on their side. If given social status and power they might become useful allies in suppressing sedition and crime. And they guessed correctly. In 1795 state-subsidized education for Catholic priests was introduced, and Maynooth, the national seminary, opened its door. As Inglis notes, on the night of the official opening, instead of being branded or castrated, the Catholic Archbishop of Dublin went to dinner in Dublin Castle.[101]

While oppressed during the seventeenth and early eighteenth centuries the Catholic Church was in no position to prevent popular festivals from being celebrated. Once it gained strength, however, it came increasingly to challenge such practices.[102] The Dean of Killaloe who provided the above description of wake amusements held that such profane fooleries grew up 'in wild luxuriance in the days of Ireland's most depressed state, and were continued till finally put down by the vigilance and influence of the Roman Catholic clergy'.[103] By the mid-nineteenth century the Irish Catholic Church had become an 'independent power bloc to which the English State had decided to bequeath the task of civilising and socially controlling the Irish people'.[104] The civilizing process transformed the lifestyle as well as customs and manners in rural Ireland. Customary folk practices, wake amusements in particular, were curbed, marriage and sexual behaviour were restrained and public order was controlled. The impact of this development will be analysed in the following chapter.

It may suffice to point out here that, with bourgeois values ruling the land, it seems quite possible that Sheila fell victim to this process – just like the Sheela-na-gig sculptures. Whether the two were related cannot be argued with any degree of certainty, but later further evidence will be examined which points in this direction.

Gig: a woman's privities

In the light of so many unconvincing etymologies – semantically unsound and comprising many alternative spellings – it seems almost incomprehensible to find that English and Scottish dictionaries of slang, obsolete or provincial English provide plausible explanations of the possible meaning of the term. *Gig* – also spelt *gigg*, *gigge* or *geig* – means:

1   A woman's privities, the vulva, or *pudenda muliebria*.[105]
2   A wanton (or flighty) girl, a giddy woman, a prostitute, a harlot.[106]
3   Anything that whirls: a whipping-top, a jig.

The first meaning is of course of singular interest here because it denotes the most obvious aspect of the sculpture. But the second, coinciding as it were with an oft-repeated interpretation of the sculpture, is no less exciting. Brocklett mentions *giglot* as another term with the same connotation. This, he argues, is supported by Saxon *geagle*, meaning 'lascivious'.[107] Particularly intriguing is the epithet 'giddy', which was used by Witt, Wright and Witkowski (see p. 54) when they referred to the Sheela-na-gig as 'Julia the Giddy'.

The third meaning is of great relevance, too, as it not only signifies the revolving motion of a dance, but also specifies the jig. In the sense of the toy the word is still contained in 'whirligig', whose etymology is generally given as: ME for whirl + obs. *Gig* whipping-top. The *gigolo* also springs to mind: 'a young man paid by an older woman to be her lover' or 'a professional male dancing-partner'. The word is formed as the masculine of French *gigole*, meaning a dance-hall woman,[108] thus combining sexual innuendo with dancing and woman.

In his study of sexual language and imagery in Shakespearean and Stuart literature, Gordon Williams quotes a number of literary examples where *gig* is used combining several of these meanings. 'Giddy wild gigs bounce like tops', 'wanton women allow their gigs to be tickled, or show it for a Pot of Ale'. And one character cited by Williams boasts, 'I told her I'd give her a Whip for her Gig', and in the next stanza 'he has "down'd with" his "Breeches"'.[109]

With some caution, I would propose that some of the meanings – woman, vulva, dance and possibly also the ship – are interconnected. Regrettably, none of the dictionaries provides entries that elucidate the whole term Sheela-na-gig. But so many avenues could be explored to find answers to the riddle of the term. I have only touched upon some of these and resisted the temptation to investigate other possibilities.

4

SHEELAS, BIRTH, DEATH
AND MEDIEVAL
RURAL TRADITIONS

There are plenty of indications that Sheela-na-gigs belong with ordinary people and rural traditions. The majority of these figures occur in small country churches and it is obvious that sculptors with varying skills turned their hands to carving them. Judging by their often very poor workmanship they must have been the work of local amateur carvers or stone masons who were not sculptors, rather than that of skilled craftsmen. It is precisely on account of the inadequate technical, often clumsy, execution that many archaeologists have refused to consider the sculptures as proper artefacts worthy of their attention. Furthermore, although Sheelas had existed in churches and other medieval buildings for centuries, scholars had no knowledge of them. When they did discover them they could not believe their eyes and many also refused to believe their ears when they first heard the name, which had been in use for a long time among the ordinary folks.

In Ireland most Sheelas remained undetected by the Ordnance Survey teams, which would indicate that the country people preferred to keep them secret. Indeed, the impression emerges that rural communities protected Sheelas even at the risk of antagonizing their clergy. Reports to that effect have reached us from Ireland as well as from England. Mary Banks reports from Ireland: 'The people seem to have regarded them with special attention and to have brought them out on occasion as charms; a priest at Barnahealy, Co. Cork, attempted to abolish this practice, but the "idol" was concealed.'[1]

Rituals involving the Ballyvourney Sheela also fell under clerical disapproval. Votaries nowadays have to reach into a dark cavity stretching their arms almost to full length in order to touch a stone three times, which forms part of the ceremony. Formerly this smooth round agate was loose and handed about for its virtues. But the priests forbade that practice, after which it was placed permanently in this small dark niche from where it may not be removed.[2]

From Binstead (Isle of Wight, England) it is reported that the Sheela was removed from the church but not replaced when it underwent some repairs during the late eighteenth century. However, 'the inhabitants were displeased at it, and procured its restoration'.[3] A more determined effort was required from the people of Dunmanway in Co. Cork. Windele observes that when the Sheela there was 'brought out occasionally for charms: the priest twice attacked it, but the people concealed it'.[4]

Finally, the fact that many Sheelas were carefully buried in graveyards or concealed in walls or gate pillars stresses the esteem in which the people held them and how unwilling they were to obey the Church's order to destroy the figures. That these orders came from the higher echelons of the Church's hierarchy is documented by Patrick Corish, a retired professor of History from Maynooth College. 'In 1631 provincial statutes for Tuam order parish priests to hide away, and to note where they are hidden away, what are described in the veiled obscurity of Latin as *imagines obesae et aspectui ingratae* – in the vernacular, sheelanagigs.'[5]

As pointed out by Corish, Sheela-na-gigs were not the only reason for Episcopal concern. Pilgrimages to holy wells and trees, traditional wakes and funerals and other time-honoured practices redolent of 'the old religion' were further occurrences the bishops wished to eradicate. Corish mentions two other diocesan edicts which specifically commanded that Sheelas be destroyed. One of these, from Ossory, is a 'diocesan regulation of 1676 ordering sheelanagigs to be burned', and the other ban which was issued by Bishop Brenan from Waterford 'was ordering exactly the same thing that same year'.[6] Corish interprets this as a sign that a 'religion older than Trent was still strong in the countryside'.

More importantly, these edicts make a nonsense of arguments based on distribution patterns or on inferences drawn from the observation that in Ireland Sheelas are more concentrated in the midlands and underrepresented or absent from certain counties in the east or the west. If there had not been just as many, perhaps even more, Sheelas in counties Waterford, Kilkenny or Galway, the bishops of these areas would hardly have ordered their parish priests to remove them. A careful study of provincial statutes might throw more light on this.[7]

Another potentially very weighty piece of information may be contained in the bishops' use of the word 'burn'. This seems to confirm what is true of many early Irish artefacts: that Sheela-na-gigs were also made of wood, although, naturally, very few wooden figures have survived.

Two crucial questions arise from all of this. First, why should the clergy begin to fulminate against the sculptures in the seventeenth century when in the preceding centuries they had accepted them as part of their church's ornamentation? Second, why was this figure so important to the people that they would not let go of it? Bearing these questions in mind, I shall take a fresh look at the material evidence in the British Isles.

If one studies the body language of the figures for signs of a possible meaning, one cannot help noticing that there is a burdensome aura about them. None of the special identifying features, such as the baldness and nakedness, the grimacing face, emaciated ribs, awkward gesture of hands, sagging vulva or the troubled posture of splayed legs, could be interpreted as either erotic or as an invitation to lovemaking. In fact, they are not even remotely indicative of sex or sexual pleasure. To my eye the posture instead suggests labour. To the obstetrician Rump this was only too obvious (see pp. 49ff). The placement of hands and legs, the size and shape of the genitals and the expression of the face signalled to him that he was looking at depictions of women giving birth.

Conceding that this rational approach which attempts to interpret what is seen with the eyes may not be congruent with the spiritual dimension the medieval contemplator intuitively might have brought to bear on the figure, I shall nevertheless take the notion of childbirth as the starting point of my argument. On the basis of this premise and in combination with the findings so far, I propose to place the Sheela-na-gig in the realm of folk deities in charge of birth. Fortunately, not so long ago a parturient

Sheela was discovered, capturing the moment when the head of the foetus appears between the open thighs of the squatting figure.

Folk deities are found in peasant societies and they belong to the common people. I shall argue that in the folk world Sheelas were associated with life-giving powers. Their assumed main task was assistance in childbirth, but they were probably also regarded as guarantors of fertility in humans, animals and crops. I shall furthermore explore the idea that Sheelas formed a link with the realm of the dead. Life and death depend on one another, are necessary and inevitable. It is this coincidence of opposites which is so remarkably represented in the sculpture itself with her skeletal upper half, suggestive of old age and death, and her fertile lower part emphasizing fertility and birth.

In agricultural societies like those in the British Isles, religious activity would have been based upon agro-pastoral life. People were directly dependent on the natural environment to produce food on which to subsist, and so religious customs and symbols long associated with production and reproduction in the vegetable, animal and human domain would have been difficult to discard. It thus makes sense to see the Sheela-na-gig as an integral part of folk religion, too important and too intimately bound up with the welfare of peasant communities to be disregarded by the Christian Church. Therefore I would attribute the preservation and prominent placement of the figures to the strong feelings which the common people entertained for them. I suggest that the early church tolerated the Sheela-na-gig in the knowledge that such a compromise would only be of a temporary nature and would in time be re-adjusted in favour of the 'true' God. By the seventeenth century and most probably earlier, the Church began to take a dim view of these figures and disposed of them wherever possible.

The hazards of medieval motherhood

Evidence to back up this claim is not easily produced. The material and documents for the study of medieval history deal almost exclusively with the upper strata of society. One runs into all sorts of problems when trying to reconstruct life in rural communities in the Middle Ages or when looking for sources that would permit us to catch the voices of the ordinary people. The rural past is full of black holes. No direct evidence in the form of personal accounts is available from the people at the centre of the investigation because they were the non-literate folk. So their viewpoint is excluded. Case studies of medieval settlements which to some extent reflect contemporary circumstances of the peasantry[8] and their villages are only beginning to emerge and are too few and far between to form a comprehensive picture of rural communities.[9] The same can be said about the material evidence: only an insignificant number of excavations of cemeteries and deserted villages have been carried out to date. Turning to studies on popular customs and religious practices one is also faced with a dearth of publications, and as Gurevich has pointed out, the few penetrating studies that were published mostly concentrate on the end of the Middle Ages and the early modern period.[10] Finally, as no proper records were kept anywhere in Europe, reliable demographic data about medieval societies are notoriously scarce.

Consequently, very little is documented about the realities of rural life, and when it comes to country women, written evidence fails us almost entirely. The first texts in early Europe were produced by men who were trained in monastic communities, and the women they wrote about were either pious, legendary or historical figures or were mentioned in connection with ecclesiastical and secular law. Later, when scholars began to explore the lives of medieval women, they focused on the feudal ladies of courtly romances, the nuns and saints portrayed in religious literature and the bourgeois wives who left diaries and letters.[11] To date, modern medievalists who have studied the conditions of ordinary working women have mainly taken urban women as their subject, which means that the experiences of their rural sisters have remained largely unexplored. So one cannot expect to catch more than a few brief glimpses of women's lives in the medieval countryside.

For the present purpose the famines, diseases and epidemics that swept through most of Europe, particularly in the sixth and fourteenth centuries, will have to be passed over and the devastating impact these would have had on the rural population remain disregarded. The focus is restricted to those sources that throw some light on the life of country women. But in order to augment the basis of evidence somewhat studies from parts of continental Europe, be they scientific, literary or linguistic, are also considered. Despite regional differences and peculiarities, the social, cultural and economic conditions of mainly Northern and Western continental Europe broadly resemble those of the British Isles. And in spite of their paucity and scattered nature, these studies give some insight into the life of country people and allow some conclusions to be drawn from the material at hand.

There is general agreement that in most of Europe the average peasant family was a small conjugal unit consisting of husband, wife and two or three children,[12] who tended to live in close proximity, often crammed into small habitations of one or two rooms. There was no rigid division of labour along gendered lines. Women shared farming tasks with the men and were full partners in the running of the holding,[13] in addition to being responsible for childcare, cooking, washing and certain other household duties.

Estimates with regard to age and incidence of medieval marriage vary. For most of the medieval period the transition from childhood to adolescence seems to have occurred between 12 and 14. This was the age when female sexual maturity was reached. Roman Law defined the marriageable age of girls as 12. The Christian Church allowed a marriage as soon as a girl had reached puberty.[14] Although referring to the ruling class, it is nevertheless illuminating to read that between 1300 and 1520, of the 41 daughters of the House of Wittelsbach, four married between the age of 12 and 13, eight at about 14 and two at about 15 years of age.[15] Ennen confirms for the mid to late medieval period in Germany that girls generally got married at the age of 12 or 13, but that gradually this was deferred to the age of somewhere between 16 and 20 in the following centuries.[16] From early Irish Law texts we learn that the 'age of choice' of a girl was 14.[17] Early marriages seem to have been still popular in Ireland in later centuries, as witnessed by Carr, who noted in 1805, 'The low Irish are not only remarkable for their early marriage but for the inviolate sanctity with which the marriage contract is kept.'[18] This was corroborated by Croker who noticed, some 20 years later, that among the peasantry courtship was generally commenced soon after the parties attained their teens, with the result that they got married and started families at a very early age.[19] In the more remote areas of Carna and Mweenisch (Co. Galway) Charles Browne observed the same practice as late as 1900: 'Men marry at a very early age, some even at sixteen years old, usually under the age of twenty-four. Girls are marriageable from fifteen years and upwards.'[20]

But medieval women did not only marry young, they also died young, and so did their children. Despite the fact that

> women have been delivering babies since time immemorial and have been dying in the process, as have their babies, it seems that no attempt was made to work out any of the statistics of either maternal or infant mortality until the second half of the eighteenth century,[21]

write O'Dowd and Philip in their history of obstetrics. And even when referring to figures from as late as the nineteenth century, they point to the fact that the risk of a mother dying in childbirth remained very high in Britain. Looking back over the past they refer to 'a deep, dark and continuous stream of mortality'.[22]

So while there are no precise figures available that would allow us to calculate mortality rates for the medieval peasantry, there are various indications from which we can deduce that death rates must have been very high indeed. A few random studies will elucidate the point.

Vilhelm Möller-Christensen, who was involved in the excavation of a Danish burial ground, examined the skeletal remains of 209 women who had been interred between 1200 and 1550. He calculated that on average their death had occurred at the age of 27.7 years.[23] An Italian study of fifteenth-century Florence found that the life expectancy of women there was then 29.8 years,[24] and one source states that in England the average life expectancy during the thirteenth and mid-fourteenth centuries was as low as 27.[25]

From autobiographical accounts of doctors in fourteenth-century central France it appears that on average women went through more than eleven pregnancies during their lifetime.[26] Simon estimates that in sixteenth-century Germany approximately one out of ten women died giving birth.[27] Jacobsen, who looked at pregnancy and childbirth in the medieval Nordic countries, observes that once a woman became pregnant, she had to face the possibility that she might die during delivery or that her health would be severely impaired.[28] 'Medieval women had to live with the uncertainty of the outcome of pregnancy. They knew that many survived; they also knew that many others did not and that very little could be done about it.'[29]

Bennett, who focused on medieval England, says that women would have spent most of their adult years either pregnant or nursing an infant child, only to bury between one-quarter to one-third of their offspring before they reached maturity.[30] Given such low expectations of life, she argues, three-generational households must have been rare because few people lived long enough to welcome any grandchildren into the world. This would have also been true for the rest of Europe according to Norbert Ohler, who asserts: 'Insgesamt bewirkte die geringe Lebenserwartung, daß wenige Familien drei Generationen umfaßten.'[31] (Thus poor life expectancy resulted in low numbers of three-generational families.) A survey carried out in a poor district in Dublin as late as the first half of the nineteenth century established very similar facts. Women went through many pregnancies: one mother in every seven had ten or more children baptized. Apart from the fact that many babies conceived would not have come to full term, of the successful births many did not survive infancy. Excluding stillbirths we find that of all the children born to these Dublin women, over 22 per cent died within the first 12 months, more than half perished by the fifth year and, by the ninth year, only 42 remained alive out of every 100 births.[32]

Arnold calls the rates of infant mortality in medieval Europe shocking. He found that in Germany one out of every two babies died during its first year. In other words, every second child was born to die.[33] Arnold traced mortality rates in infancy and childhood by compiling reports on excavations of village cemeteries. He compared figures by looking at the number of children who failed to reach their fourteenth birthday. In a Carolingian graveyard in southern Germany the figure stands at 59.9 per cent, in a late Saxon cemetery in northern Germany it is 51.1 per cent, in a tenth- to twelfth-century Slav village in east Germany it is 47.7 per cent, and exactly the same percentage was worked out for a Swedish village where the burials date back to the twelfth to fourteenth centuries.[34]

From an English study which concentrated on the sixteenth to the eighteenth centuries, it transpires that even at this stage roughly 12 to 20 per cent of children died in infancy and that another 12 to 20 per cent did not live to see their fifteenth birthday,[35] corroborating O'Dowd's and Philip's bleak picture of loss of life in Britain down to fairly recent times. Deploring the appalling maternal and infant mortality in contemporary England, a seventeenth-century royal petition states:

> That within the space of twenty years last past, above six-thousand women have died in childbed, more than thirteen-thousand children have been abort-ive and five-thousand *chrysome* infants (those in their first months of life) have been buried within the weekly bills of mortality.[36]

To conclude, a very high mortality rate prevailed among women and children in medieval and early modern times. But in actual fact the figures would have been worse for the early Middle Ages when mortality was even higher and life expectancy even lower. The main reason for this was poor nutrition. The early medieval peasant subsisted on a diet which did not provide an adequate amount of protein and was low in iron.[37] Due to advanced farming methods, the introduction of protein-rich vegetables and the growing consumption of fish and meats, as well as better cooking facilities, the medieval diet began to improve slowly from the ninth century onward.[38]

Women in particular benefited from the increased intake of iron. Before menarche and after menopause their needs are the same as those of men, but during menstrual age they require at least twice as much iron as men. Bullough and Campbell argue that the average iron intake would have been barely sufficient for males and, because of their greater need, grossly insufficient for females.[39] Being married so young and faced with so many pregnancies, many women would have been severely anaemic. And while anaemia is seldom the primary cause of death, it acts as a predisposing factor, increasing the risk of other diseases such as cardiac problems, pneumonia and bronchitis, to name but a few. Indeed, as Bullough and Campbell point out, childbirth was pro-bably the leading anaemia-related death for women in the early medieval period.[40]

So to medieval woman the prospect of motherhood must have been pretty frigh-tening, as childbirth was such a dangerous business for both her and her child. Who could she turn to? What practical help for the physical problems of birth and what spiritual guidance could she count on in her hour of need?

She certainly could not have expected much help or sympathy from the Church. According to the Christian teaching holy wedlock had been instituted by God for the generation of children. This implied not only a duty to procreate and an acceptance of all the children God might send, but a duty which had to be expiated in pain. Had not the Lord God said unto Eve: 'I will greatly multiply thy sorrow and thy conception; in sorrow thou shalt bring forth children; and thy desire shall be to thy husband, and he shall rule over thee' (*Genesis* 3:16). Peder Palladius makes this point precisely in his *Consolation and Admonition of Pregnant Women* when he says: 'You are dealing with God the Father, the Son and the Holy Ghost; they have ordered that you bring forth your child with pain and bring it up with sorrow and distress and many sleepless nights.'[41] So suffering during labour was only to be expected. Zealous Christians went even further, believing that it was in fact a deserved punishment for the original sin, a reminder as it were of woman's innate depravity as a consequence of the Fall. Intended as some kind of consolation, women were given to understand that if they died in the process of giving birth this at least afforded them the chance of atonement.[42] Quoting from a sixteenth-century sermon from Cologne, Kruse shows that some clergymen went so far as to suggest that there was nothing quite as delectable ('köstlich') as suffering and dying during childbirth.[43]

Women's helpers during labour

Most women, one would imagine, did not share this vision of ultimate bliss and had the good sense to look for help elsewhere. Small wonder then that childbirth in the Middle Ages was a woman's affair: helpers both divine and human were predominantly female. Although there are some records of men assisting their wives, in the vast majority of cases women were attended in childbed by other women, who were usually experienced neighbours or relatives, some of whom would in time become professional midwives. A circle of women around the one in travail is one of the constants of childbirth reported from all over Europe.[44] Since neither medical nor obstetric knowledge was available to medieval women they had to rely on time-honoured practices and remedies comprising herbal or animal remedies, amulets, girdles, charms and invocations, physical manipulation and various rites relating to springs and stones. Their aim was to help to accelerate the birth process and avoid the agony of a long drawn-out labour, because extended labour could result in the death of the mother from exhaustion and a dead or brain-damaged child.

Collections of cures, remedies and lists of medicinal substances survive in manuscripts mainly stored in continental monasteries. Medical texts were also found in England, but these appear to have borrowed heavily from classical sources. They represent a curious and complex mixture of Greek medicine infiltrated by Mediterranean folk practices and magical ideas imported by Christian and other agencies into North-Western Europe, where a touch of pagan Teutonic magic was added.[45] There are no medical treatises from early Ireland. Late medieval Irish texts, like their English counterparts, tend to be reproductions of Mediterranean sources, but without much change or input from native medical tradition.[46]

English manuscripts survive from the ninth or tenth century onward in both Latin and vernacular forms.[47] The two main Anglo-Saxon medical manuscripts, the *Leechbook* (c.950) and the *Lacnunga* (c.1050), both produced in monasteries, contain an assortment of pagan cures and charms with various degrees of Christianization. Purely heathen passages alternate with charms that are but superficially Christian. Northern gods and Christian saints are invoked in the same manner; Christ is treated on a par with Woden and Thor and occasionally mistaken for one or the other.[48]

Only a relatively small proportion of the materials contained in these manuscripts deals with obstetrics and gynaecology.[49] These few text passages were duplicated over and over again with the result that most obstetrical advice changed very little throughout the Middle Ages.[50] An example of a typical herbal remedy would be the following:

> In order that a woman may give birth quickly, take the seed of . . . coriander, eleven or thirteen grains, tie them with a thread in a clean linen cloth; then let a person who is a virgin, a boy or a maiden, take them, and hold them at the left thigh, near the genitalia, and as soon as all the birth is over take the medicine away, lest part of the intestines follow thereafter.[51]

While most of the cures would strike us as fairly useless they did include some herbs that had inherent beneficial properties.[52] Stoerz rightly points out that we have no way of knowing how widely these remedies were known, read or used.[53] However, looking through the list of ingredients required for the potions, such as wine and exotic herbs and spices, and studying the advice given with regard to activities that should be abstained from during pregnancy, like horse riding and having hot baths, it becomes obvious that most of these remedies were not meant for and were certainly beyond the reach of the ordinary peasant.

Some of the cures were still in circulation in the nineteenth century. James Joyce alludes to one of these collections in *Ulysses*.[54] The text in question is *Aristotle's Masterpiece*, an anonymous seventeenth-century publication which saw many editions and was reprinted as late as 1827.[55] An upper-class perspective is clearly revealed in the recipes and the dietary advice given, consisting of rare meats, fruits and oriental delicacies to be taken with a little wine. The same is true of the things to be avoided during pregnancy, which include loud noises like the discharging of great guns, immoderate laughter, coach rides on stony roads and too close lacing. But wearing a necklace of gold was deemed to be beneficial for the breasts.[56]

Before we turn to practices ordinary country people would have resorted to, two observations have to be made. First, there is an amazing homogeneity of choice and application of such obstetric remedies worldwide. Second, the efficacy of virtually all the recommended treatments depended to a large extent on sympathetic magic. This idea is based on the belief that a certain physical sympathy exists between living creatures and inanimate or animate objects, and that magical effects can be achieved by performing an associated action or using a sympathetic object. This notion implies a basic belief in the harmony of nature: the destiny of humankind is ruled by the macrocosmic forces that surround it. The human body is seen as a mirror of the great universal body, and the two worlds are interconnected. So medical knowledge depended on the study of obvious or concealed sympathies or antipathies as the case may be. The belief in such magic worked at different levels. The most basic of these, for instance, required that all knots be untied and buckles unfastened to help to open the woman's birth passage. Another type of sympathetic principle was involved when human milk was administered to women in labour, where the underlying idea was that the success of the woman who had already given birth could be transferred to one who was about to. Mythology enters yet another kind of sympathetic magic. For example, the herb artemesia was placed on the genitalia to speed birth because it bore the name of Artemis, who was the Greek goddess of childbirth.

As such these measures are, of course, pretty inadequate, even worthless, but given that every pregnancy must have been the cause for tormenting anxiety, psychologically they would literally have worked wonders. In their time of danger it must have instilled medieval women with a great sense of encouragement and reassurance to know that all was done that could be done. Traditional cures have a coherent logic of their own, and for those applying them truth was truth, whether the certainty of ritual, the abstract truth of religious belief or the hard truth of the physical fact.[57]

Stones

Among the various obstetrical aids, amulets made of precious or semi-precious stones, or of ordinary stones and pebbles considered precious by virtue of their natural form, were extremely popular everywhere, it seems.[58] They were commonly placed on or tied on a string around certain parts of the woman's body. During pregnancy they were usually put on the upper part of the body, worn as necklaces or bracelets, but at the first sign of labour they were transferred to the genital area or the legs. Of the many different types the *aetites* or eagle stone was probably the best known. It is a hollow stone which contains a pebble, sand or some other material that makes a rattling noise when shaken. The allusion to pregnancy is obvious, and it was therefore highly prized for its supposed efficacy in preventing abortion and easing childbirth. One source even claims:

> It makes women that are slippery able to conceive, being bound to the Wrist of the left arm, by which, from the heart toward the Ring Finger, (next to the little Finger) an Artery runs; and if all the time the Woman is great with Child, this Jewel be worn on those parts, it strengthens the Child, and there is no fear of abortion or miscarrying.[59]

A mid-seventeenth-century text advises applying the *aetites* to the thigh of one in labour as this definitely eases and quickens delivery.[60] Forbes's literary evidence for the use of this stone stretches back to the seventh century, but he also found its popularity attested in relatively recent times in the folklore of England, Italy, Russia, Spain, Palestine, Austria, the Faroe Islands, France and Switzerland.[61]

Used also on account of the sympathetic principle was the lodestone, now known as magnetite. The attractive power this stone has on iron was transferred to the pregnant woman, and it was believed that the stone was capable of both holding the foetus within the body, thus preventing abortion, and drawing the infant forth, thus expediting delivery. The only disagreement was over which hand, the left or the right, should hold the amulet.[62] Because of its magnetic qualities, amber too was supposed to have the ability to draw out babies and was therefore used in the same fashion. It is not entirely clear why so many other stones were thought to possess curative or protective powers, but it is likely that the custom of wearing or holding an amulet during childbirth simply afforded solace and support.

In addition to those already mentioned, agate, amethyst, borax, carnelian, coral, emerald, flint, haematite, jasper, jet, lapis lazuli, limonite, malachite, meerschaum, onyx, pearl, sapphire and turquoise were in favour from very early times. The soluble varieties were sometimes pulverized in liquid and drunk. Some were crushed, finely powdered and then mixed with other choice ingredients like red sandalwood, citron wax and cypress cones, to be eaten or applied as an ointment. The rationale behind this, Forbes thinks, is that it was believed that abortions occur when the uterus is excessively moist, and that remedies containing stone material would have a drying effect even if applied externally.[63] But because of the prohibitive cost of preparing such concoctions cures like these fall into the same category as the expensive herbal remedies and would have been confined to the upper classes.

Normally birthing stones were carefully put away and kept safe for the next occasion, and it was customary also to loan them to other women in labour. In Provence gemstones with brownish or reddish lines reminiscent of the shape and colour of a foetus were carried during pregnancy and replaced, after the birth, by others of a whitish colour called *gardo la*, which were thought to encourage the flow of milk.[64] Only a few stones bear an inscription. An interesting example was found in Ireland. It was made of amber and had ogham characters inscribed on it. Westropp informs us that it was 'used as a charm in childbirth', and had long been preserved at Ennis, Co. Clare. The ogham characters translate as 'LMCBDV', which he interprets as the initials of a formula or prayer like those on religious medals, and he appositely quotes from the sixth century *Homilies* of St Eloi of Limoges: 'let no woman hang amber round her neck . . . or have recourse either to enchanters . . . or to engravers of amulets', and 'do not tie strings round the necks of women'.[65] Another fascinating engraved birthing stone was found at a Roman-British excavation site in Hertfordshire, England. It shows among others the goddess Isis and a representation of the uterus with ligaments and Fallopian tubes, as well as a key which symbolically unlocks the pregnant uterus at term.[66]

Norse sources mention so-called 'stones of life' which were supposed to ease childbirth. One such birthing stone was listed in the inventory of the property of Hólar Cathedral in the early sixteenth century. The fact that we are dealing with a pagan stone preserved in a Christian house of worship can only be explained by assuming that the stone was sanctified for Christian use, 'because it had proved impossible to eradicate the originally heathen custom entirely'.[67]

Similar compromises appear to have been reached in the British Isles. One example is an engraved amulet made of onyx which was supposedly presented to St Alban's Abbey by Aethelred the Unready (king of the English from 978 to 1016). Kept in the church on a lavish shrine, it was especially treasured for the help it provided women in childbirth. Anyone in need of it was allowed to take it home. No request could be refused, but if the stone was removed fraudulently from the church its secret virtue was supposed to leave it. Meaney explains how it worked: 'With an invocation to St Alban, it was laid between the woman's breasts and then gradually moved down her body, for the infantulus fled the approaching stone.'[68]

A round piece of quartzite called St Olan's Cap placed on top of the ogham-inscribed pillar of St Olan's Stone in Aghabulloge parish Co. Cork, which was believed to ensure a safe delivery, was frequently borrowed as a talisman by women in travail. Another such stone known as St Columcille's Pillow was preserved on Tory Island.

Logan lists three more holy stones – Our Lady's Bed in Lough Gill, the praying altar on Inishmurray, both Co. Sligo, and St Kevin's Bed in Glendalough, Co. Wicklow – which necessitated a ritual of three rounds of prayers or the touching of the stone to ensure that the woman would not die in childbirth.[69] For the very same reason pregnant women also went to the top of the South peak on Skellig Rocks, Co. Kerry.[70] And on the Scottish island of Rona where there is a chapel dedicated to St Ronan, a big plank of wood about 10 feet in length lies on its altar. Every foot has a hole in it and in every hole there is a stone to which the natives ascribe the virtue of 'promoting speedy delivery to a woman in travail'.[71]

Girdles

As equally widespread as the use of stone amulets was the application of girdles during pregnancy and confinement. These could be pieces of string, silk threads, woollen fillets, ribbons, leather belts, bandages, in fact any thin or broad strips of material which were mostly fastened round the woman's abdomen, but also bound to her thighs or tied about her waist, wrist, neck or chest. Almost universally the popular conception prevailed that everything should be unloosened in these contingencies; thus husbands must not sit with their legs crossed, hair must be undone, knots untied and so on. Similarly, obstetric girdles were loosened and removed at the beginning of confinement with the expectation that this would expedite parturition. Following the logic of this one is inclined to understand an Irish custom whereby after a successful birth child and mother or nurse 'were girt with girdles finely plated with woman's hair'.[72]

Unfortunately space constraints do not permit a detailed analysis of the admirable amount of literary and pictorial evidence which Dilling[73] traces through the history of such girdles and their use throughout the world. So only some of the relevant aspects pertaining to the present investigation are referred to.

The sympathetic principle is the most obvious element everywhere, and this is rather charmingly demonstrated in a Japanese record of ceremonies, according to which, 'It is customary to beg some matron, who has herself had an easy confinement, for the girdle which she wore during her pregnancy; and this lady is called the girdle-mother.'[74] In many traditions a collection of magic words is written inside the belt, often containing the number three or comprising three words arranged in three rows. Others bear the well known names of divine helpers of women in childbirth such as the Egyptian Isis and the Babylonian Istar, who herself carried as her symbol the womanly girdle. Another candidate is Eilithyia, whose name means 'child-bearing' and who was invoked in ancient Greece 'to loose the parturient zone'. Also mentioned is Artemis, to whom the expression 'to unloosen the girdle' was applied and in whose temple girdles were dedicated to her. Aphrodite's name occurs, too, as do those of the Roman Lucina and Diana, who was called 'the opener of the womb',[75] the Germanic Nornen and the Norse goddess Freyja (Frigga). In Rome the goddesses of birth gradually acquired the epithet 'Solvizona' – 'the Girdle-loosing' – which is some indication of how common the girdle was as an obstetric aid.

This interrelation is further demonstrated by the fact that the Latin word 'incincta' means 'girded', sometimes 'ungirdled' and colloquially 'a pregnant woman'. From this is derived the Italian 'incincta', 'pregnant'; Spanish 'estar encinta', 'to be pregnant';

French 'enceinte', 'pregnant'; and probably German 'entbinden', 'to release' and 'to deliver'. As Dilling points out, this verbal evidence further reinforces the impression we get of the huge importance attached to girdles in pregnancy in early times.[76]

Women do not seem to have wavered in their enthusiasm for this obstetrical aid. In medieval Denmark the custom prevailed among the peasantry of tying the skin of a white worm around the waist of the parturient woman, and sometimes straps of human skin were used for the same purpose. This custom was also reported from the German countryside as late as the outgoing seventeenth century, and in France the skin of a snake fulfilled the same requirement at that time.[77]

Birthgirdles were obviously used by women of all classes. In the 'Privy Purse Expenses of Elizabeth of York' there is an entry in the year 1502 which says: 'To a monke that brought our Lady gyrdelle to the Quene in reward, vjs. viijd'. The commentator notes on this statement: 'Probably one of the numerous relicks with which the monasteries and abbeys then abounded, and which might have been brought to the Queen for her to put on in labour, as was a common practice for women, in this situation.'[78] As already noted, pagan birthing stones were sometimes sanctified and so, too, were birthgirdles. These Christianized girdles were usually connected with 'our Lady' or the name of some saint who was specially invoked in order to obtain his or her intercession for the relief of the condition. In France the girdle of St Oyan was employed for this purpose, while the Swabians held the girdle of the 'Holy Margareta with the Dragon' in high respect. Part of a ritual in her honour consisted of the symbolical loosening of the girdle along with an invocation. St Margaret also protected women in labour, and in different parts of Germany she stood definitely 'in the relation of the old girdle-loosing goddess'.[79] Comments Dilling:

> It is not difficult to understand the application of the names of Christian saints to the old pagan girdles when we reflect that the Christian priests must have found the virtues of this custom deeply impressed on the minds of their uneducated flock, and, doubtless, being unable to eradicate the superstition, they sanctified the girdles, gave them the names of their own saints, and permitted the people the use of them, thus satisfying their own consciences and the popular demands.[80]

This view is indeed corroborated in a letter of inventory of the sacred relics at the convent of St Austin in Bristow (England), dated 1536, where we find the following statement:

> I send you also our Ladies girdle of Bruton, red silk. Which is a solemn relic, sent to women travailing, which shall not miscarry *in partu*. I send you also Mary Magdalene's girdle: and that is wrapped and covered with white: sent also with great reverence to women travailing. Which girdle Matilda the Empress, founder of Ferley, gave unto them, as saith the holy father of Ferley.[81]

Some birthgirdles were explicitly the length of the image of a saint. A fourteenth-century Austrian codex advises pregnant women to measure a cord as long as the picture of St Sixtus and girdle her belly with it for a safe delivery.[82] Then there were long scrolls with the Magnificat or lengthy prayers written upon them which 'women in travail' wrapped around them.[83] Similarly, some medieval English scrolls were applied measuring about 180 cm because that was supposedly the length of Christ's body.[84] Bühler investigated prayers and invocations written on a number of such Middle English scrolls and found the wording on these to be pretty similar, all promising a quick delivery if the scroll is placed on the woman's womb. The following is a typical example:

> And if a woman trawell of childe, take this crose and lay it one hyr wome and she shalbe hastely be delyuerede with joy with-outen perell, the childe to haue Christendom and the moder purification of Haly Kirk. For Seynt Cerice and Seynt Julite, his moder, desired thes of almighty Gode, the wich He grauntede thame.[85]

Upon the dissolution of the monasteries in England many such Christianized birthgirdles came to light. The monasteries at Leicester alone yielded eleven birthgirdles in different places, all purportedly belonging to 'our Lady'.[86]

In his search for birthgirdles Dilling also found references in collections of folklore customs as well as in some more recent literary texts. For example, he came across the following passage in the 'Battle of Lora', by Ossian, i.e. James Macpherson: 'An hundred girdles shall also be thine, to bind high-bosomed maids. The friends of the births of heroes. The cure of the sons of toil'. The somewhat unreliable author adds in a footnote:

> Sanctified girdles, till very lately (1761), were kept in many families in the North of Scotland; they were bound about women in labour and were supposed to . . . accelerate the birth. They were impressed with several mystical figures; and the ceremony of binding them about the woman's waist was accompanied by words and gestures which showed the custom to have come from the Druids.[87]

Walter Scott also mentions the practice in his *Demonology and Witchcraft*. Speaking of the trial of Bessie Dunlop for witchcraft, he states that 'she lost a lace which Thome Reid (a spectre) gave her . . . which tied round women in childbirth had the power of helping their delivery'.[88]

Dilling, himself a medical doctor from Scotland and curious to find out whether such girdles still existed in his time, corresponded with several Highland medical men upon the matter. Much to his amazement he discovered that none of them had even ever heard of, never mind seen, one. The use of the girdle was obviously surrounded by secrecy. But then, by chance, Dilling himself came eye to eye with such a girdle in Dublin (Ireland) in 1906, and he gives us the following most intriguing story:

> Being called to a confinement, I, and a second student, examined the woman and decided that birth would be unlikely to occur for about an hour and a half. Shortly after my arrival, a neighbour appeared with a leather belt, old and greasy, about 1.1/8 inches broad, and long enough to pass easily round the body; it possessed an iron buckle of ordinary design, and had from my recollection no special marks on it. On demanding its purpose I was informed

that it was something which I would not understand, but that it would make the baby come more quickly. On receiving permission the neighbour fastened it round the woman's chest . . . quite loosely, and . . . without special ceremony.

The child was born within half an hour, and pondering on an explanation for this, Dilling concludes:

I was satisfied then that the girdle did have an effect, although, of course, it must have been purely a psychological one. On inquiry of the person who owned it, no information could be got, but subsequently it was ascertained that it was a belt worn by people who are members of a society of St Augustine, and helps them in times of sickness and childbirth.[89]

Charms

Word charms in which the verbal formula itself constituted the *materia medica* were evidently used throughout early Christian Europe. A charm, from the Latin 'carmen', song, served as another obstetrical aid in which folk practices and Christian elements mixed and mingled. Charms were usually learned by heart and only worked if recited in the exact same sequence. Sometimes they were written down and placed on the body or around the house. As a rule they were accompanied by some kind of ritual, and in England as many as a quarter of the 12 extant Anglo-Saxon metrical charms show some dependence on amulets to achieve the desired magical purpose.[90]

In Italy the fifty-first Psalm was written on paper with ink as far as the words 'O Lord, open thou my lips', then rinsed off, and the water was swallowed by the parturient woman.[91] From Spain one learns of an apparently very successful method whereby three grains of pepper had to be swallowed, one after the other, without touching the teeth. And with each grain one paternoster was to be said by an old woman, but instead of saying 'Deliver us from evil', she would say instead 'Deliver this woman, O Mary, from this difficult labour'.[92] From Germany it is reported that charms were sometimes cut into bread or cake which had to be eaten on an empty stomach three days in a row before any desired effect could be expected.[93] Written in the margin of an old book at the Monastery of Maria Laach, near Cologne, the following advice is noted down:

Excellent for a difficult birth: 'Elizabeth bore him who went before, Holy Mary bore the Saviour. Be thou male or female, come forth, the Saviour calls thee. May all the holy saints intercede for this woman.' Write this and tie it three fingers' [breadth] above the knee. If after this she shall not have given birth promptly, then write on another paper: 'Lazarus, come forth, the Saviour calls thee' and put it on the woman's chest.[94]

A very similar inscription on a Norwegian runestick reads: 'Mary bore Christ, Elizabeth bore John the Baptist. Be absolved in their names. Come out, child, the Lord calls you to the light.' And one formula, 'Mother Mary, lend me your key so I can open my loins', survived the Reformation in Sweden. Pregnant women recited this charm well into the eighteenth century.[95]

A wooden statue of St Brendan which was preserved on Inis Gluaire off the coast of Co. Mayo had the ability to empower anyone to assist women in labour if the following ritual was observed: the statue had to be raised three times in the name of the Three Persons of the Blessed Trinity, and those hands that had raised the statue were then capable of helping the pregnant woman by touching her.[96]

Among Catholics there generally seems to have been a great trust in the efficacy of Christian saints. Different saints were assigned to almost every part of the human body and any affliction it might befall. An early seventeenth-century text tells us that the Irish had 'saints that be good amongst poultry, for chickens when they have the pip, for geese when they doe sit, to have a happy successe in goslings: and, to be short, there is no disease, no sicknesse, no greefe, either amongst men or beasts, that hath not his physician among the Saints'. Regrettably the writer does not name which saint was invoked by pregnant women; instead he uses the ambiguous phrase that women were not 'without their *shee* saints, to whom they doe implore when they would have children, and for a quick deliverance when they be in labour'.[97]

There is a very intriguing childbirth charm in the *Lacnunga*. It requires that the pregnant woman performs three ritual acts, each accompanied by an incantation. The first incantation must be repeated three times as she steps over the grave of a dead man. Translated into modern English the charm goes as follows:

> This is my remedy for hateful slow birth,
> This is my remedy for heavy difficult birth,
> This is my remedy for hateful imperfect birth.

The verbal magic obviously lies in the triple repetition of 'this is my remedy', but the ritual of stepping over a grave cannot be explained easily. It will be returned to later. Weston thinks that the grave marks a boundary between the living and the non-living, this human world and the other: 'the woman bearing a not-yet-living child embodies a similar boundary within herself'.[98]

With the second incantation a complementary act completes her passage from potential to actual life. This time she steps over a living man, saying,

> Up I go, step over you
> with a living child, not a dead one,
> with a full-born one, not a doomed one.[99]

The third and final part of this charm places the woman within her Christian community. Knowing that her child lives she is to go to church, stand before the altar and say: 'To Christ, I have declared, this child announced.'[100]

In other charms the actual wording does not always make sense. Kruse suspects that this might be due to the censoring of the medieval scribes who, as she could prove, certainly made deletions or changes to some of the texts.[101] At times, however, one wonders whether the unintelligibility was not intended. Forbes, somewhat disrespectfully talking about 'gibberish', found the following childbirth charm in a fourteenth-century British manuscript: 'Boro berto briore + Vulnera quinque dei sint medicina mei + Tahebal ++ ghether +++ guthman +++++ Purld cramper +.' He quotes from three other British 'charmes for travailing of childe' dating from the fourteenth or fifteenth century, which also consist of a mixture of jumbled Latin, recognizable English words and seemingly meaningless utterances. In two cases the scribe had helpfully added the advice that the charm should be said three times, or better still, written down and bound to the right knee.[102] As an alternative interpretation one could of course read the 'gibberish' as examples of 'divine readings' which priests concocted to replace pagan incantations.

Forbes writes that the practice of using charms in the British Isles continued until the nineteenth century despite attempts of the Church to stamp it out.[103] He produces evidence to the effect that in the 1840s Irish women on the delivery bed still relied on the help of charms inscribed on vellum and tied on to the abdomen. This is not surprising considering that due to widespread illiteracy among the peasantry, not just in Ireland but all over Europe, obstetrical knowledge and methods of treatment would not have advanced rapidly since medieval times.

Apart from that, early Irish writing reveals a deep fear of procreation, pregnancy and childbirth. Whenever they are referred to, supernatural connotations, otherworldly elements and magic abound.[104] Davies, who scanned Irish texts for medical lore, points out that in Ireland there does not seem to have been an interest in medicine, nor even any popular interest in herbal lore.[105] All the indications are that in Irish society sickness itself – and by extension also childbirth – was ritualized. Healing was not perceived as being dependent on medicine, for it was seen as essentially irrational. So if help or a cure was needed, it was more likely to be sought through magic than through any medical treatment. And although old Irish charms indicate awareness of various ailments the remedy is always the same: put butter round a splinter or apply an all-purpose ointment and say the charm. Thus Davies concludes: 'And it was not that there was no healing tradition but rather that it was overwhelmingly magical and not at all medicinal'.[106]

Midwives

The earliest descriptions of European midwives as far as I can see are found in the *Poetic Edda*. Here we learn in 'The Plaint of Oddrun' that a woman, 'by labour o'ercome', could not give birth to her children before Oddrun came to her help. 'Stern spells she spake, strong spells she spake, for womb-bound woman witchcraft mighty', to invoke the goddesses Frigg and Freya. And in 'The Lay of Sigrdrifa' midwives are advised to 'learn help runes eke, if help though wilt a woman to bring forth her babe: on thy palms wear them and grasp her wrists, and ask the disir's aid'.[107] Apart from Frigg, Freya and the 'diser', midwives could also try to obtain the help of the norns (or Fates): they all assisted parturient women and possessed identical faculties where childbirth was concerned.[108]

Professional midwives who did not (entirely) rely on divine intervention were known in ancient Greece and Rome, and they are also referred to in the Bible.[109] Obstetrical lore did, however, suffer disruption during the Middle Ages. It was only from the seventeenth century that the training and supervision of midwives began to be re-established in Europe, but midwifery did not become a regulated profession until the eighteenth century.

In medieval rural Europe neighbouring women or female relatives were usually called upon to play the part of the midwife. Sometimes village women were chosen to be midwives chiefly because they themselves had successfully borne several children, and quite often the role of midwife was passed on from mother to daughter within a single family. With little or no formal instruction or obstetrical knowledge the craft which she brought to the delivery usually amounted to no more than a blend of hearsay, practical experience and magico-medical customs.[110]

Upon arrival at the pregnant woman's house one of the first tasks the midwife carried out was to prepare the lying-in chamber by physically and symbolically enclosing it. Doors, windows, even keyholes were shut up to exclude air and daylight, and all apertures remained tightly closed throughout the birth, thus protecting the parturient woman and her newborn child from both cold draughts and evil spirits. Candles were lit, and a special drink, the *caudle*, was brewed, which the mother drank throughout the delivery to keep up her strength. Another traditional feature was that neighbouring women would prepare a 'childbed-porridge' for the pregnant woman. This special dish was named after divine helpers at birth and called 'Sarraka-porridge' by the Lapps and 'norn-porridge' among many Nordic peoples.

In rural Ireland, Britain, France, Italy, Germany and all the Nordic countries straw played an important role. The lying-in woman was not allowed to lie in bed, but a straw bed was prepared for her on the floor. In Ireland this was called 'leaba thalúna', i.e. ground or earth bed.[111] In Nordland 'strawmother' is used for midwife, and in England 'the lady in the straw' signifies a woman in labour. Apparently in England and in Italy to give birth was simply called 'to be in the straw'.[112] Brand discovered a very interesting 'old' document entitled *The Child-bearer's Cabinet* describing how such a bed ought to be furnished:

> A large Boulster, made of linen Cloth, must be stuffed with straw, and be spread on the ground, that her upper part may lye higher than her lower. On this the woman may lye, so that she may seem to lean and bow rather than to lye, drawing up her feet unto her that she may receive no hurt.[113]

Such or similar preparations for *confinement* took place all over Europe and, in Wilson's view, amounted to the setting up of a ceremony. The lying-in chamber became a consecrated place, demarcated from the outside world and ritually distinguished from its ordinary functions as a mere room.[114] Or as Gélis put it, the room became a womb, 'kept free for a while from the evil designs of men and malevolent spirits'.[115] If there was not enough living space in the house the stable was chosen instead, offering both warmth and privacy to give birth.

The midwife was in charge of the birth. She was entrusted with the right to touch the genital parts of the mother, and she determined the course of action. She would decide whether to leave the birth to nature, or to use force, when to intervene in the birth process and what, if any, remedies or charms to use in order to facilitate the birth. She would also advise what position for delivery the woman should adopt. Unlike today where a horizontal position is almost universally practised, it was common in medieval times and, judging by sculptures and artefacts also in prehistory and early history, to bear one's child standing, squatting, sitting (semi-reclining) or kneeling.[116] The Bible in Exodus, too, mentions that women gave birth in either the squatting or sitting positions, as they did in Egypt.[117] While there is agreement that these four 'vertical' positions were those naturally adopted in earlier times by most women in labour – because they do help the expulsion – opinions differ only as to which of the positions, standing or squatting, predominated.[118]

Because the midwife knew from experience that unforeseen complications could arise at any moment during childbirth she would be strongly tempted to take a hand early on: 'the ever-present fear of an accident urged her to hasten the labour'.[119] Driven by the desire to get parturition over with as quickly as possible, her first action was to undo all knots, fastenings, girdles or buckles of the mother's clothing.

She would then proceed to smear her own fingers, hands and forearms as well as the private parts of the woman in labour with a lubricant, and immediately start to work on the vulva: she would pull, pat, stretch, widen and generally 'torment' the birth passage in order to help the baby to glide out of its mother's womb. The unguents applied for this purpose varied according to local custom and availability. Most frequently mentioned are fresh butter, vegetable oils, animal fats (hog's grease and lard) and egg whites.[120] To extend and stretch the passage midwives also prepared fumigations, channelling the vapours of herbs into the woman's womb. Others would make the woman sit over a hot cauldron because it was thought that the warmth would soften the rump and make it more yielding.[121] Yet another means was to administer a sneezing-powder made of hellebore (*Veratrum album* L.), which apparently also helped to widen the birth passage.[122]

The chief aim of all these measures was to stretch open the vulva as widely as possible. But pregnant women did not wait for the midwife to dilate their private parts – they had their own methods to work on this task themselves weeks ahead of confinement. After having abstained from sexual intercourse during the first six months after conception, women would lie with their husbands during the last months of pregnancy because this supposedly 'opens the passage, and facilitates the birth'. This was further enhanced by using 'syrups and other opening things' which assisted the operation.[123] Women themselves would start rubbing their abdomen and private parts with grease before the onset of labour. Of course such very private matters are notoriously difficult to trace, and it is therefore impossible to guess how widespread such practices were. But Gélis asserts that even eighteenth-century obstetricians still believed in the benefit of such a preparation for labour, and quotes one source as stating:

> The woman will be advised, seven or eight days before the birth, to rub her private parts with fresh butter, which will make the passage easier and more slippery; young women who have no previous child will benefit from this method. These rubbings are even more necessary in women of an advanced age who are in their first pregnancy.[124]

Midwives used to administer various herbal concoctions not only to hasten birth pangs, but also to purge stomach and bowels from contents which were regarded as obstacles to an easy birth. A full stomach and a lazy bowel made women uncomfortable and hesitant to push. Thus purgatives and vomitives were in abundant use everywhere. There are cases where midwives also tried to provoke nausea by suggesting revolting things to eat or drink, the very sight and smell of which would make the stomach heave.[125]

Few details survive about other methods and customs that were practised by the midwives. Some of their activities are alluded to in ecclesiastical and secular laws which attempted to regulate the profession in post-medieval times. In sixteenth-century England an act was passed which permitted representatives of the church to grant licenses to midwives. In 1555 bishop Bonner of London prescribed: 'A Mydwyfe (of the diocese and jurisdiction of London) shal not use or exercise any Witchcraft, Charmes, Sorcerye, Invocations, or Praiers, other then suche as be allowable and may stand with the Lawes and Ordinances of the Catholike Churche.'[126] Midwives were then required to take an oath of office before they could be licensed, and in 1584 such an oath taken at the direction of the Bishop of Chester similarly specified that they not use 'any witchcraft, charms, relics or invocation to any Saint in the time of travail'.[127] The last reference is of great interest here because it proves that from then on the Church would no longer tolerate a practice which it had condoned for quite some time, namely the invocation of Christian saints to assist women in labour.

English bishops would regularly inspect the churches in their diocese, during which they asked the clergy certain questions. These are contained in the 'Articles of Visitation', drawn up in the mid-sixteenth century. Article I asks whether any woman is acting as a midwife who has not been admitted to office by the bishop. Article II enquires whether authorized midwives are 'catholic and faithful'. Article III questions if midwives use any witchcraft, charms, sorcery or invocations, and Article VI asks if 'there be any other disorder or evil behaviour' among the midwives, their assistants or their patients.[128]

The whole thrust of the clerical interrogation does not seem to have changed over the centuries. The following questionnaire was drawn up in 1599: 'whether you knowe anye that doo use Charmes, Sorcery, Enchauntementes, Invocations, Circles, Witchecraftes, Southsayinge, or any lyke Craftes or Imaginacions invented by the Devyl, and specially in the tyme of Women's travalye'.[129] Another almost identical catalogue of vague undesirable practices is contained in a *Book of Oaths* issued in the mid-seventeenth century, where the midwife has to swear that, among other restrictions, she will not 'in any wise use or exercise any manner of Witchcraft, Charme; or Sorcery, Invocation, or other Prayers than may stand with Gods Laws and the Kings', nor 'give any counsel, or minister any Herbe, Medicine, or Potion, or any other thing, to any Woman being with Childe whereby she should destroy or cast out that she goeth withal before her time'.[130]

The striking feature of these and later documents pertaining to midwifery is that the professional competence of the midwife is not referred to at all. The most important criterion of her profession was that the midwife obeyed the laws of the Church and refrained from practices whose symbolic character smacked of paganism. We can find a description of the 'ideal' candidate in *Aristotle's Masterpiece*:

> A Midwife ought to be of a middle age, neither too old nor too young, and of a good habit or body, neither subject to diseases, fears, or sudden frights. . . . She ought to be sober and affable, not subject to passion, but bountiful and compassionate, and her temper cheerful and pleasant, that she may better comfort her patients in their sorrow. . . . But above all she ought to be qualified with the fear of God, which is the principal thing in every state and condition, and will furnish her on all occasions both with knowledge and discretions.[131]

On the continent, too, after the Council of Trent (1545–63) the church began to exert a stricter control over midwives. It kept a close and incessant check on their behaviour at work, pressurizing them into learning the formula for baptism *in extremis* and swearing oaths of loyalty to the church.[132] It is obvious that the church was deeply concerned about the practice of midwifery and thus made determined efforts to exercise authority over the profession. Even down to the end of the eighteenth century, phrases like 'Women helping one another' or 'mutual assistance' constantly recur as complaints in the writings of priests and administrators reporting on childbirth in rural France.[133]

Given that in earlier times the whole occasion of childbirth was out of men's and the Church's reach and control, and that it took place in some secrecy involving the use of quasi-magical rituals, it is small wonder that the midwife became one of the favourite targets of inquisitors during the witch-hunts instigated by Church and state, whose reign of terror acquired a terrible momentum towards the end of the Middle Ages.[134]

Sheelas and folk religion

The overwhelming impression one gets from the enquiry into medieval motherhood is that women all over Europe sought the assistance of magical means in their hour of need, and that they continued to do so well into modern times. The question now to be addressed is how the Sheela-na-gig fits into all of this, and what role she might have played in the wider pattern of rural life and folk religion.

Generally folk deities, sometimes referred to as guardian or domestic spirits (in German 'Hausgottheiten' or 'Schutzgeister'), or *Spiritus familiares*, are known all over the world as potent magic forces. They operate under the principle of magic analogy within a network of correspondences already outlined. Their domain tends to be practical rather than 'spiritual', in that they deal with more personal and immediate burdens, hazards and crises, and they preside only over certain departments of life in which they have clearly determined functions. Knowledge of their special power is transmitted orally and forms part of the folk tradition. Oral tradition supplies the stories of their wonder-working capabilities and also prescribes the ritual. People make their own images or statuettes of these proven spirits, and their invocation is usually done in conjunction with an utterance or magic formula. This type of worship is less visible and more difficult to trace because it is paid by individuals in their homes or in secret meeting places. Devotion to such spirits does not necessarily undermine the place of greater, more powerful gods or the ultimate rulers of the universe. Only these are approached in a more public and formalized context.[135] In Europe the multifarious pagan gods and goddesses were gradually replaced by the one Christian God, but the folk deities continued to co-exist with Christianity for a very long period and could only to an extent be replaced by Christian saints who were countering their magic with miracle.

Folk deities assisting at birth

Belonging as they did to the scantily researched realm of medieval country women, and with a view to the secrecy surrounding childbirth, it is hardly surprising to learn that there are no written accounts of Sheelas in action. Fortunately, however, there are plenty of clues to go on which help us to understand how they would have worked.

The most obvious clue is the seemingly grotesque-looking lower abdomen of the sculpture. The cavernous oval-shaped vulva, pointed to or held open by her hands, often shown as swollen or sagging, mostly pointing downwards, and in some cases so big as to reach the ground, finds a perfect explanation: it expresses the physical state pregnant women craved and worked for. It shows the desirable degree of dilation of the cervix immediately before, during or after childbirth. Touching a vulva so indicative of parturition surely must have filled pregnant women with the hope and energy necessary to push on with their own business. Better still if they knew the right magic formula to accompany the action. It is small wonder then to read that the genital area of those Sheelas who were placed within reach was found to have been 'rubbed'.[136] Birthing stones may also have been placed inside the genitalia. This appears to be the case with the Sheela at Church Stretton (123), whose pudenda is filled in with a pebble. The enormous pudenda of the Oaksey Sheela (139) is often said to include the clitoris, but on close inspection it transpires that this is actually a cavity – big enough for a finger or a stone.

As pointed out in the first chapter, the birth passage is usually not the only accentuated cavity. Many Sheelas have other conspicuous touch-holes mainly defining navel and anus. Women, it would appear, desired to have the bowels emptied and cleansed of all obstructions. Thus the depiction of an open anus makes sense. It is more difficult to interpret why any emphasis should be placed on the navel. Two possible explanations spring to mind. The navel was simply seen as a knot that had to be untied. Or it may have had a deeper significance, in that it represented the umbilical cord which connects mother and child, and was symbolically opened just like the birthgirdle which itself might have stood for the navel-string. Perhaps these holes were touched, perhaps they were lubricated with the same fat or grease that was used for the vagina, or perhaps they were filled with birthing stones which were ritually removed.

A few Sheelas have additional holes drilled into their head or body, the purpose of which is unknown, but it stands to reason that they were connected with some ritual. The most enigmatic is the Seir Keiran Sheela (79) because, apart from a whole ring of holes around her genital area, there are holes drilled into the top of her head and one through her throat. An even bigger hole is cut right across the throat of the Kilmokea figure (55), while Knockarley (60) shows a small hole in the top of her head and another one below the vulva. Tiny holes are also placed in the head and body of the Tullaroan Sheela (89). Stanton St Quintin (147) has two large holes drilled into the genital area and two smaller ones into the main body. Another rather interesting example is the Rosnaree Sheela (76), whose elongated cavity in the crown of the head suggests the use of libations. It is actually very reminiscent of the hollow carved into the top of the head between the two faces of the well known 'Janus figure' on Boa Island (Lough Erne), a figure which some researchers regard as a Sheela prototype.

A further morphological Sheela feature which makes a lot of sense in the light of the present argument is the posture. Whether standing, squatting, kneeling or seated, Sheelas are portrayed in the 'vertical' birth-giving pose. They are, in other words, invariably shown in one of the four universally applied positions for delivery in medieval times and, just as in real life, the first two of these are the most frequently adopted. The often conspicuously outward-turned feet also support this interpretation because parturient women adopting the vertical posture would instinctively turn their feet outwards.[137]

Then there are the objects some Sheelas are depicted with. What certainly look like birthgirdles are the band-like features between ribs and hips worn by the Sheelas from Cullahill (38), Moate (67) and Tracton (88), with Knockarley (60), who is wearing a thick band around her neck, and the Kilmokea (55) figure, showing a horizontal line across the two thighs, being further possible cases. The circular objects held by the Sheelas from Kiltinane Castle (58), Lavey (61), Lixnaw (63), Copgrove[138] (125) and Tugford (150) may also represent girdles. Girdles in the shape of scrolls are depicted on the Seir Kieran (79) and Romsey 1 (142) Sheelas. In the case of the former the rolled up scroll can be seen from the side, and in the case of the latter the open scroll seems to be the full length of the figure. An open girdle may be indicated in Clomantagh (30) and Freshford (48) where some kind of band is depicted running from the left side of the head down to the upper arm. In Stanton St Quintin (147) the two hands held close to the genital area seem to have just opened a girdle which falls to the ground.

The slender unidentified objects in the hands of several Sheelas may very well be birthing stones, but in the absence of any definite indication this remains, admittedly, mere speculation. The most conspicuous of these are the objects raised by the Sheelas from Aghadoe (2), Kiltinane Castle (58), Romsey 1 (142) and Egremont (157). Two figures wear necklaces possibly holding birthing stones. While only traces of the necklace remain in Clonoulty (36), it is clearly visible in Drogheda (41), and attached to it is a pendant of inverted cone shape.

Generally Sheelas are presented with their vulva in the specific physiological state before, during or after giving birth. What looks like a protruding amniotic sac is depicted on the Sheelas of Ballinderry (8), Ballyportry (13), Bunratty (18), Killinaboy (54), Kilmokea (55), Tracton (88), Fiddington (132) and Tugford (152), and most dramatically on the one from Taghboy (83). A groove or channel is cut vertically downwards below the pudenda in Caherelly (20) and horizontally beside it in Rathcline (71). In other cases there is an 'unexplained', roughly egg-shaped, object lying between the two open legs of the Sheela, which may represent a newborn infant, but it may also, of course, symbolize a birthing stone. These are the figures from Behy (15), Cloghan (29), Clomantagh (30), Clonmacnoise 2 (34), Dunaman (42), Redwood (73) and Romsey 1 (142). In the case of Romsey 2 (143), however, there is not the shadow of a doubt about what is depicted – the squatting female is giving birth. Hanging between her open thighs is the head of her baby, whose little face shows two eyes, a nose and a mouth.

The childbirth connection leaps to the eye in a few churches where there is a connection between the Sheela and the baptismal font. The Ampney St Peter Sheela (113) in Gloucestershire, though not on the baptismal font itself, is placed on the wall of the nave directly overlooking it.

The only extant example in the British Isles where the figure is actually sitting on the font itself is the Whitechapel Sheela at Cleckheaton (124), whose fate is quite probably indicative of other examples. Unlike structural elements like quoins, lintels or capitals on which Sheelas are predominantly placed, a baptismal font with an offensive figure can easily and untraceably be removed and replaced. There are obvious signs that attempts were made to destroy this particular old font, which was cut in half and buried, but fortunately, after an iniquitous temporary service as a garden ornament, it was returned to the church, put together again, and now stands on a new pedestal as testimony of an older tradition.[139] Forlong makes reference to a Sheela on an 'old

English font', but regrettably he omits the name of the church.[140] While he may have had Cleckheaton in mind it is equally possible that reference was made to an entirely different church.

Referring to Irish churches in the 1880s, Wakeman noted that 'in one or two instances . . . upon otherwise exquisitely designed baptismal fonts' a Sheela-na-gig is found. As a striking example he draws attention to the font taken from the ruins of the old church of Kilcarne (Co. Meath), and now preserved in the chapel at Johnstown.[141] Following up on this information, Edith Guest, who found the font obscured on one side, declared herself unable to confirm such a figure,[142] while Andersen 'strictly' rejects any notion of a Sheela because all he could make out looked like an erotic encounter between various figures.[143] What he clearly overlooked is the fact that the original pedestal of this font had been replaced with a new stand before it was returned to the church. It is difficult to imagine that Wakeman, being such an accurate observer and meticulous draughtsman, should have mistaken a Sheela for some other figure, particularly when in this very context he draws attention to other well known Sheelas elsewhere. The more likely explanation to my mind would be that the Sheela Wakeman saw was sitting on the pedestal, which was later replaced with a plain non-offensive concrete specimen.

Two other Sheelas carved on baptismal fonts do not belong to the British Isles. They can be seen in Danish churches. One of these, found at Vester Egede, near Naestved, shows an upside down Sheela who has just given birth.[144] The other example is a squatting Sheela about to give birth in the church at Vendsyssel.[145]

There may not be, and not even expected to be, any written accounts of Sheelas in use, but there is ample material from observers of the Baltic countries as well as from Central and Eastern Europe, and the entire extensive Northern Eurasian continent originating from the beginning of the seventeenth to the middle of the twentieth century, which proves beyond doubt the existence of many folk deities of birth. At first glance it may seem a little far-fetched to include evidence from areas that far away. However, the aggregation of studies and accounts from peoples living in these areas is an invaluable source of information which will allow some insight into the deeper layers of birth rituals. Furthermore, a surprisingly large number of features can be found to be common to customs in all these regions.[146] Finally, Séamas O Catháin in his extensive study of *The Festival of Brigit* has demonstrated that there were similar if not altogether identical traditional customs among the inhabitants of the British Isles, Scandinavia and various other circumpolar peoples, particularly the Sámi and the Finns. The overwhelming conformity with regard to various cultural manifestations in fact prompted him to call for a new approach to Irish folklore, literature and archaeology based on a Nordic perspective.[147]

When ethnographers of the past centuries describe folk traditions in Northern and Eastern Europe they always differentiate between two polar cult-places in the homes: that of the men and that of the women at opposite ends of the room, tent or house. Different deities were connected with the two sides indicating that a certain antagonism existed between the male and female gods. An expression of this can be seen in many taboo prohibitions which barred the representatives of one sex from trespassing on the cult-place of the other. Generally, deities of birth were considered extremely 'unclean' and therefore had to be kept as far from the deities of men as possible. Both groups of spirits were associated with different functions.

The main domain of the female deities was direct help in childbed, but interestingly they were everywhere also connected with fertility, the health of children and young domestic animals.[148] The door area was the traditional place for their cult. This is where they received libations and other sacrifices. But this area was also thought to be the critical border where all the malignant spirits bent on entering the house had to be combated, and that would seem to indicate that the deities of birth had some genetic tie with the demons of illness who were sacrificed to, not in worship but in fear.[149]

It was customary for people to make their own images of the deities of birth. Unfortunately, though often referred to there is not a lot of detailed description to be culled from the reports, but from what I can gather the idols were no Sheela-na-gig lookalikes. All we find out about them is that they were frequently small stuffed rag dolls or statuettes made of wood or clay and occasionally drawings on a piece of cloth. As a rule these idols were roughly shaped like human beings.[150] The smallest of these, described as a figurine the size of a thumb, was cut from the dried supple twigs of the birch tree, and when finished, it was adorned with a glass pearl necklace and a band tied around the waist. Not much is known about the rituals involving these little idols either. We learn that some were hugged and kissed, and some were ceremoniously fed.[151] Women made these figures themselves or inherited them from their mothers. One researcher mentions that traditionally it befitted the old women to fashion the idols.[152] Often they came in specially made containers and were to be taken out only when needed. In many traditions mothers put them up over the beds of their young daughters, a custom which demonstrates that over and above the assistance at birth these idols were associated with fertility. And this aspect is further emphasized by the fact that the figures were procured by women who were childless.[153]

The only idol which shows no human form but simply consists of a decorated three-pronged branch or stick is known as 'tul'gu-tös'.[154] In this connection it may also be noted that in several parts of Europe woodcutting used to form part of childbirth rites, and seems to have worked under the principle of magic analogy. Furthermore, 'Sar-akka', one of the Lapp deities of birth, is known as the 'dividing woman', who separates the child from its mother at birth. Her name is derived from the verb to cleave, and a synonym of her name denotes 'a piece of wood split at one end into two parts'. Mention is also made of sticks with a cloven end which belonged to this deity's ritual porridge, referred to earlier.[155]

Of the many birth customs which Ränk describes, I will have to restrict myself to picking one typical scenario. The focus is on the Yakuts, a semi-nomadic people in Siberia whose southern ancestry points to the Turkish tribes of the steppe. They worshipped Ajysyt, a household spirit who was believed personally to assist the birth by standing at the head of the lying-in woman. If she failed to turn up both mother and child would die.

As in most other areas under investigation pregnant Yakut women were hermetically closed off from the rest of the family and attended to only by other women. Sometimes special tents were erected for them or the childbed was placed at the door, which men were forbidden to use. Traditionally pregnant women made a pledge to sacrifice to Ajysyt an animal which was killed during childbirth. Certain parts of the animal were cooked and served to the deity on a table close by the childbed. Other ritual food was butter in three dishes, one for the midwife, one for the other female helpers and one for Ajysyt. During labour the midwife would cast butter on the hearth, saying: 'We thank you, Ajysyt, for what you have given and ask for it even in future.'

The deity was thought to stay in the birth house for three days, and during all this time the mother had to lie in her bed of straw on the floor at the same place where she had given birth, and the birth refuse, too, had to remain where it had fallen under parturition. When the three days had passed, the midwife would pick up the straw on which the lying-in woman had lain and deposit this together with the birth refuse on the top of a tall tree. Ajysyt was believed to take her leave with this ceremony, and only then were men allowed back into the house.[156] From O Catháin we learn, incidentally, that according to an Irish tradition, the afterbirth of a cow was also placed in a tree because it was thought that burying it might cause the calf to die.[157]

Ränk found many parallels of Ajysyt's midwifely functions and the idea that the lives of mother and child depended on the presence of the birth deity among the cults of various other peoples. Indeed, quite a few of the rituals described – the preparation of the lying-in chamber, the straw, the closed circle of women, the butter, the magical three days and three dishes – are distinctly reminiscent of the practices we learned about in medieval and early modern Western Europe.

The continuous cycle of life and death

So far the main consideration has centred on the lower half of the Sheela and its aspects of fertility and childbirth. But now the upper half of the figure, which stands in such sharp contrast to it, must come into focus. Instead of the plump breasts one would expect in connection with motherhood, Sheelas, startlingly, either have no breasts at all or are depicted as the flat and drooping breasts of old women. The impression of emaciation or death is, as pointed out in Chapter 1, further underlined by a skeletal rib-case, a skull-like head, hollow eyes, baldness and in some cases striations carved across head and body.

Beside these deathly morphological features the sepulchral context of the figure also has to be borne in mind. The country churches in Britain and Ireland which boast Sheelas are invariably surrounded by a graveyard. Wherever the figure is placed on the outside walls of the church – and the majority are – the Sheela-na-gig inevitably overlooks a burial ground. In the case of Church Stretton (123) this position is further accentuated by the fact that she is inserted above a door known as 'the corpse door', as it was used only for bringing in the dead.[158] Many Sheelas were found 'all too decently'[159] buried in graveyards and only came to light during clearance operations. Furthermore, during the early days of their scholarly discovery, Clibborn voiced the opinion that several Sheelas had been used as gravestones (see p. 20). One such more recently discovered example certainly appears to be Kilmokea (55), where an inscription on the reverse side reads: MB [initials of person] d [died] 12 March 1703 a [aged] 72. And finally there is the amazing case of Kildare (52), where a Sheela is carved on the tombstone of a bishop.

It would seem that in ancient times life and death were regarded as interrelated, as counterpart functions. Just as in the natural world around them, human existence was obviously seen as cyclic: a continuous cycle in which all things were interlinked, in which life ended in death, but death did not mean extinction because new life sprang from it. In literature and art the expression of this interconnectedness is a very old phenomenon. It can be found in many myths where gods emerge from the world of the dead every spring to bring new life to nature, or where earth mothers appear as givers and takers of life: a concept most dramatically exemplified in the Hindu goddess Kali who devours her own children. Or, as already pointed out, we see the idea embodied in the myths of Celtic goddesses in whom the powers of creativity and destruction merge into one. Ancient sculptures from all over the world portray the female as both huntress and nurturer,[160] including pre-Indo-European and Indo-European goddesses who as earth mothers and mothers of the dead protect women in childbirth and also hold the key to the grave.[161]

There seems to be a similar notion behind many old European customs and traditions surrounding birth and death. For instance, almost everywhere it appears to have been customary first of all to place newborn babies on the bare ground, and to bury the dead in the foetal position, surrounded by their food vessels, tools and ornaments, so that they might awaken to a new life.[162] In assisting women at childbirth and also attending to the laying out of corpses, midwives presided at both births and deaths.[163] Across the northern part of Europe, according to Hutton, there was a tradition of dances which involved the stylized killing and resurrection of one of the participants, embodying 'a very widespread prehistoric concern with the theme of death and rebirth and its enactment in ritual'.[164] Even Christianity presents the cyclical image in the 'earth to earth, ashes to ashes, dust to dust' prayer at internments.

Well attested throughout large parts of medieval Europe are noisy funerary dances ('Bestattungstänze') which took place in graveyards and were accompanied by singing, drinking and general merrymaking that often took the form of lovemaking.[165] In Ireland one of the principal rituals at wakes was the by all accounts lewd ceremony (see p. 32), during which several young folk were married by a mock priest. Various explanations for such seeming debauchery have been advanced, with some interpreting the custom as symbolizing the dying year and reviving spring,[166] while others see in it the survival of early fertility rituals where death offered an incitement to reproduction,[167] and according to yet another opinion it epitomized the hope of rebirth beyond the tomb.[168]

But there is a deeper, quite sinister aspect to this phenomenon. For our pre-Christian forebears there seems to have been no real boundary between this life and the next. Whereas Christianity taught them to pray *for* the souls, our ancestors prayed *to* them because they believed that the dead continued to take part in life, and, worse still, that they posed a threat to the living. By trying to ingratiate themselves with the dead the living hoped to be spared any trouble from them.

Folklore studies illustrate this anxious concern. During wakes when the corpse lay in the open coffin or was propped up on a chair the mourners would eagerly address it. In Norway old women would do the talking, saying things like: 'Now you will take this last meal in our house.'[169] In the Baltic countries relatives and neighbours would gather around the deceased, to whom, if it was a man, everybody would raise a glass of beer and hail him as 'our dear friend'. They would loudly lament his death and ask why he had died when, what with all his nice relatives, wife, neighbours, cattle etc., he had it so good.

The exact same question would be put to Irish corpses who were often supplied with clay pipes when surrounded by their smoking friends.[170] According to one (hostile) observer in the 1750s, the 'lower sort of Irish, in the most uncivilized parts of Ireland', reproach the dead body with having died, notwithstanding that he had 'an excellent wife, a Milch Cow, seven fine Children, and a competency of Potatoes'.[171] Brand, to whom we owe this report, also had it on good authority that in the higher echelons of Irish society it was customary to have a bard for the purpose of writing an elegy on the deceased, enumerating his virtues, genealogy, wealth and other assets, the burden being: 'Oh! Why did he die'.[172] Thanks to this insight I now have a somewhat different appreciation of Thomas Davis's *Lament for the Death of Eoghan Ruadh O'Neill*. Ignorant of this tradition, I had always considered it to be a somewhat pathetic question to ask a poor victim of Cromwell's treacherous means:

> We thought you would not die – we were sure you would not go, And leave us in our utmost need to Cromwell's cruel blow – Sheep without a shepherd, when the snow shuts out the sky – Oh! Why did you leave us, Owen, Why did you die?[173]

It was also customary in Norway, Bohemia, Prussia, Denmark, Sweden and England to place a large container of beer on the lid of the coffin of a dead man. The drink was shared out among those present as if it were a gift from the deceased. Afterwards a close friend or relative would speak on behalf of the corpse, thanking everybody in the name of the dead person, for the good wake they had given him.[174] This was not very different, incidentally, from funerary customs reported from the higher echelons of society, the main difference being that, instead of beer, wine was served. One such example is a lord's burial at Shrewsbury (England) in the early part of Charles II's reign:

> The Relations and Friends being assembled in the house of the defunct, the Minister . . . made a Funeral Oration, representing the great actions of the deceased, his virtues, his qualities, his title of Nobility, and those of the whole Family, &c. It is to be remarked that during the Oration, there stood upon the Coffin a large Pot of Wine, out of which every one drank to the health of the deceased.[175]

To assist the dead on their long journey, food, drink, clothes, knives, tools, even money were often put inside the coffin. From Latvia it is reported that men were buried with a glass of beer whereas women were thought to be better off with needles and thread for their journey.[176] Slain men were often buried with an ointment in their hand which was obviously thought to heal the wounds that caused their death.[177] There is plenty of evidence that in Ireland the greatest care was taken to supply the deceased with good shoes. Shoes, an unthinkable luxury among the living peasantry, were believed almost indispensable after death, when it was supposed, writes Croker, 'much walking has to be performed, probably through rough roads and inclement weather'.[178] Evans knows of one case where even two pairs of shoes were put in the coffin: 'a strong one for bad weather, a light pair for ordinary wear'.[179] Sometimes friends of the deceased availed of the opportunity by requesting him to pass on greetings to some dead relative.[180]

Ritual respect did not cease with a person's funeral. Long after interment, on certain days of the week as well as on death anniversaries, relatives commemorated the dead by putting out food and drink for them, which was placed either on the kitchen table or beside the grave. Evans found traces of this tradition on Achill Island in the middle of the twentieth century when people were still leaving plates on the graves which formerly would have held food.[181] Equally tenacious proved a custom in some parts of Prussia where people left out a chair and a towel for the deceased. Primarily this was done to assure that the dead could watch the funerary festivities in some comfort, but then both items were replaced on certain days after the death had occurred, in some areas even weeks after the funeral.[182] In many parts of the Baltic countries the souls of the dead were annually washed and cleaned on All Souls' Day, for which liquid and a towel were required.[183]

From as late as the seventeenth and eighteenth centuries, the clergy reported that in Latvia during the month of October people held a 'convivium' for their dead ancestors. The best food and drink was prepared for that occasion and laid out on the floor of the best room in the house, which was swept clean and where a fire was kept going all night. The whole family would gather there and call out the names of all their dead relatives, inviting each of them to partake in the meal. When the head of the family declared the meal to be over, he would send the souls on their way. He would ask them to go back to where they had come from, but plead with them to stick to the roads and abstain from trampling all over the newly sown corn. If the corn harvest turned out to be bad in the following year this was a sure sign that the souls were not happy with the meal they had been given.[184]

A very similar procedure took place in Ireland on All Souls' Eve. We have the following account from Co. Tyrone in 1930:

> All Souls Eve is sacred to the memory of the departed. After the floor has been swept and a good fire put down on the hearth, the family retires early, leaving the door unlatched and a bowl of spring water on the table, so that any relative who had died may find a place prepared for him at his own fireside. On that one night in the year the souls of the dead are loosed and have liberty to visit their former homes.[185]

In parts of Co. Limerick a table was laid with a place for each of the dead kinsfolk, and Danaher confirms that in those days people still believed that the souls of the dead could come to the aid of the living.[186] Generally it was thought unlucky not to make preparations for the return of the dead, such as leaving the door open, setting seats around the fire and putting out tobacco and food.[187]

The dead were clearly thought to continue in some kind of human form, and though in some cases they may have been believed to lend a helping hand, mostly they were feared. According to some reports, before a body was lowered down in Lithuania, the coffin would be opened for a last time and the bereaved would beg the deceased to stay away and not to assail them. And to lend point to their plea they would throw money, bread and beer into the coffin.[188] McPherson reports that in some parts of Scotland all the chairs in the room from which the corpse had been taken were turned upside down in order to deceive the departed in case he should return. With the chairs overturned he would not recognize the place. Another trick to confuse the corpse was to make detours with the coffin rather than head straight for the grave. McPherson had learned of a similar practice among modern Egyptians of turning the corpse round and round to make it giddy, so that it might not know where it was going.[189]

Although the dead were not everywhere welcome to return home, for years to come the bereaved would eagerly demonstrate their undiminished respect for them at the burial place. To appease and nourish their souls they would not only offer food and drink, but also continue to sing the praises of the deceased. According to one report in Ireland they used to kneel on the grave repeating former kindnesses that had passed between them. Having thus reassured the soul of the bond that still existed between them, they would proceed to ask for favours. They complained about neighbours or other villagers who had done them wrong, abused or injured them, and begged the soul to see them righted. Afterwards they would go home 'satisfied as having given an account to one that in time may redress their injuries, revenge or relieve them'.[190] These are not only signs of a belief in the continuance of life after death, but also indications that folk belief was bound up with a perpetual communication with the dead.

O Súilleabháin, who was puzzled in particular over the practice of including the corpse in the fun, games and dancing, tried to make eschatological sense of Irish wake amusements. He found that in times gone by all over the world the living feared the dead.[191] Not knowing where the dead were lurking, the greatest fear of all was that they might return and avenge themselves on those who had taken over their place or possessions. So everything was done to placate them and assure them of their popularity, particularly while their body was still around. Hence the wake. Hoping to gain their goodwill and favour the deceased were excessively praised, and of course included in the glorious send-off organized in their honour.

The reverse behaviour was sometimes demonstrated at childbirths, where the newborn babies were lamented and bewailed. In the light of our understanding of the joy expressed at wakes and funerals, this ancient and seemingly strange custom which was observed in some parts of Eastern Europe as well as in the Baltic countries[192] finds a natural explanation. It is yet another example of ensuring the ancestors' kindly feelings in the hope that they will not take revenge on the baby for having taken their place. That similar traditions must also have been prevalent in Ireland is borne out by an old Irish saying which goes: 'Sing a song at a wake, and shed a tear when a child is born.'[193]

Among the Finnish and Russian Lapps one comes across a strongly held belief which connects the birth of a child with its dead ancestors by a peculiar reincarnation. The Lapps used to give their children the names of their dead ancestors, thinking that in doing so the deceased bearing the same name would be reborn. Their firstborn was usually named after its paternal grandfather or maternal grandmother, and the second child after its maternal grandfather or paternal grandmother. Not complying with this tradition was deemed too dangerous because if 'a child is given a name not previously occurring in the sib, the dead relatives can take the child back'.[194] Further evidence for this belief comes from Central and Western Europe. From various parts of the Vosges highlands, from Switzerland and from Germany it is reported that according to an ancient belief newborn children brought back the souls of their ancestors who were awaiting reincarnation, and who were hovering in hollow stones eagerly hoping for this moment.[195]

All these sources attest to a special connection between newborn children and the souls of their ancestors. However, the deceased were not everywhere thought to be standing by for reincarnation. For example, if a newborn baby cried a lot during the night this was just a sign that the dead ancestors were making some clamorous demand which had better be dealt with. That done, the crying would stop immediately.

In rural France the souls were generally seen as waiting for the arrival of a newborn baby because this would ensure the continuance of the family line.[196] Thus the destiny of the newborn infant and that of the ancestor were interlinked, in that when one appeared the other departed. Phrases and folk idioms which Gélis collected preserve this bond. In some parts of France people believed 'that there will be a birth in the family, since there's just been a death'. In other parts the arrival of a baby meant that some old person from the same family would soon die. It was considered to be a good omen if a child was born on the same day that a very old person died because the baby was thought to live as long as the dear departed. A bad omen on the other hand was when the 'ancient' declined to take his or her departure, as that meant that the child would die instead,[197] leaving just a hint of the old threat which anthropologists had traced elsewhere in Europe.

The Northern and Eastern European deities of birth discussed earlier were generally thought to reside underground; thus libations were usually poured on to the floor. In many areas women in labour sacrificed a live dog to them, burying it in the ground. Alexander Carmichael reports from Scotland that to propitiate Briget, the Christian saint who was invoked at childbirth, people's oblational offer also consisted of a live animal, generally a cockerel or a pullet which was buried alive near the junction of three streams.[198]

As Ränk has convincingly argued, the positive, helping and healing dimension of these female deities is a more recent development. Originally they had a definite ideological connection with the dead, i.e. with the deceased relatives. Far from being benevolent protectors, they were at first evil spirits, feeling revengeful at their deaths and desirous to bring their living relatives into their own realm of the dead. This is reflected in the concerns of various Eastern European peoples who believed that the birth spirit could decide whether a child was to live or die. If favourably inclined towards the child, it would live and prosper, if not the child was sickly and would die.[199] Therefore the sacrifices made to the representatives of the land of the dead aimed in the first place at making them refrain from interfering with the health of the living. Ränk concludes:

> Even the deities of birth of the women have a double nature: on the one hand they resemble malignant demons of illness, on the other they have been turned into benevolent spirits or patrons in the popular imagination. In the former case they had to be repelled in the door area, localized in the images and placated; in the latter they were themselves active defenders of the door, and received sacrifices on this account. The borders between these two conceptions were very vague, so that it is quite difficult to say in every individual case what were the motives for their worship.[200]

Looking for further evidence for the ambivalent positive–negative roles of the deities of birth, and the ideas connecting childbirth with dead ancestors, Ränk studied the names people had given to these spirits. And we owe some intriguing insights to his linguistic analysis, which, as will soon become obvious, will prove relevant for our own inquiry. Birth spirits were generally called 'granny'. Ränk found that the basic component meaning 'old woman', 'grandmother' or 'ancestress' formed a part of all the names under investigation, and prefixes added to this root in some cases indicated even more distant ancestors, like 'great-grandmother' and '(first) ancestress'.[201] Other widely used by-names confirm that the deity of birth was a terrestrial spirit, being called 'the earth-grandmother' ('Erdalte'), and particularly stunning in the context of our own investigation is the version *bald* grandmother' ('barhäuptige Grossmutter').[202] Another by-name which clearly refers to her obstetrical functions is 'earth-mother opener' ('Erdmutter Öffnerin'). Ränk's findings are corroborated by Nahodil, whose study yielded practically the same names with the addition of 'Ur-mother' and 'venerable old woman'.[203] Gimbutas's linguistic analysis of similar figures in Slavic mythology reveals the same idea. The ancient goddess of death and regeneration, who is well preserved in folk tales as a witch, is called Baba Yaga. 'Baba' means grandmother and the second part of her name denotes her rain-making ability.[204]

Closer to our own area of investigation, the stone statue in Morbihan (France), which nowadays bears the name of 'Vénus de Quinipily' and under whose protection pregnant country women used to place themselves, was known in the seventeenth century in Breton as 'Er Groach Couard', meaning the 'Cowardly Old Woman'.[205] And finally, in the parish church St Martin of the Bellhouse in Guernsey, there is a prehistoric fertility figure made of stone. The local people revere the sculpture as an earth mother, and they call her 'grandmother', or 'La Gran'mère du Chimquière' to be precise.

These names remarkably strengthen the notion that past generations were not only linked up with the living, but were in all probability invoked at childbirth. Ränk saw this even further substantiated by the observation that the rag doll idols placed close by the lying-in woman were similar to the images several North Eurasian peoples used to make of their dead.[206] Another indication of this connection survives in the term for midwife in a number of European languages. The first human helpers at childbirth were obviously thought to represent the deities of birth. In Lapp the midwife is called 'maddar-akku', the first component of which means 'earth' and the second 'old woman'. In Denmark she is known as 'jorde-moder', i.e. 'earth mother', and similarly in Sweden she is known as 'jordgumma', i.e. 'earth grandmother'. The equivalent in German is 'Hebamme', which is derived from 'heben', in English to lift or raise, and 'Ahne', meaning Ancestress.

The message of the early Anglo-Saxon charm (see p. 82), which required that a pregnant woman first step over the grave of a dead man three times before repeating a similar ritual by stepping over a living man, now speaks loud and clearly. The first ritual act which was accompanied by the triple repetition of 'this is my remedy' was plainly meant as a tribute to the dead ancestors. Either as a mark of respect or as a gesture of appeasement, their souls were invoked before the woman could talk about 'a living child, not a dead one'.

Early on in this chapter a wider use of the Sheela-na-gig was suggested and an association with the fecundity of farm animals and field crops was alluded to. Fortunately there are two quite unusual English examples of Sheelas carved in combination with animals. One of these is the Binstead Sheela (117), who appears to be sitting on top of an animal head. It is hard to make out what kind of beast it is supposed to represent, but the traces of a halter-strap suggest that it is a domestic animal. The other example, the very dramatic Sheela set above the window on the tower of Whittlesford Church (154), is approached by a crouching male animal, or zoomorphic male figure, with an erect penis.

Beliefs that the fertility of the land and of the livestock depended on the deities of birth is referred to in practically all the studies consulted so far, and popular religious rites combining fertility rituals, invocations for favourable weather and plentiful harvests were known in many, if not all, areas of Europe. For example, in the Nordic 'diser' all these aspects are combined. The *Poetic Edda* recommends them as helpers during childbirth, but they were also traditionally associated with fertility and the harvest cult.[207] Even the church regarded rites promoting fertility in humans, animals and the fields together with weather-making ceremonies as interconnected. The papal Bulls of the fifteenth and sixteenth centuries fulminate against so-called witches because they 'blight the marriage bed, destroy the births of women and the increase of cattle; they blast the corn on the ground ... the grass and herbs of the field'.[208] Interestingly, during the witch trials both ecclesiastics and secular judges only referred to storms, snow and hail when they denounced the witches for their alleged weather-making powers, without any indication of the fertilizing aspect of their sun-and-rain-making capabilities. Gélis adds a further linguistic point to the whole aspect. He writes that in France the same word, 'brehaigne', was used to describe childless women, fields that bore no crops and female animals that produced no young.[209]

Everywhere in Europe the sanative qualities of wells were perceived to be equally efficacious in the case of animals and human beings. One early twentieth-century account from Scotland tells a typical story. A Scottish gamekeeper intent on curing a then prevalent grouse disease set out for the holy well of Melshach in the moors when, from a distance, he spied a group of women who had got there before him.

> The women, with garments fastened right up under their arms and with hands joined, were dancing in a circle round the well. An aged crone sat in their midst, and dipping a small vessel in the water, kept sprinkling them. They were married women who had proved childless and had come to the well to experience its fertilising virtues. No doubt words had been repeated, but the ... observers were too far off to hear.[210]

Apart from the shared use of the water for the benefit of humans and animals alike, this report illuminates other important aspects. It provides further evidence for the existence of the secret circle of women, the fertility dance, the magic formula and in the midst of it all we find again 'an aged crone'. The old woman would later receive gifts from those who, thanks to her, became pregnant. McPherson informs us that 'the aged crone who officiated would be rewarded by the expectant matrons, but as a rule, and this was earlier usage, the gift was deposited in the well – an offering to the presiding deity'.[211]

This is not the only case McPherson mentions where old women presided over fertility rituals in Scotland. However, before turning to Ireland to see if similar customs lingered there, I would like to refer briefly to Gimbutas, who investigated, among other things, ritual dances in connection with what she termed 'pre-Indo-European Goddesses' in the Baltic countries. She is quite definite in calling the domestic spirits or folk deities under examination here 'goddesses', but leaving aside the nomen-clatural difference, it becomes obvious that the rituals she analysed in connection with birth-giving or fertility consisted of pretty much the same ingredients. Stones were worshipped representing these goddesses who were protecting crops, animals and humans, and considered to be earth fertility incarnate and at the same time 'Mothers of the Dead'. 'Rituals to the goddesses were presided over by a priestess or grand-mother of the family; participation was restricted to women.'[212]

Searching for an Irish case I came across an interesting cylindrically shaped stone idol on Inniskea, a small island off the coast of Mayo. This idol, called 'the god stone', was kept wrapped in flannel, and 'is entrusted to the care of an old woman, who acts as priestess. It is brought out and worshipped at certain periods', writes Wright.[213] The stone, it transpires, was not only brought out for fertility rites, it also figured in wind-raising ceremonies because it had the power of controlling the wind: it could produce either storm or calm. However, it no longer exists. A priest smashed it and threw it into the sea. A very similar story comes from Scotland. At Kempoch Point, in the Firth of Clyde, is a columnar rock, locally known as 'Granny Kempoch'. Old women used to dispense favourable or unfavourable winds from there, but this granny stone was also considered to possess fertility-inducing powers and was therefore a favourite with newly married couples who walked around it 'by way of luck'.[214] And, finally, another vague and indirect reference to this reaches us from Thurles in Co. Tipperary. The local Sheela (86), now embedded in a wall overlooking the somewhat untidy yard of a car repair place, used to preside over the west gate, which bore the name 'old woman's gate'. The figure itself was known as *Síle na ghaoth* or 'Sheela of the Wind'.[215]

It seems, then, that in ancient European traditions old women are symbolically related to fertility and clement weather, but that death, winter and snowstorms also form part of this conception. Van Hamel discusses the Scandinavian notion of storm and snow as emanating from the world of the dead, and he explains that those possessing supernatural gifts, who converse with the dead, were thought to raise the power that is embodied in a thunderstorm.[216] Gimbutas, as we have already seen, also points to this connection in Slavonic tales from Eastern Europe, but there is further evidence from Northern and Western Europe. The Norns, the Eddic 'diser', our Nordic childbirth assistants, were weather-making spirits, especially connected with winds and snow, as were the Germanic Frau Holle, Frau Perchta and others who at the same time were in charge of the fertility of man and beast and the regeneration of nature.[217] In Scotland and Ireland Briget's day, 1 February, marks the beginning of spring and the return of growth to the land. Briget, the protectress of pregnant women and cattle, promoter of fertility and patron of the ale-harvest, was said to breathe life and warmth into the dead winter, 'to make him open his eyes to the returning life of spring, with its tears of showers and laughter of blustering winds'.[218] And it is of course difficult not to draw attention again to the Newfoundland Sheela who was said to command wintry snowstorms.

In Ireland the May Day celebrations in particular linked the fertility of the family with that of the cattle and the fields. Many rituals were performed which sought the protection and fecundity of all three. Of special interest here is the so-called May Baby parade which formed part of the festivities. The following is an early nineteenth-century account from Co. Louth:

On May Day, the figure of a female is made up, fixed upon a short pole and dressed in a fantastic manner, with flowers, ribbons, etc. This figure they call 'The May Baby'. . . . Around this figure a man and a woman (generally his wife) of the humble class, dressed also fantastically with straw, etc., dance to the sound of a fiddle and entertain the people with indecent shows and postures. . . . These exhibitions cause great merriment among the assembled populace; women who have had no children to their husbands also attend to see this figure and performance, which they imagine will promote fruitfulness in them, and cause them to have children.[219]

Two very interesting aspects emerge from this account. At the centre of the festivities, which were clearly meant to entertain the crowds with music and dancing or general merrymaking, we find a couple, a man and a woman, adorned with some kind of straw vestment making indecent gestures which greatly amused everybody present with the exception of the somewhat hostile observer. This 'May Baby parade' has all the hall-marks of the wake games but at the same time also that of the 'Patrick and Sheila' parade described on p. 64. The straw clothing almost certainly has to be a reference to childbirth, to being 'in the straw'.

The second point worth noting is the description of the fertility figure called 'The May Baby'. Surely, this must be the *géag* Dinneen mentions (see p. 64) as the image of a girl made on the May festival. This means that if Kohl's informant was right, and our Sheela was actually called 'Síle na géige',[220] the English translation could indeed read 'Sheela of/with the branch', but also 'Sheela of/with the Baby'. This so-called corn dolly was usually made of the last cornstalk cut at the end of the harvest. Information gathered from various districts in Scotland reveals that invariably the last sheaf was cut and gathered by the youngest person present in the field, who would bring it to the master of the house. There it was bound with three bands, dressed as a woman and usually placed in the kitchen.[221] The custom of making such corn-dollies was indeed very widespread in the British Isles and various names are recorded for them,[222] but, intriguingly, in some parts of Scotland such figurines were called the 'old Woman',[223] just as in the Baltic countries where she went under the name of 'Old woman' or 'Old woman of the Rye'.[224]

In Ireland one of the main features on the eve of St Briget's day was the procession of unmarried girls carrying an effigy of the saint which was prepared from straw.[225] Straw and rushes were also fashioned into crosses, charms, even girdles on or before her feast day, and they were hung over doors, beds and the hearth of the house and also over the entrance of the byre.

The most striking evidence of the continuing interplay between the world of the living and the world of the dead is to be found in fertility rites involving visits to the burial ground. These are reported from all over the British Isles until the twentieth century. In many parts of Scotland women used to travel to certain graveyards because within their walls were wells well known for their efficacious qualities in cases of sterility or problems with childbirth or because they contained stones, basins or so-called cradle stones which possessed virtues with 'salutary effects in connection with child-bearing'.[226] In Ireland similar documented rites demonstrate an underlying unity of the agrarian and the funerary. On Lughnasa or Lammas Sunday, the harvest festival in August, unmarried girls would decorate hoops with ribbons and flowers, and latterly, carry these to church before setting them up in the graveyard to preside over the dancing with which the day ended. 'Rites in honour of the dead seem to have marked the old Lammas festival, so that again we notice the association of ancestral spirits with the fertility of farm and family', writes Evans, who also describes a comparable custom from the Hebrides which was associated with the eating of cakes baked before a stone flag, with the killing of a lamb, visits to graveyards and a night of dance, song and love-making.[227] McPherson, who was aware of such Lammas feasts comprising pilgrimages to holy wells in Scotland, but who could not quite get himself to describe these in detail, concludes that Lammas was a celebration of the peasantry 'at one of the spots hallowed from of old, an ancient nature rite, in the old licentious way, thus bringing upon their heads the wrath of the Church'.

In Evans's view the fertility rites of wakes and the unashamed courtships carried on at great seasonal festivals make sense in terms of time and place: they occurred where the spirits of the dead were waiting to be reborn,[228] a notion which we are now quite familiar with from reports from right across Europe.

Unfortunately, this is as far as one can probe. These folkloric beliefs cannot be pursued into a more distant past because there simply are no written records. It also has to be admitted that in the course of the explorations of rural traditions so far, many sources had to be plundered and the boundaries of space and time were crossed, drawing no distinction between overlapping and coexisting cultures or between periods. Yet while all the accounts remain somewhat haphazard, fragmentary pieces of evidence which do not add up to a coherent pattern of folk religion, they nevertheless demonstrate how many common characteristics do exist in the rural beliefs and practices of the varied and widespread peoples of Western, Northern and Eastern Europe. More specifically, they attest to a quite amazing consistency and uniformity with regard to birth rituals and deities of birth.

To me the Sheela-na-gig incarnates all those ideas connected with birth spirits formerly worshipped all over Europe. She is one of those 'bald grandmothers' invoked at birth. The deathlike upper part expresses fear and respect for the ancestral spirits, and the lower part suggests fertility and childbirth.

Nowadays only the merest traces remain of the fertility and childbirth rites once enacted by countrywomen all over Ireland and Britain. The church, as has already been noted and will have to be investigated further, is partly responsible for this in that it did its utmost to suppress what it saw as superstitious and shameless practices. But the church is not solely to blame for the lack of available information. For women themselves kept these rituals secret.

Studying the sparse evidence of the past two centuries regarding Sheela-na-gigs one cannot help feeling somewhat amused by the old air of secrecy surrounding 'womanly things', which is still just as noticeable as the old antagonism between the circle of women and the local priest. The one element that seems to have happily passed into oblivion is the fear of the dead. All that survives in folklore surrounding the Sheela is associated with positive assistance with regard to fertility and childbirth.[229] Ränk had argued that the awe-inducing aspects of the birth spirits belong to the oldest stratum of European culture, and that in time the negative components gradually faded away. It is of course a truism that folk who practise rites and ceremonies which they inherited seldom know the true reason for acting as they do. The undoing of the wake tradition may serve as an example of such a development. When O Súilleabháin interviewed participants in wake-amusements in the 1950s people told him that they only joined in because it was a traditional custom and they did not want to be different from the general pattern. And they also felt that the games helped to pass away the time and keep people awake.[230] The wake tradition was kept up, but no trace now remains of the awe in which dead ancestors were held. Nor did the participants feel any need for an explanation of what the ritual represented.

Earlier in this chapter several cases in England and Ireland were referred to where people held on to their Sheela even in the face of clerical disapproval. The clergy were quite clearly frowning on customs involving the 'idol', and in some cases even attacked it, but the nature and purpose of the undesirable rituals are not revealed. All we find out is that the people brought Sheelas out frankly as charms. But to Edith Guest the fertility aspect and the pagan origin of the figure were so obvious that no further explanations were required. And she drily adds that other Sheelas must have too blatantly confessed their pagan origin because they lie lost and buried by priestly zeal in churchyards, with only a record remaining.[231]

Having visited and observed various places where the figures are found, Guest names as the typical ingredients of Sheela rites: a holy well, with its stone, bush and rag-offerings, an association with cows and other fertility symbols, or with witches, rounds and patterns. 'One or other link will generally be absent, but the chain will still be recognisable, often with its sheltering Saint at the end.'[232] Although she does not discuss the rationale behind the rag-offerings it is quite obvious that the principle of sympathetic magic is involved here. Women would take a piece of their clothing, perhaps after touching their private parts with it, dip it in the water of the well and then affix it to the bush beside it.

Guest paid special attention to the Ballyvourney figure (14) because she thought that practices attached to this Sheela more than any other reveal most palpably the pagan fertility origin. Unfortunately, she does not offer any views on two objects which are potential sources of information. One of these concerns the missing trees. Guest quotes Windele, who had observed that in his days the votaries had to pass by three trees, the bark of which was stripped off every year 'for purposes best known to the people'. At the beginning of the twentieth century there was only one tree, and when Guest visited Ballyvourney there were none.[233] The practice of stripping off the bark may be a vital clue when we consider Kohl's word that Sheela-na-gig translated as 'Julia of/with the branch'.

In many parts of Europe the folk-idea prevailed that trees were supposed to have a fertilizing effect on both women and cattle.[234] One is also reminded of the custom of cutting wood which formed part of the magic birth rites among various peoples in Europe. But there are other rituals specifically involving the removal of the bark. O Catháin mentions the old Danish custom of sending a girl around to invite women to the post-partum childbirth feast, armed with a branch from which the bark had been peeled. This she had to keep hidden until she had an opportunity to deposit it secretly with a household where either a child was greatly desired or a birth was shortly to take place.[235] From Ireland and Scotland we hear that on the Eve of St Briget's feast it was customary to place a small white branch (the bark being peeled off) in the bed together with an icon of the saint.[236]

The second object Guest makes no further comments on is the stone now strictly banished to the dark cavity. It looks like an interesting item for a number of reasons. The cavity, called 'Briget's bowl', is obviously suggestive of the pudenda. The stone inside is an agate, known for its efficacy as a birthstone (p. 77). In Ballyvourney the agate is touched three times straight after the rubbing of the Sheela, demonstrating the close magical association that exists between the two. Formerly this stone used to be 'handed about for its virtues', which tallies with what we heard about other birthing stones kept in ecclesiastical care. Finally, the idea of compromise is well demonstrated. Rather than destroying the pagan stone the clergy simply put it out of sight and (almost) out of reach. That the custom of touching the two objects has not died out yet was summed up nicely in a newspaper article only a few years ago. When an *Irish Times* journalist interviewed a pilgrim about the rubbing of the Sheela and the stone she was told: 'It is a fertility ritual, very pagan. Why not? Wasn't that here long before Christianity'.[237]

Other Sheelas are also still in use. For example, the figure at Castle Widenham (25) 'is reported to have been touched for help in childbirth within very recent years', notes Guest.[238] One of the photographs she provided in 1936 shows the figure at Castlemagner (24), on whose belly devotees had scratched a rude cross with pebbles. By comparing this with a photograph taken some forty years later, Andersen could prove that the pebble-marks have been spreading on the figure and were now appearing on other parts of the body.[239]

The late Dean of Cashel, the Very Reverend David Woodworth, who was of the opinion that Sheela-na-gigs were meant to avert the Evil Eye, became so intrigued by the figure that he planned to write a book about them. Numerous people responded to an RTÉ television programme transmitted in December 1990 during which he discussed his ideas on the subject. One correspondent is of particular interest here. A Jim Wallace of Stoneyford (Co. Kilkenny)[240] had heard from an old woman that a long time ago there used to be in his locality a Sheela-na-gig of which, incidentally, there is no record otherwise. This Sheela (96), he was told, had originally been embedded in the walls of the old church of Killinny.

> Where the church was is not known. Many years ago I was told that where the private burial ground of the Hutchinson family is now was the site of an old church. Mrs Boland (nee Hutchinson) thought that the church was nearer to Newtown. She says that there is a stile with an inscription somewhere on the boundary fence between the townlands of Killinny and Newtown.

At some stage the Sheela was removed from the church and she ended up in a cave which then became a place of pilgrimage for certain women, the

> 'cailini dana ruadh' to protect them from the evils of their ways . . . The [parish priest] got to hear about this and after he had preached a blood and thunder sermon one Sunday a group of civic minded citizens armed with sledge hammers razed poor Síle to the ground.

Jim Wallace's story, albeit minus the Sheela, is confirmed in Hogan's book on the history of Kilkenny. Here we read the following account:

The ruins of it [the church] existed near Mr Hutchinson's house down to the present century. There are persons still living who remember St Bridget's patron to be annually observed there on 1st February; and 'St Bridget's Well' still preserves for the place name of its ancient patron.

In a footnote Hogan adds this information:

A singular practice observed on the 'patron day' at Killinny church may be worth preserving. There was an artificial cave, the site of which is still pointed out near the old church in which, on the 'patron day', married women performed a 'station', which they believed to be a remedy against sterility. My informant avers that this cave ultimately became a den of ill-fame; and attained so notorious a celebrity that the parish priest of Danesfort, with a body of peasantry, on a summer Sunday, proceeded from the chapel of Kells, after twelve o'clock mass, and demolished the roof of the grotto.[241]

There are similar stories and reports attesting to a connection between Sheelas and fertility or childbirth, but most of the material is anecdotal. One such example is a newspaper article in the *Guardian* 'Weekend' supplement. John Hargreaves, a journalist who was investigating the Early Christian Church's practice of co-opting pagan customs rather than outlawing them in rural areas, was looking for examples of such a symbiosis in his 'own quiet corner of agricultural society, Shropshire'. It was then that he first discovered the Sheela-na-gig (135). A farmer he interviewed at Holdgate explained to him how a young man would take his bride round and introduce her to the Sheela to bless his marriage with plenty of children. At Church Stretton (123) he learned that the vicar, also a host to such a figure, would prefer the Sheela not to be there, but at the same time he would resist any attempt to remove her.[242] The Oxford newspaper article Murray refers to (see p. 29), stating that it had been the custom for brides to look at the Sheela on their way to the church, obviously tells the same story.

When O'Connor was in his teens, he was told by Mrs Joan de Sales La Terriere, then owner of Kiltinane Castle, that the two Sheelas in Kiltinane (nos 58 and 59) represented an ancient fertility deity and that barren women used to scrape them for their curative dust, an explanation which his own father later confirmed.[243] Weir received a report from a local woman with regard to the Drogheda figure (41), which revealed that 'Long ago when a woman was married long and had no children, as a last resort she came down to The Figure and asked for help – and she nearly always got what she wanted.'[244] Furthermore, given that the Pennington Sheela (141) in Northern England was locally known as *Freya* (pp. 25ff) – named after the Norse deity whose connection with childbirth has been referred to a few times already – we at least have a few indications that country people, whether in Ireland or England, associated fertility and childbirth with the sculpture.

I, too, learned of this tradition attached to several Sheelas. Molly Johnston, the previous owner of the Rosnaree mill house, never considered the Sheela-na-gig (76) to be anything other than a fertility figure. She herself had persuaded a barren woman to 'say a prayer to Sheela', whereupon the woman promptly became pregnant.[245] Edel McMahon, who used to live beside Clenagh Castle, told me that when she was a young girl she often observed childless couples leaving bread and apples on the ground directly beneath the Sheela (28). It was thought that if the food disappeared within a couple of days there would soon be a child, but if it was left to rot the couple would remain childless. Archaeologist Jim Higgins later confirmed this practice.[246] Even more intriguing was the outcome of a Sheela pilgrimage staged by three women artists in 1994. Veronica Nicholson, an artist and photographer from Ireland, together with Sarah Krepp and Jo Yarrington, two American professors of art, travelled the length and breadth of Ireland in pursuit of Sheelas. One of the many people the trio interviewed was the owner of Blackhall Castle, Mrs Naomi White, who told them that traditionally every year the local farmers would bring their cows and parade them past the Sheela (17) in order to ensure their offspring.[247]

The Christian Church and folk religion

When Christianity began to spread in Europe pagan gods, folk deities, cults and practices had already existed for generations, perhaps for hundreds, possibly thousands, of years. How the new religion expanded remains rather obscure because evidence of the first few centuries of Christianity is generally scarce, but least of all is known about the earliest Christians in Western Europe. 'In the West', writes Robin Lane Fox in his study of the transition from pagan to Christian, 'early Christianity has lost its history'.[248]

The Christianization of Europe appears to have been a slow and gradual process which was not completed until the fourteenth century, when Lithuania became the last part of the continent to convert. As a rule the new faith first gained a foothold in cities and towns before it spread to rural areas, and conversion started with the higher echelons of society before it reached the lower orders.[249] Of the various reasons given for this development the most consequential seems to be that the new faith presupposed convenient meeting places, and that its congregations had to finance the ongoing costs of a bishop and his staff. As a corollary of this, bishoprics were distributed by cities, so that early Christianity was essentially known in an urban setting.[250] Furthermore, for centuries the Gospels were preached in the major literary languages of culture, and not, as far as we know, in the different vernaculars spoken by the country people.[251] In the absence of a diocesan organization, then, a different ecclesiastical set-up was needed for the conversion of rural areas. For this purpose monasteries were founded as spiritual and administrative centres for both Christianizing and ruling the surrounding countryside.[252]

In the early centuries the Church's policy was obviously geared to avoid confrontation with the older religious practices and instead seek compromise where possible, allowing harmless pagan traditions to continue to co-exist with Christian rituals, the idea being that in due course the pagan elements would be eliminated. That this course of action was adopted is borne out by several documents. One of the earliest is a fourth-century letter from St Augustine, who is generally recognized as having been the greatest thinker of Christian antiquity. St Augustine explains that in an effort to win over pagans the Church would condone certain unpalatable practices which, once they had become 'true' Christians, the pagans would either want to or have to abandon: 'Jene Bräuche habe man ihnen gestattet, damit sie Christen würden; nunmehr sollten sie sie aufgeben, weil sie es bereits seien.'[253]

Another stratagem was to use ancient sacred places of worship as the preferred sites for the foundation of Christian churches. Rather than being destroyed, pagan monuments were converted and relics and building materials utilized for Christian use. Thus authority was acquired and the continuity of worship ensured. The much-quoted and in its time widely copied letter from Pope Gregory the Great to Abbot Mellitus in 607 attests to that policy. Pope Gregory delineates the rationale of his plan of action with regard to the English people:

> that the idol temples of that race should by no means be destroyed, but only the idols in them. For if the shrines are well built, it is essential that they should be changed from the worship of devils to the service of the true God. When this people see that their shrines are not destroyed they will be able to banish error from their hearts and be more ready to come to the places they are familiar with, but now recognizing and worshipping the true God. And because they are in the habit of slaughtering much cattle as sacrifices to devils, some solemnity ought to be given to them in exchange of this. So on the day of the dedication of the holy martyrs . . . let them make themselves huts from the branches of trees around the churches . . . and let them celebrate. . . . Do not let them sacrifice animals to the devil, but let them slaughter animals for their own food to the praise of God. . . . It is doubtless impossible to cut out everything at once from their stubborn minds: just as the man who is attempting to climb to the highest place, rises by steps and degrees and not by leaps.[254]

There is abundant evidence for this spirit of creative compromise. Standing stones and rocks were Christianized by a simple sign of the cross, on shaman magic drums genuine deities of birth were replaced with St Anna. Often pagan rituals were overlayed with new Christian forms or replaced with Christian elements. Sanctuaries around springs, wells, trees, hilltops and other religious foci were turned into holy centres of pilgrimage and healing, with Christian saints acting as guardians. Many Christian festivals were fixed as counter-attractions on dates already associated with major pagan celebrations. Christian saints were modelled on older deities, and accounts of their lives were often an amalgam of myth and folklore. There are even notable examples of direct continuity, like St Briget and St Gobnait.

The greatest difficulty the Church faced was to win over the peasants. As Flint points out, it proved to be an extremely arduous task to change the rooted and vigorously alive customs practised within the intimate circle of the medieval village community.[255] Peasants were unwilling to slough off ancient practices, least of all those which concerned them most deeply, like sickness, fertility and death, and consequently they tenaciously maintained these against all authority. And those missionaries, unendowed with the sagacity displayed by Pope Gregory, who reckoned they could eradicate non-Christian worship by using ruthless or even violent methods failed miserably.[256]

Recognizing that subtler, more varied methods were called for, the Church for a long time adopted a sophisticated approach which apart from the already mentioned compromises consisted of a mixture of imitating, adjusting or incorporating folk beliefs and practices. That which was objectionable was left out, and that which was acceptable retained. Examples of this *modus operandi* are the childbirth aids, the magico-medical remedies, stones, amulets, girdles and word charms referred to earlier. According to Gélis the church even went as far as actively to encourage the use of these aids to ensure a swift and successful labour, while at the same time eliminating all symbolic allusions to the sexual organs.[257] So certain folk ways were deliberately chosen to mediate a supernatural message, but in Christian ways, and for Christian ends.

Elements of pagan practices which came into the Christian Church, Flint argues, can best be understood as borrowed and encouraged not merely as a creative compromise, but in return for the elimination of such practices outside the Church. Once firmly Christianized, the Church hoped these could be rendered harmless, phased out or even put to good use.[258]

Few canons directed against the free exercise of pagan worship appear in the councils until Christianity had become the dominant religion in the different countries of Europe. From the fourth century onwards the prohibition of blatantly anti-Christian customs such as sacrifices began to be enforced, and gradually this was extended to other practices which were deemed undesirable or quite incompatible with the Christian teaching. Throughout Western Europe, from the fifth century Council of Arles onwards, the Church seriously tried to tackle what it termed idolatry by levelling laws against it. Century after century Church councils denounced non-Christian practices, in particular those which were connected with graves, trees, wells or stones. Bishops everywhere were admonished to be more zealous in checking forbidden practices, but it is obvious that it proved impossible to eradicate such well ingrained rural traditions. So for centuries to come, in popular belief and custom medieval Christianity remained intermingled with a large residuum of paganism in Europe.[259]

Church council records generally avoided naming the pagan idols and they were also careful not to be too specific about pagan customs. Terms like *phylacterium*, generally denoting a protective device like amulets, *ligatura*, i.e. knots or plaits tied in special ways, or *carmina diabolica*, i.e. frivolous songs and dances performed in graveyards, are often referred to without any designation of their specific uses.

There is a priceless eighth-century record, entitled *Indiculus superstitionum et paganiarum*, which lists thirty superstitious and pagan practices.[260] Because of its importance for the present enquiry, I shall repeat the majority of these vaguely specified 'religious errors'.

1 Of sacrilege at the graves of the dead.
2 Of sacrilege over the departed; that is, 'dadsisas'.
4 Of the little houses; that is, sanctuaries.
5 Of sacrilegious acts in connection with churches.
6 Of the sacred rites of the woods.
7 Of those things which they do upon stones.
10 Of amulets and knots.
11 Of the fountains of sacrifices.
12 Of incantations.
14 Of diviners or sorcerers.
15 Of fire made by friction from wood; that is, the 'nodfyr'.
18 Of the undetermined places which they celebrate as holy.
19 Of the bed-straw which good folk call Holy Mary's.

22 Of storms, and horns, and snail shells.
26 Of an idol made of dough.
27 Of idols made of rags.
28 Of an idol which they carry through the fields.

Regrettably, space constraints permit only a few passing comments on this extra-ordinarily revealing list. The most striking aspect appears to be that its first two items relate to funerary customs. Mannhardt, previously quoted on a number of occasions in connection with his study of Latvian-Prussian deities, also referred to practices in connection with the dead as the single most difficult problem the Church battled to overcome in the Baltic countries. One of the main grievances, apart from the wake rituals, was that the peasants would not bury their dead in cemeteries, preferring to do this in fields and groves.

A few clarifications are needed. The most likely interpretation of 'dadsisas' (2) is that it denotes a practice similar to the Irish keening-dirge. The (original) Latin word for the 'little houses' (4) is 'fanis', which were places of pagan worship made of branches of trees. By referring to the bed-straw (19) as Holy Mary's, only an oblique allusion is made to the use of straw in connection with birth giving. The idols made of rags (27) may allude to the rag dolls representing the female deity of birth invoked in so many places, but without any specific reference this has to remain a conjecture.

Summing up the evidence from the Church council records and the list of most prevalent superstitions one must conclude that contrary to the Church's expectations, peasant traditions, embedded as they were in the cyclical agro-pastoral life and linked with magical practices, proved to be not only highly durable, but also impossible to eradicate.

This is further corroborated by the medieval penitentials from Western Europe, which best disclose the idolatrous customs that had the most tenacious hold on the people. Not unlike the earlier mentioned 'Articles of Visitation', which were designed to help visiting bishops to ask the clergy pertinent questions with regard to local midwives, the penitentials contain detailed lists of sins which the priests were to consider in assisting a penitent with his or her confession. These systematic manuals also list corresponding penances to be assigned to the penitent. Thus the penitentials are concerned with the paganism of nominally Christian people. The first of these manuals appeared in Ireland and Wales, and it seems that missionary monks from these countries introduced them to the continent of Europe,[261] where they continued to appear until the sixteenth century.

Considering the repetitious questions to be asked of penitents and the unchanging areas of clerical concern, the penitentials add further proof to the evidence supplied by the Church councils, namely that within the space of a thousand years the Church did not manage to root out a host of proscribed pagan practices. Of these the so-called idolatrous ceremonies identified as relics of a pre-Christian life posed the most serious threat, such as fertility rites associated with rural prosperity, funerary rituals, worship by trees, wells or rocks and the use of amulets and charms. The descriptions of these not only confirm the accounts of folklorists as truthful renderings of traditional folk ways, but they are also testimony to the widespread nature of these. Again a few observations concerning the documents will be made.

The penitentials written by the Frankish ecclesiastics Regino in the first decade of the tenth century and Burchard of Worms a century later demonstrate that funeral rites were conducted in pretty much the same fashion in Central Europe as they were in the British Isles and Northern Europe. Both ecclesiastics anathemize merrymaking at funerals:

> Hast thou observed funeral wakes, that is, been present at the watch over the corpses of the dead when the bodies of Christians are guarded by a ritual of the pagans; and hast thou sung diabolical songs there and performed dances which the pagans have invented by the teaching of the devil; hast thou drunk there and relaxed thy countenance with laughter, and, setting aside all compassion and emotion of charity, hast thou appeared as if rejoicing over a brother's death?[262]

A revealing condition of penance comes from Bartholomew, Bishop of Exeter (England) in the late twelfth century, confirming the fear people then had of the dead taking revenge: 'He who practises divinations from the funeral of any dead person or from his body or from his clothing, lest the dead take vengeance, or in order that another not in the same house shall die . . . do penance for forty days.'[263]

Another intriguing piece of information is contained in the penitential of one Haltigar, who in the middle of the ninth century threatened anyone who 'cuts off his hair or lacerates his face with a sword or with his nails after the death of a parent'.[264] Keeping in mind that the birth of a child was thought to be linked up with the demise of a relative, we may indeed find that this practice further explains in some way the baldness and the striations frequently found in Sheelas, in that both appear to be signs of mourning for the dead ancestors at the time of birth. From the earliest times cutting off one's hair was an offering to spirits and deities, it was a sign of deep mourning and a symbol of self-sacrifice.[265] The other equally ancient tradition of lacerating face and body carried out for the same purpose is already denounced in the Bible where it says: 'Ye shall not make any cuttings in your flesh for the dead, nor print any marks upon you' (Leviticus 19:28). What springs to mind here is that, what with the idea of sacrifice being indissolubly linked to death, shedding one's hair and blood is begging the dead for forgiveness and asking them to allow birth to new life.

As was to be expected, there are no direct references to childbirth rites, Sheela-na-gigs or other birth deities. Childbirth does not figure in the penitentials except that women are occasionally referred to as unclean after giving birth, and that un-Christian burials of unbaptized children are condemned. That said, it is interesting to note that Burchard challenges the belief in the Fates who 'can . . . while any person is being born . . . determine his life to what they wish, so that no matter what the person wants, he can be transformed into a wolf, that which vulgar folly calls a werewolf, or into any other shape'.[266]

One final punishable example of sinful action, described almost lovingly and in great detail, has to do with rain-making. Generally weather-makers, especially those who could produce hail, snow and storms, are condemned in numerous Church councils, and the penalty for their activity is consistent and unusually harsh: penance for seven years, three of which on bread and water. By comparison much lighter penances could be expected for murder, fornication and other 'serious' vices.[267] Burchard sets the scene as follows:

> Hast thou done what some women are wont to do? When they have no rain and need it, then they assemble a number of girls, and they put forward one little maiden as a leader, and strip her, and bring her thus stripped outside the village, where they find the herb henbane which is called in German 'belisa'; and they make this nude maiden dig up the plant with the little finger of her right hand, and when it is dug up they make her tie it with a string to the little toe of her right foot. Then while the girl holds a twig in her hands, they bring the aforesaid maiden, dragging the plant behind her with the water and thus they hope that by their charms they shall have rain.[268]

Apart from these ecclesiastical documents a careful study of the enormous corpus of hagiography would no doubt further illuminate the persistent struggle that took place between the people and the Church. Gurevich, for example, adduces several cases from hagiographic accounts where saints were repeatedly attacked, some even killed, by peasants who would not allow the preachers to tamper with their traditions.[269]

Then there is the huge amount of local church records which would certainly contain stories of such conflicts too. The following examples come from the north-east of Scotland, where stone-worship and holy wells seem to have posed the most menacing threat. McPherson found in his study of local church records that in the case of the chapel well of Spey, from time immemorial the noted haunts of pilgrims seeking fertility and health from its waters, the Church began in 1584 to take actions against devotees using church and well for their 'idolatrous pilgrimages'. But irrespective of the penalties imposed, whether it be fines, incarceration, court orders or excommunication, the people would not be deterred from continuing with their pilgrimages. So the clergy, acknowledging that it was not in their power to put an end to the practice, demolished the chapel.[270] Even this drastic measure had no impact on the devotees, who continued to frequent the sacred waters. Some 200 years after the church's first documented interference with the practice, there was no sign of the well losing its attractive power.

The nearby well of Seggat witnessed a similar battle. In an effort to stop the pagan practices, chapel and altar were destroyed, but again this did not affect the people's continuous worship at the well. So the Presbytery ordained that the well be blocked up. But no matter how often this order was repeated, the following morning the well was found to have been cleared of its stones during the night. And according to the records it continued to be used for at least a further 150 years.[271] Still more dramatic were the events recorded from St Mary's well at Ordiquhill. When in 1632 the local minister 'interfered with some visitors to the well with the view of identifying them, his manse was attacked at night, and he himself assaulted and disfigured'.[272]

No matter how revealing such stories are *per se*, it would make tedious reading to multiply examples of this kind. Like all the other ecclesiastical documents they do not directly contribute to our understanding of the rituals performed with or around Sheela-na-gigs beyond testifying to the fact that despite the Church's complex measures to root them out, certain folk practices were belligerently firm and widespread.

More pertinent certainly are two reports, one from France and one from England, where local clergymen were entangled in a dispute over traditional fertility and child-birth ceremonies involving a statue whose function is strongly suggestive of that of the Sheela-na-gig. The first of these reports concerns the stone statue of the *Quinipily Vénus*, now in Morbihan. Until the seventeenth century the statue stood about 12 km to the north, on the grassy slope near the river Blavet at Castennec, and at that time it was known in Breton as *Er Groach Couard*, the 'Cowardly Old Woman', or as the 'good woman'. Pregnant women from around the countryside would worship this stone figure and place themselves under her protection. The pilgrimage was so popular that in 1660 the Bishop of Vannes decided to put an end to it. Alas, no matter what course of action he took, he did not succeed in stopping the rituals surrounding the idol. A year later it was ordered that it be flung into the river and a cross raised in its place. However, the statue was secretly retrieved by the local people who once again returned to their age-old worship. In 1670 the intractable bishop struck again, trying to have it smashed to pieces, but the workmen he sent to carry out the task took fright, and after slicing an arm and a breast off the statue, contented themselves with throwing it back into the river. Finally, in 1696 Count Pierre de Lannion had the statue located, restored and erected in his park at Quinipily. The story became a major *cause célèbre* in the area. The Castennec peasants protested against the removal, instigating a court case against the Count de Lannion in order to regain the 'Cowardly Old Woman'. Yet the court decided in favour of the Lord of Quinipily and the statue remained in his park. Apparently to this day peasant women still come secretly to implore its protection.[273]

Ironically, more recently it was discovered that the statue did not survive its restoration in 1696 and had secretly been replaced with a new one by Pierre de Lannion. The statue which now stands on a pedestal placed over a fountain represents a naked woman. She is well proportioned, with vibrant contours. The lower part of her body consists of straight legs which are slightly apart, and her two hands rest on her belly. The upper part reveals round breasts and ribs and a shapely head with straight hair. Her only ornamentation is two bands. One of these is tied around her head, and the other is put round her neck with both ends hanging down in front of her body, reaching down to her thighs and broad enough to cover her genital area.[274]

Pregnant women would flock to this and many other similar statues at appointed festivals – on old agricultural or on Church feast days – but if their condition would not permit them to wait for such a special day they would ignore the liturgical calendar and make the pilgrimage at a more convenient time. Walking round such statues three times, reciting charms and touching the abdomen all formed an essential part of the ritual. Often the pregnant women would bring along a band with which they would just touch the statue and then tie it around their waist, or half of which they would tie to the statue while the other half was kept on their bodies until the birth occurred.[275]

In France the Church clamped down on such pilgrimages after the Council of Trent, including all rituals surrounding the childbed. In the late seventeenth century the Abbé Thiers proscribed the use of superstitious remedies like amulets, phylacteries, protectives, letters or notes which were tied round the neck, arms, legs or other parts of the body, and a few years later the Bishop of Rouen ordered that it be forbidden to use any relics for pregnant women, including those of saints. Even prayers for use in childbirth show this 'hardening of attitudes in the Church towards women in labour, who were frequently reminded of the "humility fitting their station" '.[276]

Like the French 'Cowardly Old Woman', another statue has also already been mentioned in connection with her name. It is the Gran Mère du Chimquière in the parish church of St Martin on the island of Guernsey. This one-and-a-half metre statue of a stylized female was shaped by the carving and rubbing of a natural granite boulder, just like many Sheela-na-gigs. According to the plaque beside it the facial features, hair and buttoned cape were added in the Gallo-Roman period, and the big crack in the middle of the statue is said to have resulted from the actions of an over-zealous churchwarden who attempted to stop the worshipping of such stone idols. Close by there is a second similarly shaped statue menhir dating from the Late Neolithic or Early Bronze Age, which is left in its original state. It is locally referred to as a Mother Goddess.

Originally the Gran Mère stood inside the consecrated ground of the churchyard, and the villagers revered her by touching her head and placing offerings of flowers and coins at her base. During the nineteenth century the pagan stone was removed from the sacred territory and placed outside the gate of the church. Nevertheless, the local people continue to pay homage to this figure.[277]

In accordance with the Church's general policy, this old fertility idol was obviously kept in the churchyard in order to draw the villagers to the church with a view to removing it when the church felt in a strong enough position to do so. By analogy it would be a fair assumption, then, to suggest that in rural areas the Sheela-na-gigs were incorporated in churches and monasteries for the very same reason.

The medieval local clergy received only meagre clerical training. Many priests would have been semi-literate, probably trained locally by the previous priest, and they would have had a weak command of church ritual due to restricted access to books. Like the rest of the community the priests would have been married and would have worked the land. In other words, they lived close to the earth and were akin to their parishioners in background and needs.[278] Because of this propinquity the line between Christian and pre-Christian ritual would have been blurred anyway, but, as we have seen, the local clergy had to be very careful not to break abruptly with any old customs.

The parish church and clergy were maintained out of the land attached to the church and the tithes from the faithful. So from the church's point of view a good relationship with the peasants was absolutely vital. To draw in the country folks and attract revenue the churches and monasteries offered more than just religious services. Rural life was to a great extent focused on them: festivities were celebrated in and around the churchyard, sports and games were played here, fairs held, and the monasteries also provided healing and caring for the sick and served as infirmaries.[279]

In spite of all these efforts and the fact that with the liturgical feasts the church tried to provide a rhythm of ritual and recreation that in part supplemented, and in part reinforced, that imposed by the seasons of the agricultural year, we saw abundant evidence to show how widely the older cults which concerned the peasant community most deeply managed to survive. In the case of childbirth it is not very difficult to see why this was the case. It must have been an almost impossible task to persuade country women, who from time immemorial had resorted to traditions permeated by magic and who had depended on the support of other women in their hour of need, to place trust in a single god. To lure them away from the comfort of routine, ritual, company and practical help to the idea of a monotheistic religion, represented as three persons, Father, Son and Holy Spirit, all of whom were understood anthropomorphically as male.

Incorporating a popular pagan figure like the Sheela-na-gig as an instrument of attracting the local community, in particular women, into churches and monasteries makes sense, and it is by no means a unique occurrence. It makes sense for all the arguments outlined, but possibly also because if anything should go wrong in connection with childbirth, and we know that so many things could, the blame could be placed on the idols rather than on the Christian god.

As regards pagan deities in Christian churches, there are many other examples of local or regional idols ending up in Christian houses of worship. Bear gods, rams' heads, three-headed deities, twin brothers and a host of other divine figures, all once at the centre of cults in pre-Christian times, have been spotted and identified in and around many Christian churches in various parts of Europe by Georg Troescher.[280] Weir reports on divine non-Christian figures incorporated into Romanesque churches in France.[281] And P. Goessler, who concentrated his study on south-west Germany, found further pagan idols in many Romanesque rural churches and graveyards.[282] I myself happened to notice during a recent visit to Easter Island in the South Pacific that all the Christian icons, including statues of Jesus on the Cross and the Virgin Mary, as well as the baptismal font and the altar in the church of Hanga-Roa, were decorated with the local Tangata Manu (birdman) emblems. Catholic missionaries only arrived on the island in 1864, and this new church is a modern construction. In other words, the Christian Church obviously still syncretizes wherever necessary to win over adherents of competing religions.

The result of this investigation into the relationship between Sheela-na-gigs and local parish churches suggests that the sculptures, carved by local craftsmen and either erected in special locations or kept by certain old women, played an important role in village life. The sculptures would have been visited or brought out as fertility symbols on certain festivals, like Lammas, or worshipped individually by pregnant women. By their acceptance into the churches these folk customs were allowed to continue, albeit with a few adjustments. Sheelas were generally placed high up from the ground, making their touching, which had played such an important part in the old rituals, difficult or awkward.

The removal of existing figures and their relocation or incorporation in churches was obviously only one part of the strategy. Another policy would have been to provide new churches with ready-made Sheela-like figures on corbel tables or chancel arches, thus preventing any kind of physical contact. A general comparison between the original Sheelas on slabs or carved in the round, and the type provided by the church itself as part of the church's ornamentation, reveals that the latter show none of the old tension between the lower and the upper part, the remarkable life and death symbolism: none of the lean ribs, striations or signs of emaciation, expression of awe or otherworldly quality. These church Sheelas are smooth, of one piece, and some are even grinning, such as in Kilpeck (136) or Clonmacnoise 1 (33). And one cannot help thinking that by mixing such pagan figures with those of Christian significance, as is often the case on corbel tables, it was intended to break the old magic of walking around idols three times.

After the Council of Trent, when the Church generally exercised a stricter control over its flock, no more churches or monasteries were built with Sheelas on or in them. In fact, the Church now had existing Sheelas removed, hacked away or burnt, as the three seventeenth-century Irish diocesan edicts which Corish quoted prove (p. 69). And only castle owners continued with the tradition of employing Sheelas for many centuries to come.

Sheela precursers and similar figures

Having in medieval human and communal terms established a motive for, and in ecclesiastical terms a case against, the worship of the Sheela-na-gig, it finally remains to investigate the material evidence of precursors or antecedents.

First, it has to be said that in the archaeological record of the ancient world the most persistent feature has been the symbolism of female deities. From the stylized images of decorated caves and models from clay to sculptured statuettes, evidence of divine females dates back to prehistoric times. And whether standing, sitting or in typical birth-giving pose, everywhere in the world similar aspects, ranging from fertility, prosperity and birth to loss and death, have been associated with the magical powers of these figures.[283]

In Palaeolithic times small naked female figurines in bone, ivory, stone and bas-relief, commonly called 'Venuses', appear in Eastern Europe and Western Asia, whence they seem to have made their way into Southern and Western Europe.[284] Their most distinctive features are the grossly exaggerated maternal attributes: pendulous breasts, broad hips, rotund buttocks and excessive corpulency suggestive of pregnancy. Sometimes the entire focus is on the primary sexual organs and no breasts are indicated. Mostly they are standing upright, though some are in a squatting position. No doubt the most famous of these are the Venus from Willendorf, near Vienna, and the apparently pregnant figure carved in relief on a block of stone in a rock shelter at Laussel in the Dordogne, holding in her right hand the horn of a bison.

E. O. James sees in these Venuses antecedents of a goddess cult which he thought had developed in the Near East from India to the Mediterranean, and had spread from there in agricultural societies along the Atlantic littoral from the Iberian peninsula to North-West Europe. Contrary to Ränk's more penetrating study, James considers the close relationship between fertility and death a later development. The birth/fertility cult in his view acquired a funerary significance in France, and from there the cult made its way across the English Channel to Britain, where some evidence of it has been detected in south-west England (Dorset, Devon and Wiltshire). The most exciting specimen of the cult comes from the flint-mines at Grimes Graves in Norfolk on the east coast, where the obese figure of a pregnant woman carved in chalk was brought to light in 1939.[285]

One may not necessarily agree with the general thrust of James's reasoning process because the main purpose here is neither to investigate a universal mother goddess nor to try to crack a unitary code that would give access to a goddess cult. The continuity argument may appear to be somewhat spurious. Furthermore, one might argue that the wide distribution could be due to function rather than to diffusion. Nevertheless, the regularity and frequency with which female cult figures with life-giving attributes and a death notion in the background occur in agricultural areas all over Europe are quite overwhelming.

Hancar's careful study of the Palaeolithic Venuses reveals a further valuable dimension. First, comparing dozens of these figures from Eastern Europe with dozens of specimens from Central and Western Europe, Hancar was amazed to find no difference either in the fundamental nature of these or in their characteristic features ('im Westen und Osten völlig wesensgleich und in weitgehender äußere Übereinstimmung').[286]

On three figures he noted band-like features on wrists and around buttocks, and in connection with one of these he also discussed the possibility of a breast girdle ('Brustgürtel') because parallel running lines were indicated on chest and back of the figure.[287] Furthermore, in an effort to identify the dimensions of possible meaning within the particular society the figures came from, he noted that all the statuettes were found in non-nomadic communities. And in the Eastern European region each single example was discovered inside the living quarters of the settlements, often within a specially built niche in the house. Hancar interprets this as a cultic veneration of a mutual ancestress, most probably reflecting the need for solidarity within family groups, but also the growing importance of women in settled communities.

Most significantly, such Venuses have been discovered in ceremonial deposits of human remains in Britain. Even Hutton has to concede that

> the only divine figures to be found relatively often with the dead are the pipe-clay 'pseudo-Venuses', at St Albans and Carlisle, and at sites in Kent and Suffolk. If we understood what these figurines signified in any other situation, it would be easier to determine their funerary role.[288]

At this stage we should briefly remind ourselves of three other studies already referred to in different contexts. The first is Thomas Wright's book *The Worship of the Generative Powers*, which demonstrated that figures which could pass for Sheela's sisters were not only found everywhere in Europe, but among every people who had any knowledge of art. The second is Margaret Murray's essay on 'female fertility figures', in which she categorizes Sheela-na-gigs along with the *Baubo* under 'Personified Yoni'. She classified these as female deities concerned with childbirth and the promotion of fertility in which the secondary maternal organs were minimized and the whole emphasis was laid on the pudenda. And we can now appreciate more fully the importance of her assertion that such figurines were invariably recorded as having been found either in the inner part of houses, i.e. the women's quarters, or in women's graves, a fact which led her to believe that they were for the use of women only, employed in rites from which men were excluded.

Finally, we should return to Anne Ross. In pursuit of primitive sexual art, Ross makes a clear distinction between two Celtic art styles. First there is the sophisticated, highly complex art of the aristocratic La Tène Celt, whose precise symbolic meaning is lost to us. Full of magical and religious allusion, it abstains from overt sexual or erotic expressions. Thus goddesses are always clothed.[289] Co-existing with this sublimated Celtic cultural expression is a second, more barbaric, artistic tradition which is concerned with naturalistic forms. Frank and direct, it does not eschew portraying sexual objects and situations. This tradition is shared not only with the peoples of the Northern world, but indeed with mankind down the centuries. 'We can, therefore, say that over and above the highly sophisticated art of the La Tène aristocracy there was an archaic, and class-free art-form, with an impressive ancestry into prehistory, and a persistence equally powerful and lengthy.'[290]

Having thus extended the ambit of her investigation in time and place, Ross examined and compared sexually explicit artistic imagery throughout Europe down to Neolithic times, with the main focus on Northern European, pre-Celtic and Celtic fertility figures. The findings of her survey yielded an abundance of early portrayals of the human figure whose sexual potency and fertility associations were beyond doubt. These male, female or bisexual fertility figures were naked and came in all shapes and sizes, as rock-carvings, bronze statuettes or sculptures made of wood, stone or clay. Apart from the nakedness, in itself apparently indicative of a sacred status, their ritual significance was in many cases further suggested by linear grooves, deep holes or certain postures.[291]

As already mentioned (p. 36), it is much to be regretted that Ross decided against pursuing her investigation into one apparently widespread example of such peasant culture, namely the face-pots used throughout Britain. She described these as depicting naked females in a lewd manner and referred to their use in fertility–funerary cults, even linking them up with the Sheela-na-gigs because she sensed that the same type of religious belief had underlain both groups of sculptures.

Another sculpture that reminded Anne Ross of the Sheela-na-gig[292] is the remarkable oak carving from Ballachulish, found face-down at the bottom of a peat bog, and overlain by something resembling wickerwork, on the west coast of Scotland in 1880.[293] Standing almost one and a half metres high, this is the tallest of a small number of anthropomorphic wooden figures which have been discovered in Britain and Ireland. Recalling the seventeenth-century Irish diocesan regulation which ordered Sheelas to be burned, one suspects that other such wooden idols once existed.

The chief peculiarities of the Ballachulish example are the large size of the bald head, inset quartz eyes, large ears and a wedge nose. The trunk is straight with arms, hands and fingers outlined on the belly. The pubic area, marked with a central vertical incision, is 'much exaggerated, as well as the extent of the rima upwards'. The separated legs were joined at the lower end in a pedestal base. Of particular interest for us are two other features of the figure which draw it even closer to the Sheela. One is the shallow round hole at the crown of the head, the purpose of which is unknown, and the other is a band-like feature, described by Coles as a shoulder-strap, which hangs over the right hand shoulder and falls across the chest. The radiocarbon dates indicate that the figure belongs in the first millennium BC (728–524).[294]

A little older (1096–906 BC) and smaller (just over a metre), but otherwise quite similar, is the late Bronze Age yew wood carving from Ralaghan, Co. Cavan, in Ireland.[295] It has strong facial features and biggish ears. Like the Ballachulish figure it is also carved from a complete roundwood stem, and is much the same width from head to hips, with very little differentiation of neck, arms, waist or buttock; hands are not indicated. The legs are quite straight and not separated. The most conspicuous feature is the well defined triangular pubic region with its large central hole. Coles, who put a finger inside the hole, found that it actually widens within the body, and on the floor of the hole there is a small patch of white granular material, possibly quartz.[296]

The third figure, which is much older (2351–2139 BC) and smaller still, with a height of less than half a metre, is carved from pine wood and was unearthed in

Dagenham on the south-east coast of England.[297] The bald head is large in proportion to the rest of the body, and there are no ears, but strongly incised facial features with deep ovals cut for the eye sockets. The trunk has no arms, while waist and buttocks are deftly indicated, and the footless legs are well separated. Again the most striking feature is the central pubic hole, which, like the eyes, had been cut as a vertical oval.

Mainly because there is not the slightest indication of breasts on any of them, some archaeologists are inclined to believe that the Ralaghan and Dagenham figures might represent males, and that the hole was meant for the insertion of a now missing penis. Since the absence of breasts in female idols is familiar, such an interpretation does not naturally follow. Indeed, the stones inside the pubic hole of the Ralaghan idol and the oval shape of the hole in the Dagenham figure, strongly indicative of female representation – and ill-designed, according to Coles, to hold a penis – would tell us otherwise.[298]

Despite the fact that they span a long period, these three prehistoric sculptures are remarkably similar. Apart from the features already mentioned, Coles points to a further common aspect, namely a deliberate asymmetry. Examples of these include: left and right eyes of a different depth or size, the nose off centre, left and right shoulders at a different height, thickness between left and right leg varies, pubic triangle begins higher on one of the sides, two different feet. The Ralaghan figure is declared to be 'asymmetrical from head to toe'.[299]

In Chapter 1 attention was drawn to the many asymmetrical aspects of the Sheela-na-gigs, and it was in fact Andersen who first pointed to this kind of distortion. He says of the Errigal Keeroge Sheela 1 (44) that 'the deliberate asymmetry affecting the figure from top to bottom is a distinct feature', which to a lesser extent he also noted in one or two other figures. Ironically, he interprets precisely this asymmetry as evidence for their medieval rather than earlier pagan origin. And on account of this obviously erroneous statement, Anne Ross stands reprimanded for having included the Errigal Keeroge figure in her book *Pagan Celtic Britain*.[300] McMahon and Roberts on the other hand take the asymmetrical nature of Sheelas in general, but that of the Errigal Keeroge figure in particular, as a typical feature of Celtic art.[301]

To conclude the overview of possible precursors of Sheelas in the British Isles, it has emerged from this brief discussion of the various sources that a continuation of this line of inquiry promises to be very beneficial because there is obviously so much material to be further investigated. What is striking is the continuity of such sculptures from Palaeolithic times on. In their function as fertility idols, assisting in childbirth and paying homage to ancestral spirits, Sheelas are in no way singular or special: similar figures are found across the world and are known by many different names.

CONCLUSION

This book has been an attempt to provide the study of the Sheela-na-gig phenomenon with a fresh impetus and to open up new avenues of research. What first prompted this inquiry was what I perceived to be the inconsistency of the literature on the subject. The term Sheela-na-gig itself has been unsatisfactorily defined and applied. Moreover, the theories proffered to date, often by proponents entrenched in their positions, not only are contradictory – even mutually exclusive – but often contain their own internal inconsistencies. Thus they can be seen to be inherently flawed and to require intellectual somersaults of the reader wishing to make sense of them. So the purpose of this study was threefold: critically to review all the literature on the subject; to advance a new hypothesis consistent with all the evidence available; and to complement the corpus of Sheela-na-gigs.

My judgement in assessing the literature was guided by common sense because I can claim no expertise in the areas of either archaeology or art history. Yet I hope that, despite being highly critical of some of the experts' opinions, I have been fair in my evaluation of their works. The hypothesis I myself put forward followed almost naturally from the review of all the foregoing material which informed my own proposal. However, instead of the more discipline-driven approach which quite often results in tunnel vision, I deemed it more fruitful to adopt an interdisciplinary *modus operandi* which took into consideration the wider implications of the context in which the Sheela-na-gigs are preserved, the reasons why they were preserved and the function they fulfilled. This investigation resulted in a huge amount of primarily analogous and cumulative evidence drawn from many different places, periods and fields of research. I am very much aware that, in covering such an enormous amount of material, it was inevitable that a great deal of generalization had to occur. Naturally, specialists would have examined the various subject areas under investigation much more extensively, in more depth and detail. But the 'broad brush' approach afforded consistent and striking new insights which formed the basis of my own theory. While my contention that the Sheela-na-gig belongs to the realm of folk religion cannot be conclusively proved, I hope that I have produced sufficient evidence in support of this idea. Every so often in the course of this study, suggestions for further research have been made, and nothing would be more gratifying than to see researchers take up these recommendations.

While I thoroughly enjoyed every aspect of this investigation, the most exciting part, beyond any doubt, was my personal quest for the Sheela-na-gig. Luckily my attention was drawn to 23 Sheelas which so far had escaped the attention of all other authors who had published books on the Sheela-na-gig. Eleven of these additional figures can be found in Ireland. These are Aghagower (3), Ballinaclogh (7), Cashel Palace Hotel (23), Emlaghmore (43), Freshford (48), Kilmokea (55), Kilshane (57), Merlin Park (66), Rathcline (71), Taghboy (83) and Tullaroan (89). Nine are in England: Alderwasley (112), Cleckheaton (124), Etton (131), two figures in Lower Swell (137 and 138), Romsey 2 (143), Stanton St Quintin (147), Stoke Sub Hamdon (148) and one whose provenance is unknown (156). The latter is in a museum. Figure 160 comes from Kirknewton in Scotland, and the last two additions come from Wales, from Haverfordwest (164) and Raglan Castle (167) respectively.

Altogether I managed to look up about 85 per cent of the extant figures in the British Isles. The one regret I have, in hindsight, is that in the beginning I did not come fully prepared. Sometimes I forgot to bring my tape-measure and, worse still, I neither looked for nor closely investigated certain features whose importance I only became aware of later. What I overlooked in the initial stages were the touch-holes, the traces of girdles and the signs of objects descending from the genital area or lying between the legs of the figure.

Details on the individual figures, including setting, measurements, descriptions and observations, which I gathered during my visits to Sheela sites, were entered into the catalogue appended hereafter, which also draws on information provided by relevant publications. The catalogue incorporates all other previously published lists of Sheelas in the British Isles, but excludes from these all those figures that fail to comply with the definition laid down in the first chapter.

Plate 1 Figure no. 7, Ballinaclogh (copyright Conleth Manning).

Plate 2 Figure no. 9, Ballyfinbory (copyright Barbara Freitag).

Plate 3 Figure no. 13, Ballyportry (copyright Shae Clancy).

Plate 4 Figure no. 20, Caherelly (copyright Shae Clancy).

Plate 5 Figure no. 27, Chloran (copyright Barbara Freitag).

Plate 6 Figure no. 31, Clonbulloge (copyright Heather King).

Plate 7 Figure no. 34, Clonmacnoise 2 (copyright Barbara Freitag).

Plate 8 Figure no. 47, Fethard Wall (copyright Shae Clancy).

Plate 9 Figure no. 62, Liathmore (copyright Shae Clancy).

Plate 10 Figure no. 70, Rahara (copyright Gay Cannon).

Plate 11 Figure no. 76, Rosnaree (copyright Barbara Freitag).

Plate 12 Figure no. 77, Scregg 1 (copyright Barbara Freitag).

Plate 13 Figure no. 79, Seir Kieran (copyright Barbara Freitag).

Plate 14 Figure no. 83, Taghboy (copyright Gay Cannon).

Plate 15 Figure no. 89, Tullaroan (copyright Barbara Freitag).

Plate 16 Figure no. 130, Easthorpe (copyright Barbara Freitag).

Plate 17 Figure no. 143, Romsey 2 (copyright John Harding).

Plate 18 Figure no. 147, Stanton St Quintin (copyright John Harding).

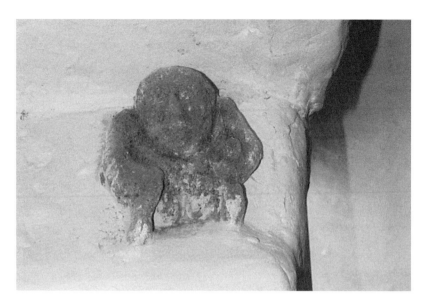

Plate 19 Figure no. 151, Tugford 1 (copyright John Harding).

Plate 20 Figure no. 154, Whittlesford (copyright John Harding).

SHEELA-NA-GIG CATALOGUE

Guest's numbers apply to her article 'Irish Sheela-Na-Gigs in 1935', and Andersen's numbers refer to those used in his book *The Witch on the Wall: Medieval Erotic Sculpture in the British Isles*, published in 1977, while McMahon/Roberts's numbering refers to their book of 2001, entitled *The Sheela-na-gigs of Ireland and Britain. The Divine Hag of the Christian Celts: An Illustrated Guide.*

Should their names be absent, it means that their list does not include the figure in question.

All measurements are approximate, and quite often because of the irregular shape and features of the carvings only the height is given. Where the width is indicated the measurements refer to the figure in its greatest dimensions.

Ireland

Extant figures

1 Abbeylara (Co. Longford)
Guest 52; Andersen 47; McMahon/Roberts 1
Location: Cistercian Abbey (thirteenth century); figure mortared into inside wall of central tower at a height of *c*.2.5 m.
Dimensions: (h) 37 cm; (w) 21 cm; projecting 10 cm from wall.
Description: Carved in the round, face and body quite badly weathered. Arms held close to sides with forearms bent forward to clasp tightly flexed knees. Posture similar to figures 5, 79 and 84. Three indentations in breast area; vulva oval-shaped with raised middle strand, and touch-hole underneath.

2 Aghadoe (Co. Cork)
McMahon/Roberts 2
Location: In private possession (Mrs Twohig), and now incorporated into a farm house near Killeagh, this figure came from Aghadoe Castle.
Dimensions: (h) 40 cm; (w) 30 cm.
Description: Carved in high relief left of centre on limestone slab. Triangular-shaped head set directly on shoulders. Centrally placed breasts and clearly indicated ribs. Left arm raised, holding indistinct object. Right arm goes under thigh with hand clutching a sagging vulva. Legs splayed, knees bent slightly, right foot and part of left foot broken off.

3 Aghagower (Co. Mayo)

Figure discovered in June 2001. Thanks to Siobhan Kavanagh, it was brought to my attention by Michael Gibbons, Clifden.

Location: In wall, some 60 cm above ground level, close to graveyard and beside holy well near ruins of medieval church and round tower.

Dimensions: (h) 25 cm.

Description: This small framed figure faces the road and is difficult to make out. Large round head, no breasts, arms akimbo, vulva a small slit, legs widely splayed.

4 Ardcath (Co. Meath)

McMahon/Roberts 4

Figure discovered in 1978 during removal of a masonry gate pier at entrance to farm where it had been intentionally concealed from view. The pillar itself was probably only *c*.200 years old.

Location: In private possession (Mr and Mrs Corry), now built into wall of farm SW of Ardcath; original provenance unknown.

Dimensions: (h) 54 cm; (w) 28 cm.

Description: Carved in false relief on limestone block, the figure fills frame formed by cut edge of stone. Big head with prominent round eyes, no neck, arms akimbo with both hands on thighs close to pudenda which is indicated as a roundish indentation. Legs slightly bent and both feet face in same direction.

5 Athlone (Westmeath)

Guest 24; Andersen 49; McMahon/Roberts 5

Location: Athlone Castle Museum. Figure formerly placed above gateway of laundry belonging to the Convent at St Peter's Port.

Description: Sculptured almost in the round. Strong face with pursed lips, and a striated pattern incised across left cheek. With arms embracing tightly flexed knees, pose quite similar to figures 1, 79 and 84. Big V-shaped vulva.

6 Ballaghmore (Co. Laois)

McMahon/Roberts 6

Figure first recorded in 1978.

Location: Ballaghmore Castle (fifteenth century). Figure situated on side of an L-shaped quoin on SW facing wall of castle, some 10 m above ground level.

Dimensions: (h) 47 cm; (w) 36 cm; projecting 7 cm from surface of quoin.

Description: Carved in bold relief in white sandstone, the figure is asymmetrical and badly weathered. Pear-shaped head with big mouth, slanted eyes and prominent ears, pressed back against head. Arms akimbo, right hand seems to rest on hip while the other touches left thigh. Vulva only slightly exaggerated. The short stumpy legs are splayed with knees bent and feet turned out.

7 Ballinaclogh (Co. Tipperary)

First recorded by Conleth Manning in 1989.

Location: Ruins of a fifteenth-century church in graveyard. Figure carved on quoin at NW corner of nave facing road.

Dimensions: (h) 45 cm (quoin: 70 cm wide).

Description: Carved in relief on large limestone quoin some 3 m from ground. Material and dressing of stone the same as all other stones in church. Triangular head with asymmetrical eyes and big jug ears; small dangling breasts on deeply incised ribs; legs apart. Left hand raised to head with hand touching ear. Right hand seems to be grasping pudenda. It looks as if lower part of figure was deliberately defaced. Figure in a standing position with feet turned outwards.

8 Ballinderry (Co. Galway)

Andersen 50; McMahon/Roberts 8

Location: Ballinderry Castle (sixteenth century); figure on key-stone of the arch over main doorway facing N.

Dimensions: (h) 25 cm (key-stone: 36 cm wide at top, 25 cm at bottom).

Description: Right upper corner and bottom of stone have small parts broken off. Beside Sheela figure there is a hexafoil rose, a marigold, a bird, a knot motif and a circle with three curved spokes. A plait-like ornament protrudes from behind both sides of Sheela's head at a right angle showing a different pattern on each side; while the right one resembles plaited hair, the other forms a guilloche. Wavy lines across forehead, ovoid eyes, strong wedge nose, a slit-mouth and prominent ears. No neck; tiny, flat breasts tucked away under arms; navel and nostrils deeply indented. Arms almost form a circle in front of body with both hands touching vulva. Figure depicted as standing with legs wide apart, and feet damaged. The most striking feature is what appears to be an afterbirth protruding from vulva and ending on the ground where it forms a heap between legs. In this respect figure similar to carvings 13, 18, 54, 55, 83, 88, 132 and 151.

9 Ballyfinboy (Co. Tipperary)

Guest 9; Andersen 51; McMahon/Roberts 9

Location: Ballyfinboy Castle (fifteenth/sixteenth century); figure in a sunk panel on a SW quoin of wall, above entrance doorway, some 4 m above ground; many features pointing to contemporaneity with castle.

Dimensions: (h) 42 cm.

Description: Boldly carved clear outline of a standing neckless female set in a frame. Relatively small, earless round head, clearly incised ribs and no breasts, disproportionally thick arms, elbows turned outwards, reaching from behind splayed legs to touch sagging pudenda. Below an upright elongated indentation, seemingly indicating the vulva, there is a further downward pointing cavity which both hands clutch. Knees and feet bent outwards.

10 Ballylarkin (Co. Kilkenny)

Guest 45; Andersen 52; McMahon/Roberts 10

Location: National Museum of Ireland, Dublin; discovered in fifteenth-century parish church of Ballylarkin, Co. Kilkenny.

Dimensions: (h) 58 cm; (w) 32 cm.

Description: Carved in relief on slab and probably most refined of all Sheelas, depicted in a squatting position. Oval head with big ears, ovoid eyes, small long nose and slit-mouth; thick neck. Tiny, pendulous breasts dwarfed by decisively carved ribcage. Arms akimbo with right hand placed on bent knee while middle finger of left hand delicately touches pudenda.

11 Ballynacarriga (Co. Cork)
Andersen 52a; McMahon/Roberts 7
Location: Ballynacarriga Castle (fifteenth/sixteenth century); figure situated above main entrance door at considerable height on E facing wall of castle.
Dimensions: (h) 45 cm.
Description: Standing figure with splayed legs and feet turned outwards; upper part of body depicted disproportionally large. Big head with huge droopy ears and asymmetrical eyes accentuated by different shape and size. Long, slightly bent arms reach down to grasp vulva from behind splayed thighs.

12 Ballynahinch (Co. Tipperary)
Guest 8; Andersen 53; McMahon/Roberts 12
Location: Ballynahinch Castle (fifteenth century); above doorway in E wall of tower house, about 6 m from the ground.
Dimensions: (h) 55 cm.
Description: Figure on rectangular slab inserted in wall. Big round head with eyes wide open; strong billowy lines across forehead; large jug ears. Lean ribs, and no breasts seem to be indicated. Arms akimbo with hands joined above pudenda, shown as a deep round hole. Squatting position, knees bent, heels touching like figure 21, and toes turned out.

13 Ballyportry (Co. Clare)
Andersen 54; McMahon/Roberts 14
Location: National Museum of Ireland, Dublin; discovered S of Ballyportry Castle (fifteenth/sixteenth century).
Dimensions: (h) 53 cm; (w) 38 cm.
Description: Crudely carved in limestone. Neckless huge head with big jug ears; deep-set round eyes raised in sockets; nose broken off. Teeth showing in slightly opened mouth. No breasts, but an over-large round navel. Hands pass behind wide open thighs; fingers tear open long deep vulva from which amniotic sac protrudes. The latter is shaped like a balloon, filling gap between widely splayed legs. Knees bent, feet turning outwards; left half foot broken off.

14 Ballyvourney (Co. Cork)
Guest 4; Andersen 55; McMahon/Roberts 15
Location: St Gobnait's Abbey; carved slantwise in the stone forming a windowhead over trefoil window in S wall of church.
Dimensions: (h) 30 cm; (w) 20 cm.
Description: Carved in false relief in ovoid depression. Below normally proportioned torso with head and arms – albeit without breasts – are two small truncated legs carved in lower relief than rest of figure. Posture probably standing; arms flexed with both hands in front of body joined to cover pudenda. General features and pose of arms strongly suggestive of Sheela, but no definite indication of pudenda. However, Guest

observed and described fertility and childbirth rites connected with this figure, re-inforcing impression that it is a Sheela.

15 Behy (Co. Sligo)
McMahon/Roberts 17
Location: Behy Castle (sixteenth century); figure built into internal wall face of out-house, i.e. in farm shed to E of castle.
Dimensions: (h) 45 cm (slab: 85 cm wide).
Description: Figure carved at extreme right hand side of large rectangular limestone slab, the surface of which is punch-dressed and has a large X picked out on left side. Irregular damage to left hand side of slab. The quoins of disused farmhouse beside shed have same pock-marks and X patterns. It would appear that quoin-slabs and carving were taken from castle of which only two dilapidated walls remain. Figure depicted as stand-ing, and is now painted pink. Vaguely triangular head with ovoid eyes, slit-mouth and conspicuously big left ear. Right ear covered by raised right hand, while left hand rests on thigh with fingers pointing at genitals. Breasts clearly indicated; vulva exaggerated and sagging. Between moderately splayed legs, underneath vulva, there is an ovoid object similar to those connected with figures 29, 30, 42, 70, 73 and 142.

16 Birr (Co. Offaly)
Andersen 57; McMahon/Roberts 18
Location: National Museum of Ireland, Dublin; presented to museum in 1956; ori-ginal location unknown (findplace neighbourhood of Birr), but thought to have come from St Brendan's church.
Dimensions: (h) 53 cm; (w) 30 cm.
Description: Figure carved on curved underside of oblong stone which might be a broken-off corbel; quite weathered. Large (now) featureless head on elongated thick neck. Thin bent arms with small round breasts under armpits. Both well shaped hands in front of body, pointing to vulva whose irregular shape looks torn. Lower part of sculpture appears to have been deliberately damaged. Legs no longer traceable.

17 Blackhall (Co. Kildare)
Guest 14; Andersen 58; McMahon/Roberts 19
Location: Blackhall Castle (fifteenth century); figure carved on rectangular slab and placed by doorway of tower house facing WSW. When part of the wall collapsed in 1999, owners of castle, Mr and Mrs White, rescued Sheela and kept her safe indoors.
Description: Carved in low relief with deep groove around head and shoulders similar to figure 28. Round head with ovoid eyes. Broad shoulders; small breasts and deeply incised ribs. Both arms pass under thighs to reach into large sagging vulva. Legs asymmetrical and widely splayed; both feet turning outwards, but right foot complete with toes and positioned higher than left foot whose toes are no longer traceable.

18 Bunratty (Co. Clare)
Andersen 59; McMahon/Roberts 21
Location: Bunratty Castle (fifteenth century); figure set by S window in hall of great keep; transferred there from inner reveal of window in top room of SW tower during twentieth-century restoration of castle.

Dimensions: (h) 22 cm; (w) 20 cm.
Description: Carved at left to middle of large rectangular slab. Triangular head with deep-set eyes, grim mouth and gritted teeth. Flat, but sizeable, pendulous breasts. Arms form circle, passing behind thighs. Legs widely splayed and set at right angles to body before bending at right angles at knees. Vulva, sagging below thighs, appears to be torn open by both hands to release some soft substance.

19 Burgesbeg (Co. Tipperary)

Andersen 60; McMahon/Roberts 22
Location: National Museum of Ireland, Dublin; figure discovered among pile of stones in SE corner of old church ruin in local graveyard in 1932.
Dimensions: (h) 62 cm (stone: 70 cm high, 35 cm wide).
Description: Figure carved in relief on block of sandstone; partly dressed to an approximately rectangular shape. Shape would suggest that figure was once built into the structure and formed part of arch of door or window. Round head with sharp chin; eyes clearly cut circles, but nose and mouth ill-defined; narrow neck. Breasts barely indicated. Arms flexed and hands grasping deeply hollowed out pudenda between widely separated thighs; prominent touchhole or anus below genitals. Knees bent; feet pointing downwards.

20 Caherelly (Co. Limerick)

Andersen 61; McMahon/Roberts 24
Location: Hunt Museum, Limerick; figure discovered by workers repairing a culvert near Caherelly Castle, near Lough Gur. It had been used as building stone in wall, and was embedded face downwards.
Dimensions: (h) 50 cm; (w) 34 cm.
Description: Figure quite skilfully carved in flat relief on local limestone; damaged, head missing, and legs from thigh downwards and left hand also broken away. Trunk and limbs unusually plump without signs of emaciation; well shaped droopy but proportional breasts. Arms passing behind legs; right hand lifting lower part of thigh. Deeply incised navel and oval pudenda; shape of latter exaggerated, and seems to be split at upper end. A groove is cut vertically downwards below pudenda. A similar channel pointing directly at vulva, but cut horizontally beside figure, can be seen at Rathcline.

21 Carne (Co. Westmeath)

Guest 63; Andersen 62; McMahon/Roberts 25
Location: National Museum of Ireland, Dublin; carving originally found in ruins of Carne Castle (sixteenth century) at Coolatore.
Dimensions: (h) 63 cm; (w) 36 cm.
Description: Carved on irregular, heavy slab; triangular head with ovoid eyes and slit-mouth. No neck, heavy shoulders and round breasts. Arms in front of body with both hands reaching into vulva, hanging between widely splayed thighs. Heels joined together and toes pointing down and outwards.

22 Cashel (Co. Tipperary)

McMahon/Roberts 27
Location: On quoin stone at SE corner of fifteenth-century Hall of the Vicar's Choral on the Rock of Cashel; high on E face, and inserted horizontally.

Dimensions: (h) 45 cm.
Description: Neckless head sitting on square shoulders; grim round face, wedge nose and slit-mouth; no breasts. Squatting figure with lower abdomen almost touching ground; vulva long narrow slit; both feet turned outwards.

23 Cashel Palace Hotel (Co. Tipperary)
Location: On wall beside entrance to bar of Cashel Palace Hotel together with a framed rubbing; figure recently transferred from boiler house which formerly served as Cashel Diocesan Library (built 1733–40). In latter it had been inserted sideways on quoin, E face of NE corner. Unrecorded figure which came to my attention in the notebooks of the late Dean of Cashel, the Very Reverend David Woodworth.
Dimensions: (h) 60 cm; (w) 35 cm.
Description: Outline of figure shallowly incised in rectangular limestone block. Big round head with huge jug ears, ovoid eyes and wedge nose; long neck. Both arms in front of body with bent elbows; hands touching vulva. Suggestion of flat droopy breasts. Oval vulva sagging between widely splayed thighs. Lower part of legs not indicated.

24 Castlemagner (Co. Cork)
Guest 34; Andersen 64; McMahon/Roberts 28
Location: On right face of holy well of St Bridget, W of Castlemagner, situated on bank of Catra stream.
Dimensions: (h) 57 cm; (w) 30 cm.
Description: Figure carved on limestone block. Standing or kneeling posture with both arms raised and legs terminating immediately below flexed knees. Neatly carved and well proportioned; no breasts and discreetly indicated vulva. Scratched pebble marks, cross-shaped, on both hands, forehead, trunk and thighs.

25 Castle Widenham (Co. Cork)
Guest 39; Andersen 65; McMahon/Roberts 29
Location: In private possession and kept in store room; it will be made available to public at some time during 2004. Originally figure was discovered lying by holy well of St Patrick on bank of Awbeg river close to Castle Widenham.
Description: Carved in flat relief at left hand side of heavy block. Some interpret incision behind head as huge headdress or hair, but head looks decidedly bald. Standing position with legs splayed, knees bent and feet turned outwards; hands pointing at oval pudenda.

26 Cavan (Co. Cavan)
Guest 1; Andersen 66; McMahon/Roberts 30
Location: Cavan County Museum, Ballyjamesduff (on loan from National Museum of Ireland); found in graveyard in 1842 and believed to have come from medieval parish church, now destroyed.
Dimensions: (h) 43 cm; (w) 23 cm.
Description: Right side damaged from top to bottom giving the impression that figure was cut off vertically. Big head; ovoid eyes with pupils; fleshy nose with clearly cut nostrils; open mouth with protruding tongue and beading round lips, possibly representing teeth. Two or three bands round forehead, and hair seems to be indicated.

No neck and no breasts; deeply incised ribbing. Arms in front of body with fingers of both hands inside huge oval vulva hanging down between splayed knees; deep touch-hole underneath pudenda. Many features very similar to figure 27.

27 Chloran (Co. Westmeath)
Andersen 66 a; McMahon/Roberts 58
Location: British Museum, London (Witt Collection); found in 1859 in field at Chloran, Killua Castle, and supposed to have belonged to a church nearby.
Dimensions: (h) 47 cm; (w) 15 cm.
Description: Roughly rectangular granite block, broken and repaired. Rectangular indentation (17.5 cm × 6 cm) carved into back, possibly for propping up figure. Huge head with asymmetrical jug ears; ovoid eyes; large, crooked nose with nostrils and very pronounced nostril channels (similar to figure 70). Open mouth showing two rows of teeth. No neck; tiny round breasts. Arms in front of body with fingers of both hands inside huge oval vulva, sagging between splayed knees. Lower right leg missing, left foot turned outwards; very deep touch-hole underneath pudenda.

28 Clenagh (Co. Clare)
Andersen 67; McMahon/Roberts 31
Location: Quoin stone on SE angle of Clenagh Castle, an enormous late sixteenth-century tower house; figure set 85 cm above ground, facing farmyard and apparently contemporary with castle.
Dimensions: (h) 50 cm; (w) 37 cm.
Description: A wide groove-like depression outlines earless head; facial features barely discernible; no neck, and breasts only hinted at. Arms close to trunk and joined around oval depression, indicating pudenda and with signs of rubbing. Squatting position with thin, spindly legs widely splayed and set at right angles, bent at knees, feet pointing outwards.

29 Cloghan (Co. Roscommon)
Andersen 69; McMahon/Roberts 33
Location: Quoin stone on SE corner of Cloghan Castle (fifteenth/sixteenth century); figure inserted horizontally, c.7 m over ground level; first came to archaeological notice in 1970.
Dimensions: (h) 60 cm; (w) 30 cm.
Description: Carved in high relief; background of stone decorated with chisel-punch technique as all other remaining quoin stones. Oval head with hair or more possibly tight-fitting cap (similar to figures 69, 113, 127, 130, 151, 152), small eyes, wedge nose and mouth with protruding tongue. Tiny breasts; arms almost form a circle in front of body with both hands grasping slit of vulva. Between flexed and splayed legs directly below genitals there is an elongated object similar to figures 15, 30, 42, 70, 73 and 142. No feet.

30 Clomantagh (Co. Kilkenny)
Guest 46; Andersen 70; McMahon/Roberts 34
Location: Quoin stone on SW corner of Clomantagh Castle (early sixteenth century); figure inserted horizontally at considerable height, just below level of fourth floor.

Description: Large figure set within recessed frame. Head rests on long, thin neck; flat, droopy breasts, and wavy lines across upper torso indicating ribs. Left arm in front of body with hand touching square cavity indicating vulva; right arm bent at elbow with lower arm raised up towards side of head. Deep groove extending from raised arm to head may indicate hand or band. A somewhat thicker band is depicted on left side of head and disappearing behind arm (similar to Freshford). Legs widely splayed; knees bent at right angle with feet turning outwards. An elongated object is placed on pudenda similar to figures 15, 29, 42, 70, 73 and 142.

31 Clonbulloge (Co. Offaly)
McMahon/Roberts 35
Location: Public Library Edenderry (on loan from Mrs Patty Lawlor); figure found in Figile river under Kilcumber Bridge near Clonbulloge in 1970s, and brought to archaeological attention by Heather King in 1993; original position unknown.
Dimensions: (h) 28 cm; (w) 44 cm (slab 20 cm thick).
Description: Figure carved in high relief at an angle into left hand corner of roughly rectangular limestone slab (possibly quoin). Large head with wavy lines running across forehead; bulbous eyes with eyebrows; clearly marked nostrils; five striations on left cheek; gaping mouth with portruding tongue. Only left ear depicted; round growth on right cheek. Small breasts above minuscule waist; thin flexed arms with big hands reaching into slit-vulva under which there is a small, deep touch-hole. Genitals carved in the lower left corner of stone leaving no room for legs.

32 Clonlara (Co. Clare)
Guest 51; Andersen 71; McMahon/Roberts 36
Location: Set into parapet of bridge across Limerick to Killaloe Navigation Canal at Clonlara; The date 1769 appears on top left hand corner, possibly indicating year when first (hump-backed) bridge was built which was replaced with modern structure in 1974. Original position unknown.
Dimensions: (h) 62 cm; (w) 47 cm.
Description: Carved on rectangular slab; figure was given a patent reveal surrounding it when inserted in new parapet. Signs of deliberate hammering below waist, thus legs and genital area only barely traceable. Bony head with grim face; arms flexed; both hands indicating or touching vulva; legs splayed.

33 Clonmacnoise 1 (Co. Offaly)
Guest 23; Andersen 72; McMahon/Roberts 37
Location: On voussoir in outer order on N side of chancel arch in Nuns' Chapel (twelfth century).
Description: Small figure cut in a lozenge; pear-shaped face with grinning mouth; without body, arms or hands; biggish, oval slit of a vulva revealed by upturned legs embracing head. Pose similar to figures 69, 127, 133 and 160.

34 Clonmacnoise 2 (Co. Offaly)
McMahon/Roberts 23
Location: In store room adjoining cathedral. It has no known provenance.
Dimensions: (h) 25 cm; (w) 21 cm.

Description: Carved in relief on one face of octagonal stone, all other sides smooth and without decoration. Huge earless head with bulbous eyes and biggish chin. Angular shoulders; clearly incised ribs, no breasts. Left hand resting on thigh, right arm raised with hand held to side of face. Deep hole indicating vulva with clitoris (?) at upper end. Legs slightly apart and bent with both feet facing the same way.

35 Clonmel (Co. Tipperary)

Andersen 73; McMahon/Roberts 38

Location: National Museum of Ireland, Dublin; figure discovered 1944 in wall in Blue Anchor Lane, Clonmel, and believed to have been associated with nearby Dominican priory.

Dimensions: (h) 62 cm; (w) 60 cm.

Description: Carved on trapezoidal-shaped stone. Broad earless head with top half of face destroyed or weathered, a fierce mouth showing gritted teeth, only facial features discernible; broad shoulders; lean ribs carved in relief below flat, droopy breasts which show striated pattern. Seated pose with legs splayed and feet turned outwards. Right hand under thigh; left arm in front of body with fingers inside large, oval, swollen-looking pudenda; touch-hole underneath.

36 Clonoulty (Co. Tipperary)

McMahon/Roberts 39

Location: GPA Bolton Library, Cashel; found in Clonoulty graveyard during cleaning up operation in 1989. Stone was buried up to neck at foot of yew tree and appears to have been placed in this position as grave marker. Given age of tree, figure must have been buried at some time prior to 1800.

Dimensions: (h) 71 cm; (w) 35 cm.

Description: Carved on irregular slab; head so damaged that no facial features survive; traces of a necklace at base of neck; ribs clearly indicated. Left arm behind left leg with fingers appearing from under thigh; right arm reaching down to vulva in front of body with hands gripping large slit-vulva. Squatting pose, legs widely splayed and bent at knees, feet turned outwards.

37 Cooliaghmore (Co. Kilkenny)

McMahon/Roberts 40

Location: Kept in Cronin Room in Rothe House, Kilkenny; unearthed during clearance work on churchyard of medieval parish church at Cooliagh (thirteenth century), and said to have been buried there in early nineteenth century, after having been discovered in a local well. Figure brought to archaeological notice by Sean O'Doherty in 1979.

Dimensions: (h) 78 cm; c.15 cm thick.

Description: Carved in the round. Earless, inverted pear-shaped head; facial expression calm, ovoid eyes, wedge nose and slit-mouth. Thin neck, round shoulders; no breasts, but slightly incised ribs. Fingers of right hand just touching vulva, indicated as vertical line and ending in very noticeable deep hole. Left hand (much larger than the other) may hold an object resting on thigh. Peculiar leg position reminiscent of Egremont; left leg almost straight with foot turned inwards, while right leg tightly flexed at knee with heel of foot pointing at pudenda.

38 Cullahill (Co. Laois)
Guest 47; Andersen 74; McMahon/Roberts 42
Location: Situated some 14 m up in masonry near W angle of S wall of Cullahill Castle (fifteenth century).
Description: Powerfully built limestone figure carved in relief. Stern, manly looking face with big ears; broad shoulders; big, limp breasts; strong, billowy lines indicating ribs across upper torso; arms in front of body, hands joined with fingers either covering or entering vulva; no legs.

39 Doon (Co. Offaly)
Guest 56; Andersen 75; McMahon/Roberts 43
Location: Quoin stone at S angle of E wall of Doon Castle (fifteenth century); figure inserted horizontally.
Dimensions: (h) 23 cm; (w) 38 cm.
Description: Huge round head with ears; bulbous eyes, wedge nose and open mouth. Round shoulders, small round breasts, lines indicating ribs running across chest; at junction of legs strongly incised oval vulva. Right hand passing behind thigh while left hand passes over thigh, extremely long fingers on both hands. Legs almost straight with both feet pointing in same direction.

40 Dowth (Co. Meath)
Guest 22; Andersen 76; McMahon/Roberts 44
Location: On outer side of S wall of medieval parish church at Dowth; this church was built on site of an earlier pre-Norman church.
Description: Figure only vaguely discernible, obscured by funerary monument. Photograph published by Margaret Murray in 1934 shows a small head, biggish, almost rotund torso and both arms reaching down to sizeable round hole, indicating vulva. Guest reported in 1936 that the 'prominent abdomen characteristic of this figure had been hacked off to accommodate a modern tombstone'. She also asserts that according to a sketch in private possession, at one time figure had splayed legs and hands directed towards lower abdomen. One of the earliest recorded Sheelas, mentioned by both Kohl and Clibborn.

41 Drogheda (Co. Louth)
Andersen 77; McMahon/Roberts 45
Location: Millmount Museum, Drogheda; taken from a Victorian house at No. 18 John Street, Drogheda, where it had been placed some 4.50 m up the front wall; thought to have originally come from nearby medieval hospital site.
Dimensions: (h) 42 cm.
Description: Carved in high relief on block of sandstone and quite weathered. Behind head of figure three contiguous hollow ovals. Large neckless head, two irregular depressions for eyes, no nose, mouth indicated by slit. No breasts; necklace with pendant pointing at long narrow slit, indicating vulva. Arms in front of body with hands touching vulva, and deep touch-hole underneath.

42 Dunnaman (Co. Limerick)
Guest 18; Andersen 78; McMahon/Roberts 46
Location: Set high up among masonry on SE wall of ruined Dunnaman Castle.

Description: Large figure on slab and set within frame. Roundish head shows several billowy lines across forehead, oval eyes, wedge nose and open mouth. Extremely long arms, with open armpits, and hands passing beneath thighs to grab vulva. Flat breasts on heavily incised ribcase which extends over abdomen. Oval-shaped vulva, hanging between widely splayed legs. Large toes touching edge of frame, and between these, directly underneath vulva, there is an egg-shaped object similar to figures 15, 29, 30, 70, 73 and 142. Pose reminiscent of Bunratty.

43 Emlaghmore (Co. Roscommon)
Location: In private possession, at the Colm Mee household, Tempe House, Emlaghmore, Donamon. Found lying in field east of house, and thought to have originally belonged to a church site. Figure brought to archaeological notice by Albert Siggins in 1990.
Dimensions: Length of figure 22 cm (block: 69 cm high; 48 cm in depth at top; 25 cm in width).
Description: Carved in high relief on front of richly ornamented limestone block; the two sides of stone show a demi-angel, an animal, foliate and floral decoration, and its top face carries tracing of an octagonal sundial with mounting holes. Front divided into three zones with Sheela in centre panel which, unlike rest of decoration, appears to have been deliberately defaced. Slightly exaggerated head with tresses of hair running down both sides of face; no facial features remain. Broad shoulders, arms in front of body, traces of hands on thighs; slit-vulva. Seated figure with thighs widely splayed and feet folded back underneath rump. Feet seem to be joined to tresses of hair.

44 Errigal Keeroge 1 (Co. Tyrone)
Guest 62; Andersen 79; McMahon/Roberts 47
Location: Ulster Museum, Belfast; figure found in old church of Errigal Keeroge (formerly church of St Dachiarog), near Ballygawley.
Dimensions: (h) 46 cm.
Description: Figure carved on slab in high relief and with all features distorted. Large head with ears at different height; big, round eyes, long, crooked nose and wide-open, slanting mouth. Left shoulder higher than the other; left breast hanging lower than the other. Thick arms with big hands close to genitals; fingers of left hand rest on thigh, just touching vulva; right hand passes underneath thigh, holding it up. Thighs splayed, lower legs barely discernible.

45 Errigal Keeroge 2 (Co. Tyrone)
McMahon/Roberts 48
Location: Ulster Museum, Belfast; concrete replica inserted into low masonry remains of old church of Errigal Keeroge (same site as no. 44). Figure published as possible tomb stone by Nick Brannon in 1981/2.
Dimensions: (h) 91 cm; (w) 42 cm.
Description of replica: Unique figure on roughly rectangular slab; neckless head indicated by recessed impression without any facial features. To left of head there is a deep, straight and vertical groove which is connected to head by a crack, giving impression of pipe-smoking. Arms reaching straight down to small, triangular pudenda. Figure in squatting position, thighs splayed, knees pulled up, feet not discernible.

46 Fethard Abbey (Co. Tipperary)

Guest 58; Andersen 80; McMahon/Roberts 49

Location: Inserted low in N face of wall adjacent to E end of Augustinian Friary (fourteenth century). Obviously not original to this position because edges of carving worked to follow lines of an arch. An architectural fluting running lengthwise at back of figure would further reinforce this.

Dimensions: (h) 50 cm; (w) 20 cm.

Description: Carved in high relief on wedge-shaped slab. Big swollen head with prominent asymmetrical jug ears, lined forehead, streaked cheeks, bulbous eyes, strong nose and small mouth. Clearly defined ribs, no breasts. Right arm missing; left arm in front of body, hand with dainty fingers on lower abdomen. Lower part of figure appears defaced, genitals no longer discernible. Spindly legs straight and wide apart; feet missing.

47 Fethard Wall (Co. Tipperary)

Guest 13; Andersen 81; McMahon/Roberts 50

Location: Situated in middle of a small section of town wall which runs NE and belongs to sixteenth/early seventeenth century. Figure overlooks Clashawley river and Watergate Bridge.

Dimensions: (h) 50 cm; (w) 20 cm.

Description: Surrounding stones of wall placed to accommodate figure which appears to be carved in the round. Biggish head with strong facial features; staring eyes, clearly incised triangular pattern starting underneath left eye and radiating towards wall, slightly open grim mouth showing clenched teeth. Emaciated neck, no breasts, deeply incised ribs and a protruding round navel. Figure is seated with short legs widely splayed; hands passing underneath thighs with fingers disappearing in vulva.

48 Freshford (Co. Kilkenny)

Location: Unrecorded figure; brought to my attention by Gay Cannon. In private possession (Mr & Mrs Dowling), now built into wall of farm on site of Balleen Castle; original provenance unknown.

Dimensions: (h) 39 cm; (w) 29 cm (slab 45 cm high and 52 cm wide).

Description: Carved within recessed frame on right hand side of roughly rectangular slab. Big, skull-shaped head with jug ears and strong facial features; thick ovoid eyes, flat wedge nose, deep striations on both cheeks, thick-lipped, open mouth displaying two rows of gritted teeth. Flat, pointy breasts at shoulder level; clearly marked ribs; big round navel. Arms in front of body with both hands reaching into vulva indicated as slit; fingers barely discernible. Legs widely splayed and bent; feet pointed outwards. A plait-like band hangs from left ear and disappears behind left shoulder (reminiscent of Clomantagh).

49 Garrycastle (Co. Offaly)

McMahon/Roberts 51

Location: Situated very high on E wall of ruined battlements of Garrycastle (fifteenth century); figure discovered in 1981.

Description: Large and unusually plump figure with round head, jug ears and simple facial features. Asymmetrical pendulous breasts; both arms in front of body, hands pulling at round vulva; legs splayed.

50 Glanworth (Co. Cork)

McMahon/Roberts 52

Location: National Monuments Depot, Mallow; figure unearthed during archaeological excavations at Glanworth Castle (thirteenth–sixteenth centuries); discovered beneath rubble in vaulted ground floor chamber, in N side of original gate tower where it appears to have been deliberately hidden in or before seventeenth century. First published by Conleth Manning in 1987.

Dimensions: (h) 55 cm; (w) 34 cm; (d) 44cm.

Description: Partially carved in the round from heavy, trapezoidal-shaped red sandstone; otherwise limestone only used in castle. Figure asymmetrical with large head and flat face, crooked wedge nose, mouth slightly to the right and consisting of horizontal line crossed by short vertical lines, possibly indicating teeth. Shoulders hunched upwards; flat, droopy breasts between which the navel is exposed; strongly incised ribs. Left arm in front of body, fingers touching vulva; right arm passing under thigh. Both legs widely splayed and flexed, left foot missing, right foot shown in relief. Swollen-looking oval vulva surrounded by thick rim of flesh and with round touch-hole underneath.

51 Holycross (Co. Tipperary)

Andersen 82; McMahon/Roberts 53

Location: Figure situated some 2–3 m up beside quoin on outer wall of W range of Holycross, a Cistercian abbey, built during thirteenth–fifteenth centuries, and restored in the 1960s–1970s. Sheela discovered in 1970.

Description: Mutilated figure on slab with traces of severe hacking. Big head, arms in front of body; slit-vulva; splayed legs with feet turned outwards.

52 Kildare (Co. Kildare)

Andersen 83; McMahon/Roberts 55

Location: Tomb of Bishop Wellesley (d. 1539) which once stood at Great Connell Abbey near Newbridge, and now re-erected in Kildare Cathedral; Sheela on underside of top slab in upper left corner, above crucifixion panel.

Description: On underside there are other carvings of foliate and human motifs, not evident on upper surface of slab. Sheela perfectly carved, with a rotund appearance. Round head with chubby face and short hair. Small round breasts, big navel and swollen-looking abdomen; pubic hair and discreet vulva; legs widely splayed, bent back at the knees with feet grasped by hands. Position of hands and legs very similar to Lower Swell 2.

53 Killaloe (Co. Clare)

Guest 37; Andersen 84; McMahon/Roberts 56

Location: Figure on ground to right of St Flannan's Well in garden of Allied Irish Bank, an area that was once within precincts of cathedral and appears to have been a graveyard.

Description: Carved on slab; head cut off; arms splayed out with hands joining over pudenda; legs widely splayed, knees bent.

54 Killinaboy (Co. Clare)

Guest 32; Andersen 85; McMahon/Roberts 57

Location: Above doorway on outer face of S wall of old church now in ruins; church had been built on site of early monastery founded by the daughter of Baoithe.

Description: Round head, very grim mouth; emaciated neck; no breasts; clearly marked ribs. Arms in front of body with hands around genitals. Something seems to pour out of pudenda. Standing position with legs apart and slightly bent at knees, feet turned outwards.

55 Kilmokea (Co. Wexford)

Location: National Museum of Ireland, Dublin. Unrecorded figure; preserved as headstone (object 40/1994/IA84/93), and brought to my attention by Conleth Manning (Dúchas, Dublin). Figure was discovered in the gardens of Kilmokea House, Great Island, Campile, and presumed to have come from adjacent cemetery.

Dimensions: (h) 48 cm (slab 84 cm high; 30 cm wide at top, and 25 cm at bottom).

Description: Wedge-shaped schistose slab with headstone inscription (reading: 'MB.D.12 March 1705.a 72') on one side and Sheela on the other. Figure crude and somewhat atypical; defined by grooves roughly describing figure of woman. Head shaped like an American football, without facial features, connected to torso by most remarkable big hole (*c.*4 cm deep). The only other Sheela with hole in that position is Seir Kieran. Angular shoulders; two neatly carved holes in chest area indicating breasts; straight arms reaching down to genital area; legs apart and straight, no feet. Traces of a horizontal and two vertical lines between legs.

56 Kilsarkan (Co. Kerry)

Andersen 87; McMahon/Roberts 61

Location: Above S window of medieval parish church.

Description: Big triangular head with rope-like hair and prominent jug ears; bulbous eyes, wedge nose and small open mouth. Body divides below neck; no arms; very broad genital area which shows signs of rubbing; legs spread horizontally, stretching out over spandrels of window; feet turned outwards; left leg slightly raised.

57 Kilshane (Co. Tipperary, SR)

Location: Inserted high up on gable-end wall of farm building, with a decorative arch placed above it. Farm yard was formerly associated with Holy Ghost Fathers' Seminary adjacent to it; both now in private hands, belonging to Finbar MacLoughlin. Unrecorded figure, brought to my attention through notebooks of the late Dean of Cashel, the Very Reverend David Woodworth.

Description: Figure carved right of centre on large rectangular slab. Big round head, earless and bald; stern face, slit-eyes and with grim cast to mouth. No neck; arms in front of body with both hands touching pudenda. Legs widely splayed and bent at knees, feet turned outwards.

58 Kiltinane Castle (Co. Tipperary, SR)

Guest 60; Andersen 88; McMahon/Roberts 62

Location: High up on N wall of small tower well-house and overlooking Clashawley river; well-house connected to castle by stairway. Not in original position; figure was put in place here in 1940, and it may have come from nearby Kiltinane Church, also home of figure 58. In private possession, belonging to Andrew Lloyd Webber.

Description: Small figure carved in high relief on slab. Well sculpted head with grim facial expression, several lines across forehead to side of head, deep-set eyes. No neck; slim torso with small breasts and deeply incised ribs. Oval pudenda; widely splayed legs tapering into stone. One of the few Sheelas with both arms raised, holding an object in each hand. Neither object clearly discernible, left hand holds up circular shape and right hand a slim, pointed shape.

59 Kiltinane Church (Co. Tipperary, SR)

Guest 59; Andersen 89; McMahon/Roberts 63

Location: Strictly speaking this Sheela should be listed under 'record only' because it was stolen from the old ruined church of Kiltinane in 1990, and despite a Wanted Poster issued by Fethard Historical Society offering a reward for her return, she is still missing today. Figure was inserted horizontally as a quoin stone in SW corner of church. A replica was carved by local artist James O'Connor. Figure was the first to be described by the Ordnance Survey in 1840.

Dimensions: (h) 81 cm; (w) 51 cm.

Description: Carved on large, but very thin, rectangular limestone slab. Whole figure asymmetrical. Triangular, earless head with bulbous eyes, long nose and open mouth, set on thin, elongated neck. Odd droopy breasts, one with two nipples, dangling on big round belly. Left arm raised, bent at elbow, big hand with fingers spreading fanwise to touch left side of face. Right arm reaches down to genitals, with fingers reaching into open vulva, indicated by a deep straight groove. Legs wide apart, sharply bent at knee with feet turned outwards. Left leg raised higher.

60 Knockarley (Co. Offaly)

McMahon/Roberts 64

Location: Figure found buried in graveyard; exact provenance unknown; first published by John Feehan in 1979.

Dimensions: (h) 55 cm.

Description: Carved almost in the round from local sandstone and considerably weathered. Small neat hole in top of head similar to hole below vulva. Earless head inclined slightly to right; flat, expressive face with ovoid eyes, eyebrows, straight nose and open mouth. Elongated neck with faint traces of a rectangular ornament in throat area; thick chain-like feature around neck. Right hand rests on abdomen, above navel, the left lies on thigh. Vulva a small incision surrounded by thick raised oval; with touch-hole underneath it. Kneeling position.

61 Lavey (Co. Cavan)

Guest 2; Andersen 90; McMahon/Roberts 65

Location: Cavan County Museum, Ballyjamesduff (on loan from National Museum of Ireland); found in graveyard at Lavey in 1842, and believed to have come from medieval parish church.

Dimensions: (slab 47 cm high; 58 cm wide; 18 cm thick).

Description: Figure flatly carved on left hand side of thick slab; upper left corner damaged. Large head set between shoulders; deeply set eyes, thick nose, open mouth showing gappy teeth. No breasts or ribs, but navel clearly incised. Thick arms reaching down in front of body; fingers of both big hands touch raised rim of vulva which is depicted as vertical groove with small, round touch-hole underneath. Short, stumpy legs wide apart, feet with extremely long toes turned outwards. On or under left arm (measuring 11 cm in diameter) figure holds round object whose outline is incised on top of arm. Lixnaw holds object in similar position.

62 Liathmore (Co. Tipperary)
Guest 61; Andersen 91; McMahon/Roberts 67
Location: Figure lies horizontally on E impost of N doorway of the larger of two churches on old monastic site; though placed in fifteenth-century work, figure appears to be of twelfth century.
Dimensions: (h) 10 cm; (w) 45 cm.
Description: Figure carved in low relief on sandstone; lower member is a ball or pellet ornament; at feet a decorative foliate motif, now defaced. It is a good deal stylized. Triangular head with big round eyes, strong nose and slit-mouth. Breasts flat but well proportioned; both arms in front of body, hands touching large pudenda, indicated as long vertical slit with surrounding raised rim, and hanging between straight legs.

63 Lixnaw (Co. Kerry)
Andersen 93; McMahon/Roberts 68
Location: National Museum of Ireland, Dublin; found in bed of River Cashen near medieval castle at Lixnaw.
Dimensions: (h) 29 cm; (w) 15 cm.
Description: Carved in relief on one face of roughly rectangular block of coarse feldspathic grit, possibly old red sandstone, and badly weathered. Large head with pointed chin (somewhat damaged); bulbous eyes outlined by pecked groove. Pendulous, clearly marked breasts; broad shoulders. Flexed arms pass behind widely splayed thighs with both hands grasping swollen-looking, sagging pudenda from below, small touch-hole underneath. Legs splayed and bent with feet turned outwards. Figure holds a raised oval object under left arm in similar position as Lavey.

64 Maghera (Co. Derry)
Guest 42; Andersen 95; McMahon/Roberts 71
Location: About 6 m above ground level in wall of tower on N side of medieval church.
Dimensions: (h) 30 cm.
Description: Lower part of figure damaged. Big round head with jug ears; arms reaching down in front of body with hands close to or touching pudenda.

65 Malahide (Co. Dublin)
Andersen 96; McMahon/Roberts 72
Location: On quoin at springing of gable, NE angle of choir of ruined medieval church in ancient cemetery E of Malahide Castle. Not in primary position, lower part of stone cut off to fit position.
Dimensions: (h) 48 cm; (w) 25 cm.
Description: Figure carved in false relief on red sandstone and set within frame. Big, earless head, flat face with downcast eyes, drooping gash of a mouth; short neck; squat

body. No ribs or breasts, but navel clearly indicated. Only left arm discernible, held straight with hand resting on thigh. Long vertical slit-vulva hanging between straight legs. No feet, presumably cut off together with lower edge.

66 Merlin Park (Co. Galway)
Figure discovered in 2002. Thanks to Chris Corlett (Dúchas, Dublin) it was brought to my attention by Martin Fitzpatrick, Athenry.
Location: Figure on second floor of sixteenth-century Merlin Park Tower House, on decorated spandrel above opening in S wall.
Description: Unusual figure because sitting upside down, below decorative motif; in opposite corner there is a six-petal marigold. Round head with facial features discernible; breasts indicated; both arms straight and in front of body, hands joined to touch long vertical slit indicating vulva.

67 Moate (Co. Westmeath)
Guest 64; Andersen 97; McMahon/Roberts 73
Location: Resting on top of pointed gateway of farmyard behind Moate Castle; wall was rebuilt in seventeenth century; Sheela not in original position.
Dimensions: (h) 28 cm.
Description: Carved in an oval impression of roughly rectangular slab. All features asymmetrical. Huge head, wavy lines across forehead, ovoid eyes (left empty, right with eyeball), puffy cheeks, grim open mouth showing teeth. Tiny breasts; protruding belly; arms reaching down in front of body with fingers of both hands grabbing oval vulva. Of legs only left thigh is discernible. A belt passes obliquely round abdomen.

68 Newton-Lennon (Co. Tipperary)
Andersen 100; McMahon/Roberts 76
Location: National Museum of Ireland, Dublin; found on surface of ancient churchyard of ruined medieval church.
Dimensions: (h) 37 cm; (w) 27 cm.
Description: Crude sandstone figure carved in the round. Triangular head without ears; round eyes (right lower and larger than left), small nose, open mouth; no neck, no breasts. Arms in front of body reaching for deeply cut pudenda. Legs not discernible.

69 Rahan (Co. Offaly)
Andersen 102; McMahon/Roberts 78
Location: Castle Museum, Athlone; figure found in 1971 during grave-digging in cemetery S of St Carthach's Church.
Dimensions: (h) 28 cm; (w) 21 cm (block 37 cm high, 35 cm wide and 25 cm deep).
Description: Carved in high relief on block of hard blue-grey limestone; top slightly damaged. A singular V-shaped groove starting in forehead of Sheela runs across top of head through to rear of block, and is inclined downwards towards back of stone (a V-shaped cut-out on underside surface also found on figure 70). Big head with hair or tight-fitting cap, wavy lines across forehead, prominent brow ridges, broad wrinkled nose and beading round upper lip, possibly representing teeth. Powerful shoulders; both arms somewhat mutilated. V-shaped vulva with indented ring around it. Wide open thighs; legs bent and held back behind body by hands. Pose similar to figures 33, 127, 133 and 160.

70 Rahara (Co. Roscommon)

McMahon/Roberts 79

Location: Roscommon County Museum, Roscommon Town; figure found buried face downwards in ground during clean-up campaign of old graveyard and ruined medieval church of Rahara; original provenance unknown. First published by Albert Siggins in 1990.

Dimensions: (h) 40 cm; (w) 32 cm; (d) 32 cm.

Description: Carved in low relief on wedge-shaped stone which appears to have served as keystone, a function further reinforced by V-shaped cut-out on underside surface. Figure unique because of huge hair plaits, executed in a three-strand interlace pattern flowing down to elbows. No ears; almond-shaped eyes, wedge nose and very pronounced nostril channels between nose and lip. Dangling small breasts under armpits; pronounced navel; arms splayed and bent, hands placed behind thighs and coming up underneath to open slit-vulva with three fingers of each hand. Directly underneath pudenda, between widely splayed legs, bent at knees, lies vertical object, similar to figures 15, 29, 30, 42, 73 and 142.

71 Rathcline (Co. Longford)

Figure came to my attention in notebooks of the late Dean of Cashel, the Very Reverend David Woodworth.

Location: On S facing bevel of W ogee-headed window of ruined church.

Dimensions: (h) 29 cm; (w) 8 cm.

Description: Skilfully carved, stylized and unusual figure in that it forms part of window; small groove in window pointing directly at vulva. Triangular head with indication of short hair; no ears, ovoid eyes, grim mouth; no breasts; hands clasped over abdomen. Vulva swollen looking, two vertical lines ending in deep round hole; legs straight and slightly apart with feet turned outwards; left leg slightly longer.

72 Rattoo (Co. Kerry)

Guest 21; Andersen 104; McMahon/Roberts 81

Location: Placed at great height on inside left hand corner of upper N facing window of eleventh/twelfth-century round tower, and discovered in 1880/1. Plaster cast in National Museum of Ireland, Dublin.

Dimensions: (h) 29 cm; (w) 14 cm.

Description of plaster cast: Flat figure with big head, pronounced forehead and strangely formed, almost rectangular ears; depression indicating eyes and mouth, but no nose, pointed chin; thin neck. Angular shoulders; no breasts. Arms flexed with left hand on thigh; hands not visible in plaster cast, but extension of arm pointing in direction of pudenda; right arm held at right angle; if original delineates hand it would be on abdomen. Thighs and calves of figure well rounded; both feet pointing outwards.

73 Redwood (Co. Tipperary)

McMahon/Roberts 82

Location: Very high up on wall in masonry E over doorway on rear of Redwood Castle (thirteenth–fifteenth centuries).

Description: Figure carved on irregular slab. Because of extreme height precise details difficult to make out. Large shapeless head set on spindly body. Face shows round eyes and huge, slightly open, big-lipped mouth. Downward grooves beside head and body. Tiny breasts; arms reaching down in front of body with both hands pointing at or touching genitals. Sagging pudenda with deep, round hole between splayed and slightly bent legs; feet turned outwards. There is a vertical feature directly below pudenda not unlike object depicted between legs of carvings 15, 29, 30, 42, 70 and 142.

74 Ringaskiddy (Co. Cork)
Guest 21; McMahon/Roberts 83
Location: Public Museum, Cork; figure possibly one of two Ringaskiddy figures, stated to be in a private garden, but not located by Guest.
Description: Carved in raised relief on large, roughly rectangular stone slab. Small ears; lines across forehead, circular eyes set closely together, a deep incision representing mouth. Thin small neck; round shoulders; lean torso without breasts, but navel indicated. Right arm slightly bent, left straight; both hands resting close to genitals which look swollen with a deep cut down the middle. Straight legs and both feet turning inwards with toes almost touching.

75 Rosenallis (Co. Laois)
McMahon/Roberts 85
Location: National Museum of Ireland, Dublin; found in Church of Ireland graveyard in 1992.
Dimensions: (h) 51 cm; (w) 31 cm.
Description: Heavy looking figure carved on irregular sandstone slab and quite weathered. Facial features discernible; short hair indicated. Heavy, round shoulders; small breasts, a few ribs. Decidedly swollen abdomen, possibly indicating pregnancy. Arms slightly bent; both hands touching oval pudenda. Squatting position, legs splayed and bent, feet turned outwards.

76 Rosnaree (Co. Meath)
Guest 15; Andersen 106; McMahon/Roberts 86
Location: In private possession; belonging to Barbara and George Heise, owners of old water mill-house on bank of river Boyne. Figure formerly built into wall beside door of mill (not original location), removed and at present kept safe in store. Present mill-house occupies site of earlier mill run by Cistercian monks of Mellifont, from twelfth century onwards. Owners kindly allowed me to examine Sheela.
Dimensions: (h) 54 cm; (w) 40 cm; (d) 20 cm.
Description: Crudely carved on irregular stone slab; widest at bottom part which is cut straight, allowing figure to sit firmly on ground. Elongated, deeply hollowed out groove in crown of head (presumably for libations) further indication of figure originally free-standing. Left side defaced, and some damage also to chin, right forearm, right foot and lower part of leg. Large head, no ears, big owl-like eyes with eyebrows, clearly marked nostrils, jagged incision indicating mouth and possibly teeth. Four striations on right cheek running down to side of slab. No neck or breasts, but clearly marked navel. Right arm reaches under leg which is widely splayed, but no hands or fingers traceable. Genitals indicated by deep semi-circular depression.

77 Scregg 1 (Co. Roscommon)

McMahon/Roberts 87

Location: Positioned *c*.3 m from the ground on gable wall towards right extremity of gable of carriage building (built *c*.1760) which belongs to Scregg House, a Georgian country residence. Not in original position, and thought to have come from ruined Scregg Castle at back of house. First published by Albert Siggins in 1990.

Dimensions: (h) 30 cm; (w) 25 cm.

Description: This larger of the two Sheelas is carved in false relief on a keystone shaped stone. Flat areas on side of stone decorated in chisel-punch fashion, as is area between legs of figure. Whole carving asymmetrical; prominent splayed ears, big, almond-shaped eyes with eyeballs, wedge nose and scowling mouth with pointed tongue sticking out. Small breasts, strong rib bones. Arms splayed and bent, fingers of both hands touching round pudenda; further hole underneath. Legs splayed, feet turning outwards.

78 Scregg 2 (Co. Roscommon)

McMahon/Roberts 88

Location: Same as figure 77, but at left hand side of gable.

Dimensions: (h) 10 cm (stone: 35 cm high; 20 cm wide).

Description: Carved in high relief on upper half of rectangular slab; quite weathered; compact little figure with round head, no ears, indistinct facial features apart from wide open mouth. No breasts; arms reach down in front of body with both hands close to pudenda. Round abdomen and swollen-looking genital area; wedge-shaped, open vulva. Legs splayed almost horizontally and not bent; feet pointing upwards.

79 Seir Kieran (Co. Offaly)

Guest 3/27; Andersen 107; McMahon/Roberts 89

Location: National Museum of Ireland, Dublin; believed to have come from E gable of old church of St Kieran (now destroyed); illustrated and vaguely described in *Dublin Penny Journal* 3 in 1834/5 as 'a grotesque figure in freestone' projecting from wall.

Dimensions: (h) 43 cm; (w) 27 cm.

Description: One of the best known Irish Sheelas because of ring of holes drilled around genital area and additional holes in throat and top of head, suggestive of having served some pagan ritualistic function. Round head with ears, hollow ovoid eyes, small nose, round, wide open mouth and striations on cheeks. Heavy shoulders, flat pointy breasts resting on deeply incised ribcase. Seated on her haunches with knees pulled up and splayed, held back by elbows. Right hand close to pudenda, fingers pointing downwards, left hand holds round object at height of pudenda. Feet turned outwards.

80 Shanrahan (Co. Tipperary)

McMahon/Roberts 90

Location: High up on W wall of (church) tower below closed up window. Tower seems to have been used, for a time, as residence; remains of cylindrical corner tower (SE) and bawn wall in surrounding graveyard; unlikely original position.

Description: Carved on red sandstone, seemingly in the round; details difficult to describe because of height. Big head with prominent jug ears, colour of eyes different (brighter) from rest of carving, open mouth; very thick neck. Arms akimbo forming two circles, left hand rests on pudenda, right seems to be close to it. Legs apart; feet may both turn in same direction.

81 Stepaside (Co. Dublin)

Guest 43; Andersen 109; McMahon/Roberts 91

Location: Situated beside old well in laneway of public golf course; site formerly early monastery.

Dimensions: (h) 80 cm (stone 1 m high).

Description: Stone shaped irregularly as stunted cross. On W face circular shape with two vertical bands; Sheela carved in high relief on E face. Heavy round figure, with head set low between shoulders and slightly towards left; no ears; facial features and navel indicated. Arms in front of body; hands joined over pudenda represented, or covered by worn square object.

82 Swords (Co. Dublin)

Andersen 110; McMahon/Roberts 93

Location: National Museum of Ireland, Dublin; found serving as gatepost at Drynam House, Swords Glebe; original location unknown.

Dimensions: (h) 67 cm; (w) 28 cm (pillar 1.5 m high).

Description: Carved in high relief on pillar stone and weathered. Facial features worn away; thick neck; round shoulders; small breasts, navel indicated. Arms slightly splayed with hands reaching for small oval pudenda; touch-hole underneath. Legs splayed and bent; feet turned outwards; right leg raised.

83 Taghboy (Co. Roscommon)

Figure brought to my attention by Eddie Geraghty (Dúchas, Athenry).

Location: On apex stone crowning W gable of medieval parish church, a multi-period edifice of twelfth and seventeenth centuries, standing on early Christian site. Church was burnt to ground, but partially restored in 1995.

Dimensions: (h) 21 cm.

Description: Figure carved on triangular gable top. Big, round head with jug ears; ovoid eyes showing eyeballs, wedge nose and slit-mouth. Droopy flat breasts attached to collar bone. Arms splayed in front of body with both hands grabbing wide open vulva. Figure depicted in squatting position. Legs widely splayed and bent. Amniotic sac protruding from pudenda, partially lying on ground.

84 Taghmon (Co. Westmeath)

Guest 65; Andersen 111; McMahon/Roberts 94

Location: Over trefoil window in N wall of fifteenth-century church; not in original position.

Description: Figure carved on slab in seated position. Big head without ears; pained expression on face, with mouth wide open, baring two rows of teeth. Two indentations for eyebrows and clearly marked nostrils. Big hands clasping tightly flexed knees. Lower legs held apart, revealing big oval pudenda with round hole in middle. Pose similar to figures 1, 5 and 79. Lower part of carving missing.

85 Tara (Co. Meath)

Guest 30; Andersen 112; McMahon/Roberts 95
Location: Free-standing stone (known as St Adamnan's pillar) in churchyard.
Dimensions: (h) 43 cm.
Description: Carved in high relief on lower half of stone, and because much worn difficult to interpret in detail. Big jug ears; facial features simple indentations. Arms in front of body, joined together in vaguely discernible gesture towards lower abdomen; left leg nearly straight, the other bent inwards.

86 Thurles (Co. Tipperary)

McMahon/Roberts 96
Location: St Mary's Famine Church; for many years figure was embedded in old town wall at Slibhnamon Rd in yard of car tyre firm; original location unknown.
Dimensions: (h) 51 cm; (w) 53 cm.
Description: Carved in high relief on slab, badly weathered. Skull-like head with round hollow eyes, long pointed chin. Angular shoulders; flat droopy breasts; arms widely splayed, revealing armpits; right hand touching pudenda. Lower part of body deliberately defaced; right leg missing and genital area mutilated. Left hand passes under thigh.

87 Toomregan (Co. Cavan)

Andersen 114; McMahon/Roberts 99
Location: Deposited inside doorway of Church of Ireland chapel at Ballyconnell for safe keeping; found in ditch; original location unknown. Doubtful Sheela.
Dimensions: (h) 59 cm; (w) 86 cm.
Description: Carving on arch-stone; long head with prominent ears, ovoid eyes with eyeballs, lower part of face mutilated. Figure with arms and legs, but no body. Sagging, apple-shaped genitalia indicated between widely splayed legs. Both hands hold an identical unidentifiable object.

88 Tracton (Co. Cork)

Guest 41; Andersen 115; McMahon/Roberts 100
Location: Public Museum, Cork; found at site of Cistercian abbey.
Dimensions: (h) 36 cm; (w) 30 cm.
Description: Carved on sandstone block, curved section cut from lower left hand corner to fit architectural setting. Triangular, earless head with big, round eyes. Arms slightly splayed with hands hanging at sides of body; legs splayed exposing large, deeply cut almost rectangular-shaped pudenda from which a V-shaped object is protruding. There is a band-like feature partly across the flank.

89 Tullaroan (Co. Kilkenny)

Thanks to Anne Coogan, figure was brought to my attention. Found in 1992 among rubble from demolished wall of old schoolhouse in Tullaroan (erected in 1842).
First published by Ellen Prendergast in 1992.
Location: In private possession, owned by Noel Coogan, Rathealy.
Dimensions: (h) 62 cm; (w) 25 cm (slab 75 cm high, 35 cm wide at top, 25 cm at bottom).

Description: Carved in false relief on wedge-shaped slab of pure crystalline limestone. Round head, set slightly to left; damaged nose; large projecting ears hollowed out from centre; eyes similarly hollowed out cavities; left eye has small punctured hole placed near centre of pupil. Three similar holes along horizontal slot form outline of mouth, one further hole in chest area, close to left arm. Thin neck; angular shoulders; tiny breasts attached to collar bone. Very pronounced ribcase extending over abdomen; navel indicated by circle. Arms lie close to body and pass behind legs with hands grabbing extremely long slit-vulva hanging between widely splayed thighs. Right leg longer with big foot and toes turning outwards; other foot not clearly discernible.

90 Tullavin (Co. Limerick)
Guest 19; Andersen 116; McMahon/Roberts 101
Location: High up on quoin of S face of Tullavin Castle (fifteenth century) at E side; inserted horizontally.
Description: Carved in high relief on corner stone. Left arm raised to head, depicted with some kind of head-dress and arresting facial features. Long torso with small breasts, ribs and navel; very long, contorted right arm passes under thigh with at least two fingers touching slit-vulva. Legs widely splayed; big toes turned outwards.

Record only

Reference is made to Guest's and Andersen's lists only.

91 Ballynamona Castle (Co. Cork)
Guest 38; Andersen (unnumbered, p. 145)
Sheela destroyed about 1820.

92 Barnahealy Castle (Co. Cork)
Guest 16; Andersen 56
Sheela now missing.

93 Carrick Castle (Co. Kildare)
Guest 44; Andersen 63
Sheela no longer located, supposedly transferred to Cambridge Museum of Archaeology and Ethnology.

94 Cloghan Castle (Co. Offaly)
Guest 6; Andersen 68
Sheela no longer to be found, but supposedly preserved in a museum in the south of Ireland.

95 Kells (Co. Meath)
Guest 53; Andersen (unnumbered, p. 149)
Church Sheela no longer to be found.

96 Killinny (Co. Kilkenny)
Figure was removed from old church, and later demolished by local parish priest. Church no longer exists. The story is referred to in Chapter 4, pp. 104ff.

97 Kilmacomma (Co. Waterford)

Andersen 86

Figure found in sandpit by farmer who inserted it in gable of his barn around end of nineteenth century. His son removed and hid it, and was later unable to relocate it.

98 Kilmainham (Co. Meath)

Guest 54; Andersen (unnumbered, p. 149)

Figure buried in churchyard near railway station in the 1890s.

99 Kirkiston (Co. Down)

Andersen (unnumbered, p. 149)

H. C. Lawlor refers to three Sheelas built high up into the wall of Savage's Castle at Kirkiston (*MAN*, XXXII, 1932, no. 49), but they have all disappeared.

100 Lemanaghan Castle (Co. Offaly)

Guest 5; Andersen 92

Sheela known from a drawing (1870) belonging to Thomas Cooke of Birr. Neither drawing nor stone can now be found, and castle mostly demolished in 1950s.

101 Lusk (Co. Dublin)

Guest 10; Andersen 94

Figure was seen in church and described by antiquarian Austin Cooper in 1783, but by 1844 it had already been buried by Rev. Mr Tyrrell.

102 Moycarky Castle (Co. Tipperary)

Guest 28; Andersen 98

Sheela said to be on S wall of castle. A nineteenth-century sketch of figure preserved in the RIA Library, Dublin (shown in Andersen, p. 150).

103 Portnahinch Castle (Co. Laois)

Guest 50; Andersen 101

Castle now ruined, but Sheela was saved and re-erected in garden wall of private house together with the Sheela from Tinnakill. Photographs of both figures were published by H. C. Lawlor (*MAN*, XXXII, 1932, no. 49, p. 45). Due to an accident both figures were knocked down and later re-used as building material (according to Mrs Fennelly, owner of house). All attempts to find missing figures have failed.

104 Ringaskiddy (Co. Cork)

Guest 31; Andersen (unnumbered, p. 151)

Two Sheelas stated to have existed in private garden could not be found by Guest during her visits in 1934 and the following year. One of the figures (74) appears to be in Public Museum, Cork.

105 Rochestown (Co. Tipperary)

Guest 7; Andersen 105

Figure used to be in gable of old church, but is now missing. A nineteenth-century sketch survives (shown in Andersen, p. 151).

106 Shane Castle (Co. Laois)

Guest 48; Andersen 108

O'Donovan refers to this Sheela in *Ordnance Survey Letters* of 1840 (see Chapter 2, p. 17). Castle was destroyed in 1650, and rebuilt as private residence in eighteenth century. Figure now missing.

107 Shane's Castle (Co. Antrim)

Andersen (unnumbered, p. 152)

H. C. Lawlor, who published information on figures 99 and 103, in same article also mentions this Sheela, known locally as the 'Luck Stone of the O'Neills'. Figure no longer exists.

108 Summerhill (Co. Meath)

Guest 55; Andersen (unnumbered, p. 152)

In 1911 figure was seen in rock garden of Lord Longford's estate, now a derelict ruin. Figure cannot be found.

109 Timahoe Castle (Co. Laois)

Guest 26 and 36; Andersen (unnumbered, p. 152)

In the 1890s one or possibly two Sheelas were reported from this castle, but none can now be found.

110 Tinnakill Castle (Co. Laois)

Guest 49; Andersen 113

Figure was discovered in garden wall of private house together with Portnahinch Castle Sheela, but met with same fate as the latter.

England

Extant figures

111 Abson (Avon)

McMahon/Roberts 1

Location: High on S facing wall of fourteenth/fifteenth-century tower of church of St James the Great; inserted horizontally at base of unidentifiable effigy.

Description: Due to height details extremely difficult to make out. Big head set on round shoulders; arms splayed and bent with hands on genital area; legs splayed and bent with feet pointing outwards. A band-like feature seems to lie on right flank and another unidentifiable object on chest. A little doubtful because vulva not clearly visible from ground.

112 Alderwasley (Derbyshire)

Figure came to my attention through Internet (http://www.jharding.demon.co.uk/SheelaAlderwasley.htm), accessed 13 December 2000.

Location: On corner stone of old chapel in village.

Description: Figure very weathered and somewhat doubtful. Described as having hunched up knees, folded arms, and cleft in lower abdomen.

113 Ampney St Peter (Gloucestershire)
Andersen 12; McMahon/Roberts 2
Location: Inside church on S wall of nave; 2 m off ground; overlooking font.
Dimensions: 38 cm.
Description: Carved on slab in high relief; lower part of figure defaced. Large, round head on broad neck; no ears; hair or tight-fitting cap; open thick-lipped mouth; well marked, high, rounded breasts; indication of ribs. Mutilated abdominal area suggests that pregnancy may have been indicated; outline of pudenda still showing. Thin arms reach down to genital area; legs small and broken, and clearly splayed.

114 Austerfield (South Yorkshire)
Andersen 13; McMahon/Roberts 3
Location: St Helen's church; placed at corner of capital in twelfth-century N arcade of nave.
Dimensions: (h) 28 cm; (w) 32 cm.
Description: Foliate ornament behind figure; no facial features, tool marks suggest deliberate mutilation; plumpish body in seated position. Right arm in front of body; hand touches slit-vulva; left arm joined to widely splayed thigh, hand possibly beneath it.

115 Bilton 1 (Bilton-in-Ainsty, North Yorkshire)
Andersen 14; McMahon/Roberts 5
Location: St Helen's church (twelfth century); at top of wall inside vestry; prior to construction of vestry, this was an outside wall and figures decorated eaves of chancel.
Dimensions: (h) 20 cm; (w) 25 cm.
Description: Figure on corbel; round head without ears; facial features discernible; no neck, no breasts. Big, soft shoulders; arms in front of body; both hands in vulva, indicated as simple hole. Huge haunches; squatting position with legs wide apart.

116 Bilton 2 (Bilton-in-Ainsty, North Yorkshire)
Andersen 15; McMahon/Roberts 4
Location: Situated beside figure 115.
Description: Shape similar to figure 115, but this specimen shows many signs of mutilation. Left leg hacked away; right arm passing beneath splayed leg; hole indicating vulva.

117 Binstead (Isle of Wight)
Andersen 16; McMahon/Roberts 6
Location: Church of the Holy Cross; situated above arch of doorway leading to churchyard; doorway was N entrance to former nave.
Dimensions: (h) 60 cm.
Description: Figure quite weathered; unshapely head with large droopy ears; no breasts; arms splayed and bent with both hands in big cavity indicating vulva. Spindly legs widely splayed and bent. Animal head below figure; halter-strap across snout suggests domestic animal; paw-like projections at eye level on either side of head.

118 Bridlington (East Yorkshire)
Andersen 18; McMahon/Roberts 8
Location: Priory Church; on reconstructed fragments of twelfth-century cloister arcade in N aisle.
Description: Weathered figure spanning space between W end of twin colonnettes. Hair may be indicated (possibly ears); no neck, angular shoulders, no breasts. Arms in front of body, hands grasping wedge-shaped vulva. Thin legs widely splayed and bent.

119 Bristol
Andersen 19; McMahon/Roberts 9
Location: Among roof-bosses in church of St Mary Redcliffe.
Description: Not visible from ground. According to McMahon/Roberts figure wears curious head-dress, has a large nose, sunken eyes and both hands gesture towards vulva.

120 Buckland (Buckinghamshire)
Andersen 20; McMahon/Roberts 10
Location: All Saints' Church (thirteenth century); in outer S wall of nave, inserted at a height of 3 m above priest's door.
Description: Figure on roughly rectangular slab, badly weathered and brittle, with cracks in face and upper torso. Unshapely head, round eyes, big mouth wide open, possibly showing teeth. No neck, no breasts. Arms reach down in front of body; long fingers of both hands in huge depressed area indicating pudenda. Figure seated with legs raised to both sides of head.

121 Bugthorpe (East Yorkshire)
Figure came to my attention in Weir and Jerman (1993, p. 116).
Location: Church of St Andrew; among figures of a rude kind, on S respond of arch at entrance to chancel.
Description: Details difficult to make out because lower part of figure filled in with plaster and whitewashed. Large skull-like head with round eyes, nose and open mouth. No neck, big shoulders. Squatting position; legs wide apart and knees tightly flexed; arms pass beneath thighs.

122 Buncton (Sussex)
McMahon/Roberts 11
Location: All Saints' Chapel (twelfth century); situated on N impost of chancel arch.
Description: Among abstract forms standing figure with earless head; facial features not discernible. Angular shoulders; slim torso; arms splayed with hands resting on thighs; fingers close to huge vulva, hollowed out from centre and hanging almost to the ground. Legs straight and apart, feet turned outwards.

123 Church Stretton (Shropshire)
Andersen 21; McMahon/Roberts 12
Location: Church of St Lawrence; inserted on outer wall above N door, apparently known as corpse door because it was used only for bringing in the dead.
Dimensions: (h) 60 cm.

Description: Carved in niche-like depression in roughly rectangular stone. Standing figure with shapeless head; no ears; thick neck; arms widely splayed; no breasts. Hands close to deeply hollowed out vulva. Slightly apart, heavy legs, with protruding knees and big feet.

124 Cleckheaton (West Yorkshire)

Information kindly supplied by John Billingsley, editor of *Northern Earth*.
Location: On baptismal font in White Chapel. Font was used as pedestal for font in early eighteenth-century building, it was cut in two and buried, and now stands on new pedestal.
Dimensions: (h) 61 cm.
Description: Sheela among abstract motifs and male figure; quite worn. Oval eyes, running into triangular wedge nose; no neck. Traces of scratchings that may indicate ribs. Arms clearly indicate and pull open oval vulva; straight legs, no feet.

125 Copgrove (North Yorkshire)

Andersen 22; McMahon/Roberts 14
Location: Church of St Michael and All Angels; inside in NE corner of nineteenth-century extension. Figure originally in outer N chancel wall where it served as corner-stone, 1.5 m above ground, overlooking graveyard. Known locally as the Devil's Stone.
Dimensions: (h) 40 cm; (w) 48 cm.
Description: Flatly carved in niche-like depression; big, round head set on thick, long neck; tiny torso without breasts; left arm widely splayed and bent; hand touches huge, long vulva hanging between straight legs; left leg worn away; right hand holds circular object at vulva level. A tau cross, tool or capital 'T' is carved above right shoulder.

126 Croft-on-Tees (Durham)

Andersen 23; McMahon/Roberts 14
Location: Church of St Peter; set in wall immediately inside S entrance of church.
Dimensions: (h) 50 cm.
Description: Carved on rectangular slab; large earless head with crude facial features; no neck; clearly indicated navel. Left arm splayed and bent, hand reaching for vulva, indicated as small deeply incised slit. Right arm raised with hand placed on top of head.

127 Darley Dale (Derbyshire)

McMahon/Roberts 16
Location: St Helen's Church; inside modern extension to church on keystone over archway of old main door.
Description: Figure much worn. Tight-fitting cap on head; arms reaching round buttocks, and legs raised above head. Pose similar to figures 33, 69, 133 and 160.

128 Diddlebury 1 (Shropshire)

McMahon/Roberts 17
Location: St Peter's Church; badly weathered or defaced figure on S facing outer wall of tower, inserted some 4 m above ground, just below a string-course; most probably not in original position. It came to my attention through Holdgate church leaflet

which refers to other Sheelas in local area, mentioning Church Stretton, Tugford and Diddlebury. A little doubtful.
Description: Head with hair and pleasant-looking face. Arms possibly reaching down in front of body; figure seems to be seated with legs raised high; mouth-shaped vulva.

129 Diddlebury 2 (Shropshire)
McMahon/Roberts 18
Location: inserted to right of figure 128; also somewhat doubtful.
Description: Badly weathered or defaced and too high up to describe in detail. Head and torso visible; legs may be raised to head.

130 Easthorpe (Essex)
Andersen 24; McMahon/Roberts 19
Location: Castle Museum, Colchester; previously built into nave wall above S doorway of St Mary's Church, Easthorpe, and removed in 1922.
Description: Asymmetrical figure carved in clunch stone (builders' term for chalk building stone, occurring as large lumps). Big head with hair or tight-fitting cap, jug ears and primitive facial features; no neck; clearly incised ribs. Arms splayed and bent with both hands grasping pudenda hanging between thin, splayed legs. Pudenda huge, touches ground and has long vertical rim running halfway down the middle. Inscription to right of figure reads ELUI.

131 Etton (Cambridgeshire)
All information kindly provided by John Harding (www.sheelanagig.org) and Keith Jones.
Location: Local church; figure inserted horizontally on corbel table on S face of tower.
Description: Big head with facial features; thick, long neck. Arms reaching down in front of body with hands close to big oval-shaped vulva. Standing pose, straight legs slightly apart, feet turned outwards.

132 Fiddington (Somerset)
Andersen 25; McMahon/Roberts 21
Location: St Martin's Church; figure situated on quoin stone at SE corner of nave on outside some 2.8 m above ground level.
Dimensions: (h) 30 cm (stone: 33 cm high, and 39 cm wide).
Description: Carved in low relief on reddish-purple sandstone. Round, earless head; wavy lines across forehead, bulbous eyes; right arm splayed and bent with hand resting on thigh; left arm raised to side of head, hand holding an elongated unidentified object. Traces of a few holes in torso extending from lower abdomen up to chest area. Something seems to pour out of vulva, but difficult to determine because genital area looks deliberately defaced.

133 Haddon Hall (Derbyshire)
Andersen 26; McMahon/Roberts 22
Location: Figure was placed above doorway to stables of Elizabethan estate, but has been moved to inside of stable. Said to have been found in field nearby; original provenance unknown.

Description: Figure consists of head, arms and legs, but no body. Legs raised above head; hands reaching from below to grab vulva, indicated as square-shaped depression. Pose similar to figures 33, 69, 127 and 160.

134 Hellifield (Yorkshire)
Andersen 27; McMahon/Roberts 23
Location: In private possession; discovered in 1967 in use as garden ornament; no other history. First published by Sidney Jackson, in 1973.
Dimensions: (h) 51 cm.
Description: Carved in coarse sandstone. Large head without ears; grim looking face; no neck; arms in front of body with hands joined in genital area. Standing pose, legs straight and slightly apart.

135 Holdgate (Shropshire)
Andersen 28; McMahon/Roberts 24
Location: Holy Trinity Church; placed high up above door and beside window on S facing chancel wall outside; does not appear to be in primary location. Church brochure refers to a *shiela-na-gig*, calling it a 'pagan fertility figure'.
Description: Carved nearly in the round and protruding from wall. Large head with ears and a vexed expression on face; mouth consists of two deep holes. No neck, no breasts. Legs pulled up, knees turned inwards, hands appearing underneath them to grab vulva, shown as large depression.

136 Kilpeck (Herefordshire)
Andersen 30; McMahon/Roberts 25
Location: Church of St Mary and St David (twelfth century); on corbel table on S wall of nave, in the company of animals, human figures and Christian symbols.
Description: Big triangular head without ears; rimmed eyes with eyeballs and eyebrows, wedge nose, smirking mouth. No neck, no breasts, short body. Arms, widely splayed and bent, pass behind legs; big hands pull open enormously exaggerated vulva hanging between open legs; feet turned outwards.

137 Lower Swell 1 (Gloucestershire)
Figure came to my attention through Internet (http://www.jharding.demon.co.uk/SheelaNaGigIndex.htm), accessed 7 March 2001.
Location: St Mary's Church; figure on N side and one of 26 carved stones surrounding outer edge of Norman chancel arch.
Description: Big head, oval eyes, long nose and slit-mouth; no ears, no neck, no breasts; round, soft shoulders, lean body; arms splayed and bent a little, hands on thighs, fingers touching oval vulva. Short stumpy legs, splayed with feet turned outwards.

138 Lower Swell 2 (Gloucestershire)
Figure in same location as figure 137, but seems to have escaped detection so far. Placed on capital of outer respond supporting chancel arch.
Dimensions: 9.5 cm.
Description: Big head with facial features similar to figure 137. No ears, neck or breasts. Big sagging, apple-shaped vulva. Legs widely splayed, bent back at knees, feet grasped by hands. Pose very similar to figure 52.

139 Oaksey (Wiltshire)
Andersen 32; McMahon/Roberts 26
Location: All Saints Church; situated on N external wall beside window E of porch, *c*.2.5 m from ground.
Dimensions: (h) 33 cm; (w) 15 cm.
Description: Carved in low niche on slab; round head, upper part damaged, traces of nose and mouth, but no ears. Thick neck; dangling breasts under armpits, slim trunk. Arms widely splayed and bent; hands with long fingers pass underneath thighs to grab rim of enormous, lozenge-shaped pudenda with touch-hole at lower end. Standing pose, genitals fill out entire space between splayed legs; feet turned outwards.

140 Oxford (Oxfordshire)
Andersen 33; McMahon/Roberts 27
Location: St Michael's Church; formerly on W wall of eleventh-century tower at third floor level, by Saxon window; removed 1928 to vestry; now on display on first floor.
Dimensions: (h) 30.5 cm; (w) 30.5 cm.
Description: Figure set in square niche-like frame; round earless head with facial features but no neck; arms splayed, left hand reaches from behind thigh, the other from in front, gesturing towards pudenda which is sagging between splayed, straight legs.

141 Pennington (Cumbria)
McMahon/Roberts 28
Location: Kendal Museum; figure discovered in 1925 during repair work to SE corner of St Michael and All Angels, Pennington.
Dimensions: (h) 34 cm.
Description: Carved on quoin stone and slightly damaged. Very angular figure with pointed ears, elbows and knees; angular shoulders; straight trunk with narrow, droopy breasts. Arms in front of body, both hands touching deeply hollowed out, oval-shaped vulva hanging between open thighs. Feet missing.

142 Romsey 1 (Hampshire)
Andersen 36; McMahon/Roberts 29
Location: Abbey Church of St Mary and St Aethelflaed; high up on outside W wall of N transept, above window. This is the third church on site (first abbey founded in 907).
Description: Set in square relief; figure has wavy lines across forehead and striations on left cheek; no neck, no breasts. Arms splayed and both hands hold object; right hand holds band-like feature; object in left hand looks like pair of shears. Small, but clearly indicated vulva. There is a further unexplained shape lying on ground between widely splayed legs. Feet turned outwards.

143 Romsey 2 (Hampshire)
Figure brought to my attention by John Harding (www.sheelanagig.org); information kindly provided by Frank Green (TVBC Heritage officer, Romsey).
Location: Corbel figure on N wall W of transept and close to figure 142; one of the various corbels reconstructed between 1860 and 1890 at the behest of the Reverend

Edward Berthon, wishing to restore this part of the church back to its Romanesque appearance; carving quite possibly copy or replacement of older corbel.

Description of figure in photograph: Big round head with pleasant facial features. Figure is seated and giving birth. Knees pulled up, hands grasping lower legs, baby's head showing eyes, nose and mouth hanging upside down between open thighs.

144 Royston (Hertfordshire)

Andersen 37; McMahon/Roberts 30

Location: On wall opposite bottom of modern tunnel to Royston cave, set between a horse and a sword. Cave is some 6000 years old; figures carved by Knights Templars in fourteenth century.

Description: Small figure with few identifiable features. Arms hanging at sides of quite rotund body; slightly sagging, wedge-shaped vulva between straight, wide-apart legs.

145 St Ives (Huntingdonshire)

Andersen 38; McMahon/Roberts 31

Location: In private possession; formerly at St Ives Priory; found in garden S of priory; traces of burning on figure. H. J. M. Green published discovery in 1958.

Description: Carved in high relief on rectangular block of Barnack stone. Figure crudely shaped, with arms, legs and top part of head deliberately omitted. Simple facial features; trunk plumpish, breasts and navel indicated; big cavernous genital area.

146 South Tawton (Devon)

Andersen 39; McMahon/Roberts 32

Location: St Andrew Church; on boss in fifteenth-century wooden roof, facing altar.

Description: Boldly carved in wood; very clear contour of female figure with head bent backwards emerging from decorative background. Torso without breasts; arms splayed and bent with hands on upper thighs around slit-vulva. Legs widely splayed, bent at knees with feet turned outwards.

147 Stanton St Quintin (Wiltshire)

Figure brought to my attention through Internet (http://www.sheelanagig.org/sheelastantonstquintin.htm), accessed 26 November 2003; also mentioned in Katy Jordan's *The Haunted Landscape* (Bradford on Avon: Ex Libris Press, 2000, p. 48).

Location: Church of St Giles; situated high on exterior N side of church tower; not in primary location.

Description: Carved in high relief on slab. Round head with wide mouth; circular breasts at shoulder level, arms akimbo. Torso has four holes drilled into it: two large ones in genital area, and two smaller ones at navel level. Legs straight and wide apart. Left foot turned outwards, right foot missing. Hands around genital area hold a band-like feature consisting of two stripes hanging down to ground.

148 Stoke Sub Hamdon (Somerset)

Figure brought to my attention through Internet (http://www.sheelanagig.org/links2.htm), accessed 26 November 2003.

Location: St Mary's Church; figure on corbel.

Description: Big, round head with ovoid eyes, strong nose with nostrils and open mouth. Squatting position; pudenda indicated by cleft with some indication of hands pulling at it.

149 Studland (Dorset)
McMahon/Roberts 33
Location: Church of St Nicholas; twelfth-century Norman building imposed on earlier church of same size and plan; Sheela on corbel table in company of beard-pullers, phallic males, coupling pairs etc., similar to sequence of motifs at Romsey and Kilpeck, but lacking charm of latter.
Description: Grotesque treatment of figure. Head with weathered facial features; no trunk; gap between widely splayed legs filled with huge, round pudenda (clitoris?), pulled open with over-sized left hand; stylized fingers of right hand spread out behind right leg.

150 Torksey (Lincolnshire)
Andersen 41; McMahon/Roberts 34
Location: Church of St Peter; figure inside church, set high up on S wall; not in its original location.
Description: Figure fits into a pointed arch-like frame; small and very worn standing figure with thin, straight legs; pose of arms suggest gesture towards pudenda.

151 Tugford 1 (Shropshire)
Andersen 42; McMahon/Roberts 35
Location: Church of St Catherine (late twelfth century); inside church, left of S doorway on stonework supporting rear arch.
Dimensions: (h) 15 cm.
Description: Carved in high relief, very nearly in the round. Squatting figure with big head, depicted with tight-fitting cap or hair and no ears. Vexed facial expression, ovoid eyes, strong nose, grim mouth showing teeth and tongue sticking out. No neck, no breasts; arms passing behind legs, knees pulled up, both hands pull open wedge-shaped vulva; indistinct feet. Figure holds an unidentified, round object under her left arm.

152 Tugford 2 (Shropshire)
Andersen 43; McMahon/Roberts 36
Location: Same as figure 151; on opposite side of doorway.
Dimensions: (h) 15 cm.
Description: Features similar to figure 152, but different pose. Half-reclining figure whose right arm covers chin area with hand touching lower left side of face while left arm passes under left leg with hand in genital area; both knees splayed and slightly pulled up. Swollen vulva from which what appears to be an amniotic sac is protruding.

153 Wells (Somerset)
Andersen 44; McMahon/Roberts 37
Location: St Andrew's cathedral; two Sheelas said to be among roof bosses in the cloisters, but not visible from the ground. Somewhat doubtful.

Description: According to McMahon/Roberts one figure is grasping her legs and exposing vulva, while second figure has arms and legs bent back exposing her whole body.

154 Whittlesford (Cambridgeshire)
Andersen 45; McMahon/Roberts 38
Location: Church of St Mary and St Andrew; below clock on S side of tower.
Description: On irregular block forming arch of Norman window, a seated Sheela beside a standing (feline?) animal with erect penis. Sheela has big round head with bulbous eyes, wedge nose and small mouth; no neck. Heavy body quite weathered, details difficult to make out. Right hand passes under buttocks with fingers touching deeply incised, wedge-shaped vulva. Thighs widely splayed; lower legs and feet not traceable.

155 Unknown provenance
Andersen 46
Location: In private possession; somewhat doubtful. First published by Sidney Jackson in 1973.
Dimensions: (h) 9 cm.
Description: Small figure on fine-grained reddish stone. Handsome head with parted hair, ovoid eyes, slim long nose and pouting mouth. Broad shoulders; small droopy, pointed breasts; navel clearly incised. Hands joined in front above genital area; no legs.

156 Unknown provenance
Published in *Celtic Stone Sculptures*, with an introduction by Martin Petch (London: Karsten Schubert and Rupert Wace Ancient Art, 1989, pp. 32–5).
Dimensions: (h) 25 cm; (w) 18 cm.
Description: Carved in sandstone. Figure is referred to as 'Sheelagh-na-gig fertility figure' and described as 'vulgar and sexually explicit', with intentional damage to face, and correct anatomy not adhered to. Huge round head; body seems to consist mainly of large oval pudenda with a vertical line running through it and a touch-hole underneath; right hand holds head, long fingers of the other pull at vulva; no legs.

Record only

157 Egremont (Cumbria)
Figure discovered during demolition of oldest part of Egremont Church in 1880; it was described, discussed and photographed by Parker (see pp. 24ff), but has since disappeared.
Dimensions: (h) 47 cm.
Description: Carved on quadrangular block, in relief on sunk background. Large head; small torso with droopy breasts under armpits, and navel. Very long, splayed arms; left hand, turned upwards, rests on thigh, while right hand holds pair of blunt-pointed shears. Right leg straight with foot turned inwards; left knee bent, heel of foot pointing at pudenda; leg pose similar to figure 37.

Parker makes reference to two further possible Sheelas in the same article. Egremont, in his opinion, 'is not so rude as the figure on the Cross Canonby slab, nor as that on a similarly-shaped block at that place, on which is also rudely cut a cross and a kind of thunderbolt . . . done for practice or amusement, as this may have been' (Charles A. Parker, Early Sculptured Stones at Gosforth, Ponsonby, St Bridget's, Haile, and Egremont, *Transactions of the Cumberland and Westmorland Antiquarian and Archaeological Society*, 2 (1902), 84–98).

Scotland

158 Iona (Mull, Western Isles)
Andersen 29; McMahon/Roberts 41
Location: On lintel above window of medieval nuns' refectory.
Description: Figure badly weathered. Recorded details include splayed arms, small legs and sagging pudenda.

159 Kilvickoen (Mull, Western Isles)
McMahon/Roberts 42
Location: Beside doorway of medieval parish church. Carving thought to be a Sheela, but in the absence of detailed description and/or photographs, this figure remains doubtful.

160 Kirknewton (West Lothian)
Figure came to my attention thanks to John Harding (www.sheelanagig.org).
Location: Museum of Scotland, Edinburgh; originally from doorway of medieval church demolished in 1780.
Description: Label for carving reads as follows: 'Architectural stone or voussoir showing a woman giving birth'. Truly remarkable carving which appears to depict a woman with her midwife. Both figures nude and seated; each grabs pudenda of pregnant woman with one hand. Assisting woman holds her left hand up to ear of other figure.

161 Kirkwall (Orkney)
Andersen 'addendum', p. 153; McMahon/Roberts 43
Location: Cathedral of St Magnus; high up on capital of second pillar on S side of nave.
Description: Seated figure with damage to right side; big head with mouth wide open; left hand held over ear; small droopy breasts; open oval-shaped vulva; thighs widely splayed and bent at knees with feet turned outwards.

162 Rodil (Isle of Harris, Western Isles)
Andersen 35; McMahon/Roberts 44
Location: St Clement's church; set on central panel of S wall of tower.
Description: Badly weathered figure; seated with legs widely splayed and knees bent. A child or animal (?) seems to be held above her knee; rectangular object with spout (?) in upper right hand corner.

163 Taynuilt (Strathclyde)

Andersen 40; McMahon/Roberts 45

Location: Muckairn parish church; preserved in S wall of church (built in 1829), but thought to have come from nearby ruined church of Killespickerell.

Dimensions: (h) 35.5 cm.

Description: Carved in sandstone; figure much weathered and mutilated, mainly consisting of head and body.

Wales

164 Haverfordwest (Pembrokeshire)

Thanks to Richard Avent (CADW), figure was brought to my attention by Sian E. Rees (CADW). It was discovered during early 1990s.

Location: CADW artefact store, Crickhowell; originally Haverfordwest Priory. Figure on capital from thirteenth-century cloister arcade, dismantled during fourteenth/fifteenth century and reused for new build.

Dimensions: (h) 8 cm; (w) 12.5 cm (capital 25 cm high; 27 cm wide at top).

Description: Figure seems to have hair or wear tight-fitting cap. With legs raised above head and arms reaching round buttocks, pose similar to figures 33, 69, 127 and 133. Small vulva and anus indicated.

165 Llandrindod Wells (Radnorshire)

Andersen 31; McMahon/Roberts 39

Location: Radnorshire Museum, Llandrindod Wells; figure discovered about 1894, buried in church floor of Old Parish church (thirteenth century).

Description: Figure cut in low relief on thick, irregular slab. Big head with ears; hair indicated; wavy lines across forehead, slit-eyes, strong nose with very pronounced nostril channels between nose and lip; thin, open mouth revealing teeth. Round breasts almost under armpits; incised ribs and navel. Hands on thighs and fingers of both hands touching genitals; exaggerated somewhat shapeless pudenda with rim of hair; lower legs defaced. A cross crosslet cut on side of stone.

166 Penmon (Anglesey)

Andersen 34; McMahon/Roberts 40

Location: Inside Church of St Mary, Penmon priory; removed from outer face of W wall of S transept where it had been inserted at comparatively modern date; original location unknown.

Dimensions: (h) 46 cm.

Description: Carved in fine sandstone; head in the round, rest of body in high relief. Figure badly weathered, facial features obliterated. Angular shoulders; no breasts. Legs widely splayed and bent back. Left hand on thigh; right arm stretched down to hold lower right leg. Balloon-like feature with slit fills space between open legs; may represent amniotic sac.

167 Raglan Castle (Monmouthshire)

Figure brought to my attention by Conleth Manning (Dúchas, Dublin); Richard Avent (CADW) kindly provided information and directions.

Location: In external display of sculptural fragments within castle grounds; original location not recorded; first appears in photograph of 1860s, on display on plinth at foot of Grand Stair leading up to apartments in Fountain Court.

Description: Very worn figure on almost trapezoidal block; vertical channel cut in back; upper left side of face and parts of left arm and leg cut off (presumably to fit architectural setting). Right ear very pronounced and splayed; vaguely indicated eyes; other facial features mutilated; chin damaged. Broad, round shoulders; no neck and no breasts. Arms splayed; hands on thighs, close to but not touching pudenda; legs splayed exposing wedge-shaped vulva.

Sheela-na-gigs in Ireland and England arranged by counties

Ireland

Co. Antrim
(Record only)
107 Shane's Castle

Co. Cavan

26 Cavan	61 Lavey	87 Toomregan

Co. Clare

13 Ballyportry	18 Bunratty	28 Clenagh
32 Clonlara	53 Killaloe	54 Killinaboy

Co. Cork

2 Aghadoe	11 Ballynacarriga	14 Ballyvourney
24 Castlemagner	25 Castle Widenham	50 Glanworth
74 Ringaskiddy	88 Tracton	

(Record only)

91 Ballynamona Castle	92 Barnahealy Castle	104 Ringaskiddy

Co. Derry
64 Maghera

Co. Down
(Record only)
99 Kirkiston

Co. Dublin

65 Malahide	81 Stepaside	82 Swords

(Record only)
101 Lusk

Co. Galway

8 Ballinderry	66 Merlin Park

Co. Kerry

56 Kilsarkan   63 Lixnaw   72 Rattoo

Co. Kildare

17 Blackhall   52 Kildare

(Record only)
93 Carrick Castle

Co. Kilkenny

10 Ballylarkin   30 Clomantagh   37 Cooliaghmore
48 Freshford   89 Tullaroan

(Record only)
96 Killinny

Co. Laois

6 Ballaghmore   38 Cullahill   75 Rosenallis

(Record only)
103 Portnahinch Castle   106 Shane Castle   109 Timahoe Castle
110 Tinnakill Castle

Co. Limerick

20 Caherelly   42 Dunnaman   90 Tullavin

Co. Longford

1 Abbeylara   71 Rathcline

Co. Louth

41 Drogheda

Co. Mayo

3 Aghagower

Co. Meath

4 Ardcath   40 Dowth   76 Rosnaree
85 Tara

(Record only)
95 Kells   98 Kilmainham   108 Summerhill

Co. Offaly

16 Birr   31 Clonbulloge   33 Clonmacnoise 1
34 Clonmacnoise 2   39 Doon   49 Garrycastle
60 Knockarley   69 Rahan   79 Seir Kieran

(Record only)
94 Cloghan Castle   100 Lemanaghan Castle

Co. Roscommon

29 Cloghan
77 Scregg 1

43 Emlaghmore
78 Scregg 2

70 Rahara
83 Taghboy

Co. Sligo

15 Behy

Co. Tipperary

7 Ballinaclogh
19 Burgesbeg
35 Clonmel
47 Fethard Wall
58 Kiltinane Castle
68 Newton-Lennon
86 Thurles

9 Ballyfinboy
22 Cashel
36 Clonoulty
51 Holycross
59 Kiltinane Church
73 Redwood

12 Ballynahinch
23 Cashel Palace Hotel
46 Fethard Abbey
57 Kilshane
62 Liathmore
80 Shanrahan

(Record only)
102 Moycarkey Castle

105 Rochestown

Co. Tyrone

44 Errigal Keeroge 1

45 Errigal Keeroge 2

Co. Waterford

(Record only)
97 Kilmacomma

Co. Westmeath

5 Athlone
67 Moate

21 Carne
84 Taghmon

27 Chloran

Co. Wexford

55 Kilmokea

England

Avon

111 Abson

119 Bristol

Buckinghamshire

120 Buckland

Cambridgeshire

131 Etton

154 Whittlesford

Cumbria

141 Pennington

(Record only)
157 Egremont

160

Derbyshire
112 Alderwasley   127 Darley Dale   133 Haddon Hall

Devon
146 South Tawton

Dorset
149 Studland

Durham
126 Croft-on-Tees

Essex
130 Easthorpe

Gloucestershire
113 Ampney St Peter   137 Lower Swell 1   138 Lower Swell 2

Hampshire
117 Binstead   142 Romsey 1   143 Romsey 2

Herefordshire
136 Kilpeck

Hertfordshire
144 Royston

Huntingdonshire
145 St Ives

Lincolnshire
150 Torksey

Oxfordshire
140 Oxford

Shropshire
123 Church Stretton   128 Diddlebury 1   129 Diddlebury 2
135 Holdgate   151 Tugford 1   152 Tugford 2

Somerset
132 Fiddington   148 Stoke Sub Hamdon   153 Wells

Sussex
122 Buncton

Wiltshire

139 Oaksey   147 Stanton St Quintin

Yorkshire

114 Austerfield   115 Bilton 1   116 Bilton 2
118 Bridlington   121 Bugthorpe   124 Cleckheaton
125 Copgrove   134 Hellifield

NOTES

1 THE SHEELA-NA-GIG PHENOMENON

1 The other two churches are Bristol (119) and Wells (153). The figures in parentheses refer to the numbers used in the Sheela-na-gig Catalogue.
2 From Tickhill Castle, Yorkshire.
3 Jørgen Andersen, *The Witch on the Wall. Medieval Erotic Sculpture in the British Isles* (London: George Allen & Unwin, 1977), p. 145.
4 These are Sheelas number 2, 7, 9, 10, 12, 17, 26, 27, 29, 30, 34, 35, 36, 37, 38, 39, 42, 46, 47, 48, 50, 54, 58, 77, 79, 88, 89.
5 Edith M. Guest, 'Irish Sheela-na-gigs in 1935', *JRSAI*, 66 (1936), 107–29, 109.
6 A. L. and G. E. Hutchinson, 'Distribution of Sheela-na-gigs in Great Britain', contained in 'The "Idol" or Sheela-na-gig at Binstead', *Proc. Isle of Wight Nat. Hist. & Arch. Soc.*, 1(4) (1969), 240–9.
7 James A. Jerman, 'The "Sheela-na-Gig" carvings of the British Isles: suggestions for a reclassification, and other notes', *J. Co. Louth Arch. & Hist. Soc.*, 20(1) (1981), 10–24, 13.
8 With one hand under the thigh and the other in front of the body this figure could also qualify for group IV.
9 Jerman, pp. 13–15 and map 1.
10 Edith Guest, 'Some notes on the dating of Sheela-na-gigs', *JRSAI*, 67 (1937), 176–80.
11 Ibid., p. 180.
12 According to Jerman (p. 19), there were two main types, one consisting of tails, snouts, beards, tongues and other limbs lapping over a roll molding, and a second which shows mainly birds' heads.
13 Jerman himself, it has to be said, does not express any disappointment.

2 SHEELAS AND ACADEMIC RESEARCH

1 Thomas O'Conor, Nenagh, 3 October 1840; in John O'Donovan, Letters containing information relative to the Antiquities of the County of Tipperary Collected during the progress of the Ordnance Survey in 1840. RIA Dublin, handwritten MS.
2 Homeopathic medicine.
3 John O'Donovan, Nenagh, 18 October 1840.
4 James O'Connor tells a very similar story. He grew up in the vicinity of Kiltinane church, and at the age of six, his initial enquiries about the Sheela 'met an embarrassed adult silence but subsequently the following profile emerged. Sheela was a local "loose woman" who fraternized with Cromwell and his castle garrison. . . . As a result of her supposed immorality and treachery she came to a sticky end, murdered horribly. She was rendered as a hag in stone and placed on the ruined church to annoy her ancestors and to warn off all collaborators.' James O'Connor, *Sheela na gig* (Fethard: Fethard Historical Society, 1991), p. 9.
5 According to O'Donovan this castle was erected by the O'Mores of Leix about the beginning of the reign of Queen Elizabeth. It was destroyed in 1650, and rebuilt as a private

residence in the eighteenth century. Obviously still *in situ* in O'Donovan's time, the figure is now missing.

6 Ashley Montague in his introduction to *Sexual Symbolism. A History of Phallic Worship* (New York: The Julian Press, 1957), p. iii.

7 S. J. Connolly, ed., *The Oxford Companion to Irish History* (Oxford: Oxford University Press, 1998), entry on *censorship*.

8 John G. A. Prim, 'Olden Popular Pastimes in Kilkenny', *JRSAI*, ii (1853), 334.

9 See Robert Craig MacLagan, *Our Ancestors. Scots, Picts, & Cymry and What Their Traditions Tell Us* (London & Edinburgh: T. N. Foulis, 1913), p. 28.

10 P. J. Lynch, 'Liathmore-Mochoemog', *JNMA*, 3 (1914), pp. 73–91, 85.

11 The County Laois Survey was carried out in 1838.

12 E. Clibborn, 'On an ancient stone image presented to the Academy by Charles Halpin, MD', *PRIA*, 2(1) (1840–4), pp. 565–76, 566.

13 Although giving detailed descriptions of the round tower of Rattoo, Petrie fails to mention the Sheela-na-gig placed on the inside of an upper window. George Petrie, *The Ecclesiastical Architecture of Ireland, Anterior to the Anglo-Norman Invasion, Comprising an Essay on the Origin and Use of the Round Towers of Ireland* (Dublin, 1845).

14 W. R. Wilde, *A Descriptive Catalogue of Antiquities in the Museum of the Royal Irish Academy, Volume I, Articles of Stone, Earthen, Vegetable, and Animal Materials, and of Copper and Bronze* (Dublin: RIA House, 1863). Apart from the 'three grotesque female figures' in the museum, Wilde refers to other figures still *in situ*, i.e. at Rochestown, Dowth, Kells, Ballynahinch Castle, Moycarkey Castle, Kiltinan Castle, Abbeylaragh and on the old church on White Island.

15 Edith Guest no. 29 (fig. 15).

16 Johann Georg Kohl (1808–78), who considered himself a 'polyhistorian' and a chronicler of his time, spent a large part of his life travelling and making a name for himself as a travel writer. Although his main interest concerned the history of manners and morals, customs and everyday life, his most significant publications are on the historical geography and cartography of the Western hemisphere. American geographers have called him the 'foremost Americanist of the nineteenth century'. See *Progress of Discovery. Johann Georg Kohl. Auf den Spuren der Entdecker*, ed. Hans-Albrecht Koch, Margrit B. Krewson and John A. Wolter (Graz: Akademische Druck- und Verlagsanstalt, 1993).

17 Johann Georg Kohl, *Reisen in Irland* (Dresden und Leipzig: Arnold, 1843), 2 vols, Volume 2, pp. 205ff.

18 Ibid., p. 208.

19 Clibborn, pp. 565ff.

20 The Sheelas from Lavey, Cavan and Seir Kieran.

21 Apart from the Lavey figure, he specifically mentions the Sheelas at Rochestown, Kiltynan [*sic*] Castle, Lusk, Dowth, Ballinahinch, Moycarkey Castle and on White Island church.

22 The British Museum, London, has an illustrated manuscript record (Museum Secretum) by William Simpson. On page 65 there is a drawing of the Sheela-na-gig on the Nuns' Church, (Clonmacnoise) transformed into a beautiful young lady with a lovely set of hair and elegantly shaped legs. The caption reads: 'From a drawing by Edw. Clibborn, Esqu., Secty. to Roy. Irish Academy'. Clibborn may have taken up drawing these figures later; he certainly made no mention of it during the debate. Intriguingly, Simpson scribbled 'not reliable' beside it.

23 Clibborn, p. 566.

24 Ibid., p. 573.

25 I. Webber-Smith, *An Essay on the Round Towers of Ireland. As Compared with Other Monuments* (Dublin: Milliken & Son, 1838), p. 36.

26 Roger Stalley, *Irish Round Towers* (Dublin: Town House and Country House, 2000), p. 10.

27 Henry O'Brien, *The Round Towers of Ireland or the Mysteries of Freemasonry, of Sabaism, and of Buddhism* (London and Dublin: Whittaker & Co., and J. Cumming, 1834), p. 91.

28 For an in-depth discussion of the round tower theories, see Joep Leerssen, *Remembrance and Imagination. Patterns in the Historical and Literary Representation of Ireland in the Nineteenth Century* (Cork: Cork University Press, 1996), pp. 112–34.

29 Clibborn, pp. 567ff.

30 Richard Hitchcock, 'Notes made in the Archaeological Court of the Great Exhibition of 1853', *JKAS*, 2(2) (1852–3), p. 283.

31 Windele's manuscript preserved in the RIA, 'Cloyne and Ross', p. 448.

32 For a good overview of the Evil Eye phenomenon see Pierre Bettez Gravel, *The Malevolent Eye. An Essay on the Evil Eye, Fertility and the Concept of Mana*. American University Studies Series XI, Anthropology and Sociology, Volume 64 (New York: Peter Lang, 1995).

33 Caroline, Countess of Dunraven and Edwin, Earl of Dunraven, *Memorials of Adare Manor* (Oxford: Parker, 1865), pp. 200ff.

34 George V. Du Noyer, 'Remarks on ancient Irish effigies sculptured on the walls of the ancient church on White Island, Lough Erne, Parish of Magheraculmoney, County of Fermanagh', *JRSAI*, n.s., 3(6) (1860–1), pp. 62–9.

35 See note 14.

36 Thomas Wright, *The Worship of the Generative Powers during the Middle Ages of Western Europe* (1866); reprinted, together with Richard Payne Knight, *A Discourse on the Worship of Priapus* (1786) as *Sexual Symbolism. A History of Phallic Worship* (New York: The Julian Press, 1957), pp. 35ff.

37 Wright, p. 42.

38 Especially plate VII, figs 4 and 5, 45.

39 See Leerssen, pp. 120ff; Montagu, p. iii.

40 Illustrated were the Sheelas from Rochestown, Lavey, Ballynahinch (which he wrongly calls 'Ballynahend'), Cavan, White Island, Seir Kieran and Chloran. His illustration of the last bears no resemblance to the figure, but it has been copied many times, including by J. Andersen and Jack Roberts.

41 These are George Witt's Scrapbook in the Witt Collection, which furthermore includes excerpts from letters, and William Simpson's manuscript (see note 22).

42 Richard Rolt Brash, *The Ecclesiastical Architecture of Ireland, to the close of the twelfth century, accompanied by interesting historical and antiquarian notices of numerous ancient remains of that period* (Dublin: W. B. Kelly/London: Simpkin, Marshall, & Co., 1875), p. 60.

43 W. F. Wakeman, 'The Church of White Island, Lough Erne, Parish of Magheraculmoney, County of Fermanagh', *JRSAI*, 5(4) (1879–82), pp. 276–92, 284.

44 Wakeman added a few 'new' Sheelas to the existing list. These included the figures on O'Gara's fortress (Co. Sligo), on a town gateway in Athlone (Co. Westmeath) and on a font at Kilcarne (Co. Meath).

45 Robert Macalister, *The Archaeology of Ireland* (London: Bracken Books, 1996), pp. 358ff (first published in 1928 by Methuen & Co. Ltd, London).

46 FRSAI, 'Figures known as Hags of the Castle, Sheelas, or Sheela na gigs, with supplemental list of carved female figures found in early churches, castles, &c.', *JRSAI*, 24 (1894), pp. 77–81, 392–4.

47 James Grove White, *Historical and Topographical Notes, etc. on Buttevant, Castletownroche, Doneraile, Mallow, and Places in Their Vicinity* (Cork: Guy and Co., 1905), 4 vols, Volume I, pp. 85–90.

48 Some of the figures included in this list were mistakenly identified as Sheelas.

49 Grove White, p. 78.

50 See note 6.

51 The chapel in question is the so-called Käppeli-Joch in Basel which was built in 1226. Unfortunately the figure fell victim to major restoration work which was carried out about 100 years after Boswell's visit. In the absence of any other document on the figure, Boswell's attitude is all the more regrettable. See Frederick A. Pottle, ed., *Boswell on the Grand Tour: Germany and Switzerland* (1764) (Melbourne/London/Toronto: William Heinemann, 1953), pp. 202–3.

52 Lewis transformed the figure into a man, explaining him as 'a fool opening his heart to the devil'. Geo. R. Lewis, *Illustrations of Kilpeck Church, Herefordshire: In a Series of Drawings Made on the Spot, with an Essay on Ecclesiastical Design, and a Descriptive Interpretation* (London: William Pickering, 1842), pl. 9.

53 Jørgen Andersen, *The Witch on the Wall. Medieval Erotic Sculpture in the Britsh Isles* (London: Allen & Unwin, 1977), p. 11.

54 Review of Frederick Thomas Elworthy, *The Evil Eye: An Account of This Ancient and Widespread Superstition* (London: John Murray, 1895), in *The Reliquary and Illustrated Archaeological Journal* (1895), pp. 247–51.

55 Charles A. Parker, 'Early sculptured stones at Gosforth, Ponsonby, St Bridget's, Haile, and Egremont', *Transactions of the Cumberland and Westmorland Antiquarian and Archaeological Society*, 2 (1902), pp. 84–98, 87.

56 Ibid., p. 88.

57 Quoted in A. L. and G. E. Hutchinson, 'Distribution of Sheela-na-Gigs in Great Britain', contained in 'The "Idol" or Sheela-na-gig at Binstead', *Proc. Isle of Wight Nat. Hist. & Arch. Soc.*, 1(4) (1969), 240–9.

58 Brian Branston, *The Lost Gods of England* (London: Thames and Hudson, 1957), p. 15.

59 Ibid., p. 28.

60 Quoted in Alfred Fell, *A Furness Manor: Pennington and Its Church* (Ulverston: Kitchin & Co., 1929), pp. 57ff.

61 *The Barrow News* (14 September 1929), p. 9.

62 Ibid.

63 The article in question was by M. A. Murray and A. D. Passmore, called 'The Sheela-na-gig at Oaksey'. It had appeared in *MAN*, no. 86 (September, 1923), pp. 140–1.

64 See Dina Portway Dobson, 'Primitive figures on churches', *MAN*, 31(3) (January 1931), pp. 3–4.

65 Robert Macalister, *The Archaeology of Ireland* (London: Methuen, 1928).

66 Quoted from a private letter by W.J. Hemp, 'Some unrecorded "Sheela-na-Gigs" in Wales and the Border', *Archaeologica Cambrensis*, 93 (1938), pp. 136–9, 139.

67 *The Barrow News*, p. 9.

68 See Fell, pp. 211–31.

69 Richard N. Bailey, 'Apotropaic figures in Milan and north-west England', *Folklore*, 94(1) (1983), pp. 113–17.

70 Branston, p. 155.

71 Brian Branston, 'Sheela-na-gig', *Irish Times* (24 September 1977).

72 See Chapter 1, note 3.

73 Portway Dobson, pp. 3–5.

74 For years her study on *The Witch Cult in Western Europe* was regarded as the epoch-making book on the medieval witch hunt in Europe.

75 Margaret A. Murray, 'Female fertility figures', *JRAI*, 64 (1934), pp. 93–100, and plates, 94.

76 Ibid., p. 94.

77 According to this legend *Baubo* cheered up the mourning Isis by assuming the attitude represented in the figures, thus making Isis laugh and stop lamenting for her husband Osiris.

78 Murray, p. 99. Judging by the substantial number of lesbian erotic headings on the Sheela-na-gig websites, the figure indeed seems to appeal to homosexual women. There is a pornographic novel by Bridget Doyle, called Sheela-na-gig (London: Sapphire, 2000), in which a Sheela excites women's sexual desires.

79 Murray, p. 99.

80 See note 47.

81 Guest, 'Irish . . .', p. 107.

82 Ibid., p. 122.

83 Ibid.

84 Thomas Johnson Westropp, 'The earthworks, traditions, and the gods of South-Eastern Co. Limerick, especially from Knocklong to Temair Erann', *PRIA*, 34, sec. C (1918), pp. 129–83, 135.

85 Marcus Keane, *The Towers and Temples of Ancient Ireland: Their Origin and History Discussed from a New Point of View* (Dublin: Hodges, Smith and Co., 1867), pp. 69ff.

86 J. G. R. Forlong, *Faiths of Man. A Cyclopaedia of Religions* (London: Bernard Quaritch, 1906), 3 vols, volume 3, pp. 302ff.
87 Rev. Canon J. F. M. ffrench, *Prehistoric Faith and Worship. Glimpses of Ancient Irish Life* (London: David Nutt, 1912), p. 146.
88 Robert A. S. Macalister, *Tara: A Pagan Sanctuary of Ancient Ireland* (London: Charles Scribner's Sons, 1931), p. 52.
89 Macalister, *The Archaeology* . . . , p. 364.
90 Ibid., p. 360.
91 Ibid., p. 361.
92 Ibid., p. 365.
93 Ibid., pp. 358–60.
94 Ibid., p. 365.
95 Vivian Mercier, *The Irish Comic Tradition* (London/Oxford/New York: Oxford University Press, 1969).
96 Ibid., p. 4.
97 Ibid., pp. 49–52.
98 Ibid., p. 56.
99 Ibid., pp. 5, 54.
100 Marie-Louise Sjoestedt, *Gods and Heroes of the Celts* (London: Methuen & Co., 1949); transl. of *Dieux et Heros des Celtes* (Paris: Presses Universitaires, 1940).
101 Proinsias Mac Cana, 'Aspects of the theme of king and goddess in Irish literature', *Études Celtiques*, 7 (1955/6), pp. 76–114, 356–413. See also his *Celtic Mythology* (Feltham: Newnes Books, 1983), pp. 82–121.
102 See Proinsias Mac Cana, 'Women in Irish mythology', in M. P. Hederman and R. Kearney, eds, *The Crane Bag Book of Irish Studies (1977–1981)* (Dublin: Blackwater Press, 1982), pp. 520–4; Muireann Ní Bhrolcháin, 'Women in early Irish myths and sagas', in Hedermann and Kearney, *The Crane Bag* . . . , pp. 525–32.
103 See Alwyn Rees and Brinley Rees, *Celtic Heritage. Ancient Tradition in Ireland and Wales* (London: Thames and Hudson, 1978), pp. 336–8.
104 See Maire Bhreathnach, 'The sovereignty goddess as goddess of death?', *Zeitschrift für Celtische Philologie*, 39 (1982), pp. 243–60.
105 Sjoestedt, p. 35.
106 Sjoestedt, however, does not refer to Sheelas at all.
107 Mercier, p. 55.
108 Ibid., p. 54.
109 'Togail Bruidne Dá Derga', in R. I. Best and Osborn Bergin, eds, *Lebor na Huidre. Book of the Dun Cow* (Dublin: RIA, 1929), pp. 207–45. The principal scribe of this manuscript died in 1106, but there are later interpolations by a scribe placed by Thurneysen in the thirteenth century. For a discussion of these interpolations see Introduction, p. xvii.
110 Translation from Tom Peete Cross and Clark Harris Slover, eds, *Ancient Irish Tales* (New York: Barnes & Noble, 1936) pp. 93–126, 107.
111 Ibid., p. 103.
112 Ibid., p. 107.
113 Ibid., p. 108.
114 'Togail Bruidne Dá Derga', p. 210.
115 Ibid., p. 232.
116 Ibid., p. 238.
117 Cross and Slover, p. 116.
118 'Togail Bruidne Dá Derga', p. 234. For a discussion of these interpolations, see Rudolf Thurneysen, *Die irische Helden- und Königsage bis zum 17. Jahrhundert* (Hildesheim: Georg Olms Verlag, 1921), p. 647.
119 For a discussion see Rees and Rees, p. 338.
120 See *Dictionary of the Irish Language. Based Mainly on Old and Middle Irish Materials* (Dublin: RIA, 1913–76), under heading *fés*.

121 Cross and Slover, p. 120.
122 Ibid., pp. 510ff.
123 Anne Ross, *Pagan Celtic Britain* (London: Routledge and Kegan Paul/New York: Columbia University Press, 1967).
124 Ibid., p. 229.
125 Ibid., p. 204.
126 Ibid., p. 205.
127 Ibid., p. 229. Another intriguing point is that Ross talks about the 'extraordinary group of sculptures from Ireland' without any reference to British examples.
128 Ibid., p. 232.
129 Anne Ross, 'Celtic and northern art', in Philip Rawson, ed., *Primitive Erotic Art* (New York: G. P. Putnam's Sons, 1973), pp. 77–106.
130 Ibid., p. 104.
131 Ibid.
132 Although I do not wish to make too much of it, Ross makes no reference to Mercier's book. It also has to be pointed out that she claims to be quoting from Cross and Slover's *Ancient Irish Tales*. These two editors, however, do not use the word *pudenda*. The object in question is referred to as the 'lower lip' in the case of the first hag, and 'lower hair' is used for the second hag.
133 Anne Ross, 'The divine hag of the pagan Celts', in Venetia Newall, ed., *The Witch Figure. Folklore Essays by a Group of Scholars in England Honouring the 75th Birthday of Katharine M. Briggs* (London and Boston: Routledge and Kegan Paul, 1973), pp. 139–64.
134 Ross, 'The divine hag . . .', p. 148.
135 Ross, 'Celtic and northern art', p. 104.
136 Ross, 'The divine hag . . .', pp. 148ff.
137 John Sharkey, *Celtic Mysteries. The Ancient Religion* (London: Thames and Hudson, 1975).
138 Ibid., p. 8.
139 Barry Cunliffe, *The Celtic World* (London: The Bodley Head, 1979), p. 170.
140 Ibid., p. 72.
141 James H. Dunn, 'Síle-na-Gcíoch', *Eire-Ireland. A Journal of Irish Studies*, 12 (1977), pp. 68–85.
142 Ibid., p. 70.
143 Douglas Fraser, 'The heraldic woman: a study in diffusion' in Douglas Fraser, ed., *The Many Faces of Primitive Art. A Critical Anthology* (Englewood Cliffs, NJ: Prentice Hall, 1966), pp. 36–99, 44ff. Fraser was referring to the *Irish Comic Tradition*.
144 Dunn, pp. 74ff.
145 Ibid., p. 74.
146 Patrick K. Ford, 'Celtic women: the opposing sex', *Viator*, 19 (1988), pp. 417–38.
147 Ibid., p. 432.
148 Frank Battaglia, 'Goddess religion in the early British Isles', in Miriam Robbins Dexter and Edgar C. Polomé, eds, *Varia on the Indo-European Past: Papers in Memory of Marija Gimbutas* (Washington, DC: Journal of Indo-European Studies Monograph Number 19, 1997), pp. 48–82.
149 Jack Roberts and Joanne McMahon, *The Sheela-na-gigs of Britain and Ireland. An Illustrated Map/Guide* (Bandia Publishing Ireland, 1997); Joanne McMahon and Jack Roberts, *The Sheela-na-gigs of Ireland and Britain. The Divine Hag of the Christian Celts – An Illustrated Guide* (Cork/Dublin: Mercier Press, 2001). McMahon has to be commended for her superb drawings. Both publications are not only extremely useful for locating Sheelas, but they also represent the most complete listing of these carvings. They include all formerly published figures plus some only recently discovered.
150 McMahon and Roberts, *The Sheela-na-gigs* (2001), p. 68.
151 Ibid., p. 74.
152 Ibid., p. 68.
153 Jack Roberts, Sheela-na-gigs (www.whitedragon.demon.co.uk/sheela/htm), accessed 12 March 2002.

154 McMahon and Roberts, *The Sheela-na-gigs* (2001), p. 57.

155 Ibid., p. 59.

156 Ibid., p. 10.

157 The Welsh mythic tradition, which is more vague and veiled, is contained in thirteenth- and fourteenth-century compilations. See Miranda Green, *Celtic Goddesses. Warriors, Virgins and Mothers* (London: British Museum Press, 1997), pp. 13–14.

158 Kim McCone, *Pagan Past and Christian Present in Early Irish Literature* (Maynooth: An Sagart, 1990), p. 5; Green, p. 12.

159 James Carney, *Studies in Irish Literature and History* (Dublin: Dublin Institute for Advanced Studies, 1979), p. 277.

160 Ibid., pp. 277–9, 298–301.

161 Ronald Hutton, *The Pagan Religions of the Ancient British Isles. Their Nature and Legacy* (Oxford: Blackwell, 1991), p. 148.

162 Eoin MacNeill, *Celtic Ireland* (Dublin: The Academy Press, 1981) (repr. of Dublin: Martin Lester, 1921), p. 26.

163 Thurneysen, p. 72.

164 MacNeill, p. 40.

165 McCone, p. 257.

166 Ibid., pp. 68ff.

167 Ibid., p. 72.

168 Máire Herbert, 'Goddess and king: the sacred marriage in early Ireland', in Louise Olga Fradenburg, ed., *Women and Sovereignty* (*Cosmos. The Yearbook of the Traditional Cosmology Society*, 7, Edinburgh: Edinburgh University Press, 1992), pp. 264–75.

169 See R. A. Breatnach, 'The lady and the king. A theme of Irish literature', *Studies,* vol. 152 (Autumn 1953), pp. 321–36; Diane E. Bessai, 'Who was Cathleen Ni Houlihan?' *The Malahat Review*, 42 (April 1977), pp. 114–29; Kevin P. Reilly, 'Irish literary autobiography: the goddesses that poets dream of', *Éire-Ireland*, 16(3) (1981), pp. 57–80.

170 Herbert, 'Goddess and king', p. 268.

171 She examined Baile in Scáil, and two versions of Echtra mac Echach Mugmedóin.

172 Ibid., p. 270.

173 Ibid., p. 272.

174 Green, p. 74.

175 Ibid., pp. 104–14.

176 Herbert, 'Goddess and king', p. 265.

177 Etienne Rynne, 'A pagan celtic Background for Sheela-na-gigs?', in Etienne Rynne, ed., *Figures from the Past. Studies on Figurative Art in Christian Ireland. In Honour of Helen M. Roe* (The Glendale Press and the Royal Society of Antiquaries of Ireland, 1987), pp. 189–202, 190.

178 Ibid., p. 191.

179 Ibid., p. 194.

180 Ibid., pp. 198ff.

181 Ibid., p. 199.

182 Ibid., p. 195.

183 David M. Wilson, 'An Irish mounting in the National Museum, Copenhagen', *Acta Archaeologica*, 26 (1955), 163–72, 166ff.

184 Andersen, *The Witch* . . .

185 René Crozet, *L'art roman en Saintonge* (Paris: A. & J. Picard, 1971); Jan Svanberg, *Gycklarmotiv I romansk konst. Acrobates, dompteurs et autres jongleurs dans l'art roman* (Stockholm: Antikvariskt arkiv, 41, 1970).

186 Ibid., pp. 47–9.

187 Ibid., pp. 56–7.

188 Ibid., p. 56.

189 Andersen wrongly assumes that Ireland is the only country where Sheelas are found on castles. See Andersen, *The Witch* . . . , pp. 70–1, 96, 113.

190 Ibid., p. 64.

191 Ibid., p. 68.
192 Ibid., p. 113.
193 Ibid., p. 113.
194 Ibid., pp. 73–7.
195 Ibid., p. 77.
196 Ibid., pp. 85–8, 93.
197 He refers to visions drawn from the Bible as that of the *Physiologus*, and there is reference to Rabelais and La Fontaine.
198 Andersen, *The Witch* . . . , p. 70.
199 Ibid., p. 137.
200 Ibid., pp. 91, 103, 133.
201 Frans Carlsson, 'Naked truth still veiled?', *ICO, Den Iconographiske Post*, 3 (1978), pp. 30–7.
202 Andersen is referring to a corbel acrobat from Champagnolle. See *The Witch* . . . , p. 53.
203 Carlsson, pp. 33–4.
204 Ibid., p. 34.
205 Ibid., p. 35.
206 And how would this interpretation relate to the corbel devils brandishing their genitals?
207 Andersen, p. 108.
208 Anthony Weir and James Jerman, *Images of Lust. Sexual Carvings on Medieval Churches* (reprinted London: Routledge, 1999).
209 Jerman, The "Sheela-na-gig", p. 11.
210 Weir and Jerman, pp. 20–2.
211 Anthony Weir, 'Sheila-na-gig', *The Irish Times*, 30 September 1977.
212 Weir and Jerman, *Images of Lust*, pp. 15–17.
213 Ibid., p. 139; Anthony Weir, 'Exhibitionists and related carvings in the Irish midlands: their origins and functions', in H. Murtagh, ed., *Irish Midland Studies: Essays in Commemoration of N. W. English* (Athlone: Old Athlone Society, 1980), pp. 57–72, 62.
214 Weir and Jerman, p. 138.
215 Ibid., p. 39.
216 Ibid., p. 17.
217 Ibid., p. 150; Jerman, p. 11.
218 Weir and Jerman, p. 144.
219 Ibid., pp. 11, 17.
220 Weir, 'Exhibitionists . . .', p. 67.
221 Weir and Jerman, p. 141.
222 Ibid., pp. 7–9, 141.
223 Ibid., pp. 9, 37–9.
224 Weir, 'Exhibitionists . . .', p. 61.
225 Ibid., p. 62.
226 Anthony Weir, 'Potency and sin: Ireland and the phallic continuum', *Archaeology Ireland*, 4(2) (1990), pp. 52–6.
227 Weir and Jerman, pp. 17, 21, 29, 144.
228 Ibid., p. 148.
229 Anthony Weir, 'Sheila-na-gig', italics added.
230 Erling Rump, 'Sheela-na-gig diagnostik', *ICO, Den Iconographiske Post*, 3 (1978), pp. 38–43, 38.
231 Erling Rump, '"Mater Ecclesia" (Moder Kirke): "Jeg er vejen, sandheden, og livet" (Johs. XIV, 6)', *ICO, Den Iconographiske Post*, 1/2 (1976), pp. 40–8, 46.
232 John (14:6); Matthew (6:27); John (3:3–5).
233 Rump, 'Mater Ecclesia . . .', p. 46.
234 Weir and Jerman, p. 17; Jerman, 'The Sheela-na-gig carvings . . .', p. 11.
235 Rump, 'Sheela-na-gig diagnostik', p. 42.
236 Ibid., pp. 39ff. See also Rump, 'Mater Ecclesia . . .', pp. 41ff.
237 In some places it is seen as a bad omen.
238 Rump, 'Sheela-na-gig . . .', p. 40.

239 Georges Colonna-Ceccaldi, 'Découvertes en Chypre. Les fouilles de Curium', *Revue Archéologique*, n.s., 33(1) (1877), pp. 177–89, 189.

240 See Christen Noerrelykke, 'En sheela fra Vendsyssel', *ICO Den Iconographiske Post*, 2 (1977), pp. 34–7; and Carlsson, 'Naked . . .', pp. 35ff.

241 Seamus Heaney, 'Sheelagh na Gig at Kilpeck', *Station Island* (London: Faber and Faber, 1984); Michael Longley, 'Sheela-Na-Gig', *The Ghost Orchid* (London: Cape Poetry, 1955); John Montague, 'Sheela Na Gig', *Collected Poems* (Wake Forrest: UP, 1995). See also Robin Robertson, 'Sheela-na-Gig', *A Painted Field* (reprinted in *The Sunday Times Bookshop*, 2 March 1997, p. 9).

242 Austin Clarke, *The Bright Temptation* (Dublin: Dolmen Press, 1965), pp. 248ff, and more prominently in Lindsay Clarke, *The Chymical Wedding* (London: Macmillan, 1989).

243 Painter Michael Mulcahy painted a series of pictures entitled *Pilgrimage to the Sheela-na-Gig*, which featured in the art magazine *Portfolio*, 1 (1991), cover, pp. 20–3; James O'Connor, author of the above-mentioned booklet called *Sheela na gig* (see Chapter 2, note 4), was commissioned to carve a replica of the Kiltinane Church Sheela, which had been stolen in 1990; New York artist Nancy Spero evoked Sheela-na-gigs in her large scroll paintings; see Josephine Withers, 'Nancy Spero's American-born Sheela-na-gig', *Feminist Studies*, 17 (1991), pp. 51–6; Greg and Geraldine McGarry combined their talents to produce a book which unites poetry with artistic impressions of artefacts in County Donegal called *Sheila na Gig. A Celtic Treasure Hunt* (An Inis, Contae Dhun Na nGall: Preas An Phuca, 1993); Sheelas are more and more used as a subject for jewellery, and many shops nowadays display pendants, rings, earrings, brooches etc. which are based on the figure. The National Museum in Dublin even sells T-shirts with the Seir Kieran Sheela printed on them.

3 THE PROBLEM OF THE NAME

1 Eamonn P. Kelly, *Sheela-na-Gigs. Origins and Functions* (Dublin: Country House, 1996), p. 5.

2 Síle is the Irish version of the French personal name Cecilia (English: Julia). To this is added gen. pl. of def. article, plus gen. pl. of 'cíoch' (breast or pap); the 'c' of cíoch is eclipsed by 'g'; and only the eclipsing letter is pronounced.

3 Bob Quinn, *Atlantean. Ireland's North African and Maritime Heritage* (London: Quartet Books, 1986), p. 170.

4 V. C. C. Collum, 'Female fertility figures', *MAN*, 35 (1935), pp. 62–3.

5 Edith Guest, 'Irish Sheela-na-gigs in 1935', *JRSAI*, 66 (1936), p. 127.

6 H. C. Lawlor, 'Two typical Irish "Sheela-na-gigs"', *MAN*, 31(4) (1931), pp. 5–6.

7 Brian Branston, 'Sheela-na-gig', *Irish Times* (24 September 1977).

8 Brian Branston, *The Lost Gods of England* (London: Thames and Hudson, 1957), p. 154.

9 P. J. Lynch, 'Liathmore-Mochoemog', *JNMAJ*, 3 (1914), pp. 83–4.

10 Robert A. S. Macalister, *The Archeology of Ireland* (London: Methuen, 1928), rev. ed. in 1996 by Bracken Books, London, p. 358.

11 E. Clibborn, 'On an ancient stone image presented to the Academy by Charles Halpin, MD', *PRIA*, series 1, II (1840–4) (8 April 1844), p. 565.

12 Ibid., p. 575.

13 Ibid., p. 570. M. V. Duignan in *The Shell Guide to Ireland* repeats this belief when he refers to the Rochestown Sheela as the first of these carvings to be published and the one that 'has given its name to the entire series'. Quoted in Jørgen Andersen, *The Witch on the Wall. Medieval Erotic Sculpture in the British Isles* (London: George Allen & Unwin, 1977), p. 11.

14 FRSAI, 'Figures known as Hags of the Castle, Sheelas, or Sheela na gigs', *JRSAI*, 24 (1894), p. 77, italics added.

15 James Grove White, *Historical and Topographical Notes on Buttevant, Castletownroche, Doneraile, Mallow, and Places in Their Vicinity* (Cork: Guy and Co., 1905), 4 vols, p. 85.

16 Andersen, p. 23.

17 See, for instance, James O'Connor, *Sheela na gig* (Fethard: Historical Society, 1991), p. 15; Joanne McMahon and Jack Roberts, *The Sheela-na-gigs of Ireland and Britain. The Divine*

Hag of the Christian Celts – An Illustrated Guide (Cork/Dublin: Mercier Press, 2001), pp. 20–1.

18 Johann Georg Kohl, *Reisen in Irland*, 2 vols (Dresden und Leipzig: Arnold, 1843), p. 207.

19 Clibborn, p. 566.

20 O'Donovan's spelling did not vary, but on three occasions he used a hyphen between 'ny' and 'Gigg'.

21 There is no *y* in the Irish alphabet anyway, but O'Donovan was something of a purist when it came to the Irish language. For instance, he would have preferred the Irish spelling *tír* (meaning 'land' or 'county') to be adopted in Anglicized place names instead of *tyr* as in Tyrone. See Patricia Boyne, *John O'Donovan (1806–1861): A Biography* (Kilkenny: Boethius, 1987), pp. 10ff.

22 Used in O-surnames of females where it is an abbreviation of Ní Uí.

23 In other publications one can encounter two more variations of Sheela, namely Sheila and Sheelagh.

24 George V. Du Noyer, 'Remarks on ancient Irish effigies sculptured on the walls of the ancient church on White Island, Lough Erne, Parish of Magheraculmoney, Co. of Fermanagh', *JRSAI*, n.s., 3(6) (1860–1), pp. 62–9.

25 The Irish for branch is *géag*. Kohl renders two translations into German, i.e. *Caecilie vom Zweig* and *Caecilie mit dem Zweige*. See Kohl, pp. 206ff.

26 He also gives the spelling *Shelah-na-gig* on the same page.

27 Thomas Wright, *The Worship of the Generative Powers during the Middle Ages of Western Europe* (1866); reprinted in *Sexual Symbolism. A History of Phallic Worship* (New York: The Julian Press, 1957), p. 36.

28 G. J. Witkowski uses this version in his book *L'Art profane à l'église: ses licences symboliques, satyriques et fantaisistes* (Paris: Jean Schemit, 1908), according to Andersen, p. 56.

29 Guest, 'Irish Sheela-na-gigs . . .', p. 127.

30 Mary M. Banks, 'Female fertility figures', *MAN*, 35 (1935), p. 63.

31 William Simpson, p. 65 (see Chapter 2, note 22).

32 Georges Colonna-Ceccaldi, 'Découvertes en Chypre. Les fouilles de Curium', *Revue archéologique*, n.s., 33(1) (1877), pp. 177–89.

33 Robert Craig MacLagan, *Our Ancestors: Scots, Picts, and Cymry and What Their Tradition Tells Us* (London & Edinburgh: T. N. Foulis, 1913), pp. 28–9.

34 Quoted in Alfred Fell, *A Furness Manor: Pennington and Its Church* (Ulverston: Kitchin & Co., 1929), p. 58. In Scotland 'Seelie' are the good fairies. 'Seel' means happiness, good fortune, opportune time, and is probably cognate with Old English 'Sael', or Old Norse 'Sele', from which Silbury, meaning Seleburgh, has derived its name. Perhaps the Canon had this in mind, but unfortunately he does not elaborate on the matter.

35 T. C. Lethbridge, *Gogmagog: The Buried Gods* (London: Routledge and Kegan Paul, 1957), pp. 14ff.

36 William Borlase, *The Dolmens of Ireland, Their Distribution, Structural Characteristics, and Affinities in Other Countries, Together with the Folk-lore Attaching to Them; Supplemented by Considerations on the Anthropology, Ethnology, and Traditions of the Irish People* (London: Chapman & Hall, 1897), p. 1115.

37 Robert Hunt, ed., *Popular Romances of the West of England. Or The Drolls, Traditions, and Superstitions of Old Cornwall*, 3rd rev. edn (London: Chatto and Windus, 1881), pp. 464–5.

38 William Battersby, *The Three Sisters at the Well. A Detection of Roots and Branches* (Navan: William Battersby, 1991), pp. 26–7.

39 Meaning 'daughter of Baoth', who was the first Abbess and the name in the placename Killinaboy Cill Inghine Bhaoithe.

40 Quoted in FRSAI, 'Figures known as . . .', p. 78.

41 MacLagan, pp. 28–9.

42 Thomas J. Westropp, *Folklore of Clare. A Folklore Survey of County Clare and County Clare Folk-Tales and Myths*, ed. Maureen Comber (Ennis: Clasp Press, 2000), p. 37.

43 Britta-Juliane Kruse, *Verborgene Heilkünste. Geschichte der Frauenmedizin im Spätmittelalter* (New York: de Gruyter, 1996), pp. 68–9.

44 A. Aymar, 'Le sachet accoucheur et ses mystères', *Annales du Midi*, 38 (1926), pp. 273–347.

45 Martin Martin, *A Description of the Western Islands of Scotland* (London: printed for Andrew Bell, at the Cross-Keys and Bible, in Cornhill, near Stocks-Market, 1703), pp. 288–9; and Martin Martin, *A Late Voyage to St Kilda The Remotest of all the Hebridies, or Western Isles of Scotland* (London: printed for D. Brown and T. Goodwin: At the Black Swan and Bible, 1698), pp. 135–43.

46 St Mark (15:34).

47 *Tales, By the O'Hara Family (i.e. John and Michael Banim): Containing (Crohoore of the Bill-Hook). (The Fetches, and John Doe)*, in 3 vols, volume 1 (London: Simpkin and R. Marshall, 1825), pp. 187–8. The first title was later reprinted as: Michael Banim, *Crohoore of the Billhook* (New York: Sadlier, 1881).

48 *Scotch and Irish Dances* (n.d.) The National Library of Ireland, JM 5763, 37, 40.

49 James Aird, *A Selection of Scotch, English, Irish and Foreign Airs. Adapted to the Fife, Violin, or German Flute* (Glasgow: Aird, 1782–1801), 6 vols, volume 5, p. 96.

50 *Forty Eight Original Irish Dances Never before Printed with Basses for the Piano-Forte and with Proper Figures for Dancing* (Dublin: Hime's Musical Circulating Library, College Green, No. 34, books 1 and 2, tune No. 22).

51 I owe this information to John Cullinane, University College, Cork.

52 *Encyclopaedia Britannica* (USA, 1979), under heading *jig*.

53 J. C. O'Keeffe and Art O'Brien, *A Handbook of Irish Dances, with an Essay on Their Origin and History* (Dublin: O'Donoghue and Co., 1902), p. vi.

54 Nóra Ní Shúilliobháin, 'Sheela-na-gig', *Irish Times* (20 October 1977).

55 Hugh Popham, *A Damned Cunning Fellow* (Par: Old Ferry Press, 1991).

56 Ibid., p. 11.

57 David Lyon, *The Sailing Navy List. All Ships of the Royal Navy – Built, Purchased and Captured – 1688–1860* (Conway: Maritime Press, 1993), p. 232. Also Sir William Laird Clowes, *The Royal Navy. A History* (Boston: Little, Brown & Co., and London: Sampson Lowe, Marston & Co., 1899), p. 111; and David Hepper, *British Warship Losses in the Age of the Sail* (Rotherfield: Jean Boudriot Publications, 1994), Section: 11 May–19 June 1781.

58 While most documents agree on this date, there are some which state 30 May 1781.

59 Popham, p. 11.

60 Public Record Office, Kew, ADM 1/314. The date is shown as 29 June, but this is crossed out and 22 substituted, which is the date of the 'clean' letter. This draft contains pencilled in corrections which are incorporated in the letter. Confusingly, the date given in the newspaper (see below) is 29 June.

61 *The Hibernian Chronicle*, 14(65) (13 August 1781).

62 Public Record Office, Kew, ADM 12/28B.

63 Public Record Office, Kew, ADM 1/2485.

64 Public Record Office, Kew, ADM 1/2593; ADM 6/90; ADM 9/2; ADM 12/28A; ADM 14/63.

65 The author, Hugh Popham, has passed away since the publication of the book, so unfortunately I could not establish by whom and where this version was used.

66 Kerby A. Miller, *Emigrants and Exiles. Ireland and the Irish Exodus to North America* (New York: Oxford University Press, 1985), p. 139.

67 *The Hibernian Chronicle* (18 January 1781), p. 6. Captain Rodney is not to be confused with Admiral Rodney.

68 Colman O Mahony, 'Shipbuilding and repairing in nineteenth-century Cork', *JCHAS* (1989), pp. 74–86, 74.

69 James E. Doan, 'The Irish in the Caribbean', paper presented at the IASIL Conference (July 1995).

70 Ibid.

71 Herman J. Viola, 'Seeds of change', in Herman J. Viola and Carolyn Margolis, eds, *Seeds of Change. Five Hundred Years Since Columbus* (Washington, DC: Smithsonian Institute Press, 1991), p. 13.

72 For example, the *Hibernian Chronicle* occasionally makes reference to shipping news culled from the *St Lucia Gazette or, General Intelligencer*, which suggests that newspapers in the West Indies did indeed print a very similar type of information.

73 Wright, p. 196; Thomas J. Westropp, 'A study of the folklore on the coasts of Connacht, Ireland. XIV. Calendar customs and social customs', *Folklore*, 34(4) (1923), pp. 333–49, 348–9.

74 Barbara G. Walker, *The Woman's Encyclopedia of Myths and Secrets* (San Francisco: Harper, 1983), under heading *ship*.

75 Jacob Grimm, *Deutsche Mythologie* (Graz: Akademische Druck- und Verlagsanstalt, 1968), 3 vols, pp. 214–20.

76 Walker, under heading *ship*.

77 All quoted in Josef Weisweiler, *Heimat und Herrschaft. Wirkung und Ursprung eines irischen Mythos*. Schriftenreihe der Deutschen Gesellschaft für keltische Studien, hrsg. von L. Mühlhausen, Heft 11 (Halle/Saale: Max Niemeyer Verlag, 1943), pp. 30–1.

78 Diane E. Bessai, 'Who was Cathleen Ni Houlihan?', *The Malahat Review*, 42 (April 1977), p. 115.

79 A typical heading would be, 'A letter from Sheelagh to John Bull on Irish affairs' (1805), The National Library of Ireland, JP 308.

80 'Sheelah (i.e. Ireland)' Faustus, Doctor, pseud.: 'State of Sheelah's pulse, by Doctor Faustus' (1813), The National Library of Ireland, JP 368.

81 Herbert Halpert, 'Ireland, Sheila and Newfoundland', in Alison Feder and Bernice Schrank, eds, *Literature and Folk Culture: Ireland and Newfoundland* (St John's: Memorial University of Newfoundland, 1977), pp. 147–71, 149.

82 Ibid., p. 151.

83 Ibid.

84 Ibid.

85 Ibid., p. 152.

86 Ibid., pp. 155–7.

87 Ibid., p. 163.

88 Patrick S. Dinneen, *Foclóir Gaedhilge agus Béarla* (Dublin: The Educational Company of Ireland, 1927), under heading *géag*.

89 Halpert, p. 160.

90 Ibid., p. 154.

91 Ibid., p. 166.

92 *Caubeen*, an old hat; *treheens*, a pair of stockings with only the legs.

93 Halpert, p. 170.

94 Ibid., pp. 169–71.

95 Footnote in Thomas Dinely (or Dingley), Gent. in theYear 1681, *Observations in a Voyage through the Kingdom of Ireland: Being a Collection of Several Monuments, Inscriptions, Draughts of Towns, Castles etc.* (Dublin: Printed at the University Press, by M. H. Gill, 1870), pp. 33–5.

96 John Carr, *The Stranger in Ireland, Or, A Tour in the Southern and Western Parts of that Country, in the Year 1805* (London: printed for Richard Phillips, 1806), p. 260.

97 Nicholas Flood Davin, *The Irishman in Canada* (Shannon: Irish University Press, 1969; Toronto, 1877).

98 Ibid., p. 144.

99 The text is contained in The National Library of Ireland, JM 3346, and was written by one Wm Upton, but there is no date mentioned.

100 Tom Inglis, *Moral Monopoly. The Catholic Church in Modern Irish Society* (Dublin: Gill and Macmillan, 1987), pp. 98–165.

101 Ibid., p. 97.

102 Elizabeth Malcolm, 'Popular recreation in nineteenth-century Ireland', in Oliver MacDonagh, W. F. Mandle and Pauric Travers, eds, *Irish Culture and Nationalism, 1750–1950* (London: Macmillan, 1983), pp. 40–55, 46.

103 Footnote in Thomas Dineley, p. 35.

104 Inglis, p. 98.

105 Sir William A. Craigie, *A Dictionary of the Older Scottish Tongue from the Twelfth Century to the End of the Seventeenth* (Chicago: University of Chicago Press, 1937); Eric Partridge, *A Classical Dictionary of the Vulgar Tongue* (London, 1976); *The Routledge Dictionary of Historical Slang* (London, 1973); E. Coles, *Dictionary* (1676); Eric Partridge, *A Dictionary of Slang and Unconventional English* (London: Routledge, 1984); Thomas Wright, *Dictionary of Obsolete and Provincial English* (London: Henry G. Bohn, 1857).

106 Apart from the above mentioned dictionaries see also John Trotter Brockett, *A Glossary of North Country Words with Their Etymology and Affinity to Other Languages* (London and Newcastle: Emerson Charnley, 1866); A. Warrack and W. Grants, *A Scots Dialect Dictionary* (London, 1911); Sherman M. Kuhn, *Middle English Dictionary* (Ann Arbor: University of Michigan Press, 1963); Alexander Warrack, *A Scots Dialect Dictionary* (London: Chambers, 1911).

107 Trotter Brockett, p. 187.

108 R. E. Allen, *The Concise Oxford Dictionary of Current English* (Oxford: Clarendon Press, 1990).

109 Gordon Williams, *A Dictionary of Sexual Language and Imagery in Shakespearean and Stuart Literature* (London: The Athlone Press, 1994), volume 2 (G–P), pp. 596–7.

4 SHEELAS, BIRTH, DEATH AND MEDIEVAL RURAL TRADITIONS

1 Mary M. Banks, 'Female fertility figures', *MAN*, 35 (1935), p. 63.

2 Edith M. Guest, 'Ballyvourney and its Sheela-na-gig', *Folklore*, 48 (1937), pp. 374–84, 375–6.

3 Richard Worsley cited in Jørgen Andersen, *The Witch on the Wall. Medieval Erotic Sculpture in the British Isles* (London: Allen & Unwin, 1977), p. 30; also A. L. and G. E. Hutchinson, 'Distribution of Sheela-na-gigs in Great Britain', contained in 'The Idol or Sheela-na-gig at Binstead', *Proc. Isle of Wight Nat. Hist. and Archaeol. Soc.*, 6(4) (1970), p. 246.

4 Quoted in Edith Guest, 'Irish Sheela-Na-Gigs in 1935', *JRSAI*, 66 (1936), p. 112.

5 Patrick J. Corish, *The Catholic Community in the Seventeenth and Eighteenth Centuries* (Dublin: Helicon, 1981), p. 37.

6 Ibid., pp. 65–6.

7 Corish was not specifically looking for Sheela-na-gigs and he obviously only studied Catholic documents. A look at Protestant documents might also yield results.

8 The terms 'peasant' and 'peasantry' are used here simply to denote country folk belonging to the agricultural class which depends on subsistence farming.

9 Judith M. Bennett, *Women in the Medieval English Countryside. Gender and Household in Brigstock Before the Plague* (Oxford: Oxford University Press, 1987), p. 10.

10 Aron Gurevich, *Medieval Popular Culture: Problems of Belief and Perception*, trans. János M. Bak and Paul A. Hollingsworth (Cambridge: Cambridge University Press, 1988), p. xv.

11 Bennett, p. 3.

12 Ibid., p. 62; Henrietta Leyser, *Medieval Women. A Social History of Women in England, 450–1500* (London: Weidenfeld and Nicolson, 1995), p. 143; Edith Ennen, *Frauen im Mittelalter* (Munich: Beck, 1984), p. 226; Lisa Bitel, *Land of Women. Tales of Sex and Gender from Early Ireland* (New York: Cornell University, 1996), p. 5.

13 Leyser, p. 5; Bitel, pp. 4–11; Mary O'Dowd, 'Property, work and home: women and the economy, *c.*1170–1850', in Angela Bourke, ed., *The Field Day Anthology of Irish Writing V. Irish Women's Writing and Traditions* (Cork: Cork University Press, 2002), pp. 464–71, 467.

14 August Knoch, 'Die Ehescheidung im alten irischen Recht', in Rudolf Thurneysen, ed., *Studies in Early Irish Law* (Dublin: RIA, 1936), pp. 235–68, 264.

15 Ibid., p. 264.

16 Edith Ennen, 'Die Frau in der mittelalterlichen Stadt', in Bernd Herrmann, ed., *Mensch und Umwelt im Mittelalter* (Stuttgart: Deutsche Verlags-Anstalt, 1986), pp. 35–52, 37.

17 Kathleen Mulchrone, 'The rights and duties of women with regard to the education of their children', in Thurneysen, pp. 187–206, 189.

18 John Carr, *The Stranger in Ireland, Or, A Tour in the Southern and Western Parts of that Country, in the Year 1805* (London: printed for Richard Phillips, 1806), p. 405.
19 T. Crofton Croker, *Researches in the South of Ireland. Illustrative of the Scenery, Architectural Remains, and the Manners and Superstitions of the Peasantry* (London: John Murray, 1824), pp. 234–5.
20 Charles R. Browne, 'The ethnography of Carna and Mweenish, in the Parish of Moyruss, Connemara', *PRIA*, 6 (1900–2), pp. 503–34, 522.
21 Michael J. O'Dowd and Elliot E. Philipp, *The History of Obstetrics and Gynaecology* (New York: The Parthenon Publishing Group, 1994), p. 183.
22 Ibid., p. 186.
23 Vilhelm Möller-Christensen, 'Umwelt im Spiegel der Skelettreste vom Kloster Aebelholt', in Herrmann, pp. 129–39, 131.
24 Ennen, 'Die Frau . . .', p. 36.
25 Norbert Ohler, *Sterben und Tod im Mittelalter* (Düsseldorf: Artemis Verlag, 1990, ppb-Ausgabe Patmos Verlag, 2003), p. 28.
26 Klaus Arnold, 'Die Einstellung zum Kind im Mittelalter', in Herrmann, pp. 53–64, 61.
27 Manuel Simon, *Heilige. Hexe. Mutter. Der Wandel des Frauenbildes durch die Medizin im 16. Jahrhundert* (Berlin: Dietrich Reimer Verlag, 1993), p. 124.
28 Grethe Jacobsen, 'Pregnancy and childbirth in the medieval north: a topology of sources and a preliminary study', *Scandinavian Journal of History*, 9 (1984), 91–111, 92.
29 Ibid., p. 102.
30 Bennett, pp. 115–16.
31 Ohler, p. 29.
32 Thomas Willis, *Facts Connected with the Social and Sanitary Condition of the Working Classes in the City of Dublin* (1845), newly edited under the title *The Hidden Dublin* (Dublin: Trinity History Workshop, 2002), pp. 50–1, 71.
33 Arnold, p. 60.
34 Ibid., pp. 60–1.
35 Bennett, p. 68.
36 Quoted in Thomas Rogers Forbes, *The Midwife and the Witch* (New Haven, CT: Yale University Press, 1966), p. 141.
37 Vern Bullough and Cameron Campbell, 'Female longevity and diet in the Middle Ages', *Speculum*, 55(2) (1980), pp. 317–25, 319.
38 Ibid., p. 319; Gisela Grupe, 'Umwelt und Bevölkerungsentwicklung im Mittelalter', in Herrmann, pp. 24–34, 28.
39 Bullough and Campbell, p. 323.
40 Ibid., p. 323.
41 Quoted by Jacobsen, p. 106.
42 Simon, pp. 124–35.
43 Britta-Juliane Kruse, *Verborgene Heilkünste. Geschichte der Frauenmedizin im Spätmittelalter* (Berlin: de Gruyter, 1996), p. 66.
44 O'Dowd and Philipp, p. 167; Jacobsen, 103; Adrian Wilson, 'Participant or patient? Seventeenth century childbirth from the mother's point of view', in Roy Porter, ed., *Patients and Practitioners. Lay Perceptions of Medicine in Pre-industrial Society* (Cambridge: Cambridge University Press, 1985), pp. 129–44, 135; Marilyn Deegan, 'Pregnancy and childbirth in the Anglo-Saxon medical texts: a preliminary survey', in Marilyn Deegan and D. G. Scragg, eds, *Medicine in Early Medieval England* (Manchester: Manchester Centre for Anglo-Saxon Studies, 1989), pp. 17–26, 18; Jacques Gélis, *History of Childbirth. Fertility, Pregnancy and Birth in Early Modern Europe* (trans. of *L'arbre et le fruit*, 1984) (Polity Press, 1991), p. 99; Noragh Jones, *Power of Raven. Wisdom of Serpent* (Edinburgh: Floris Books, 1995), p. 78.
45 J. H. G. Grattan and Charles Singer, *Anglo-Saxon Magic and Medicine. Illustrated Specially from the Semi-pagan Text 'Lacnunga'* (London: Oxford University Press, 1952), 2 vols, volume 1, p. 4.
46 Wendy Davies, 'The place of healing in early Irish society', in Donnchadh O Corráin

et al., eds, *Sages, Saints and Storytellers. Celtic Studies in Honour of Professor James Carney* (Maynooth: An Sagart, 1989), pp. 43–55, 43.

47 Monica H. Green, 'Obstetrical and gynecological texts in Middle English', *Studies in the Age of Chaucer*, 14 (1992), pp. 53–88, 53ff; Fiona Harris Stoerz, 'Suffering and survival in Medieval English childbirth', in Cathy Jorgensen Intyre, ed., *Medieval Family Roles. A Book of Essays* (New York: Garland Publishing, 1996), pp. 101–20, 104.

48 Grattan and Singer, p. 7.

49 Deegan, p. 18.

50 Ibid., p. 104.

51 Quoted in Audrey L. Meaney, *Anglo-Saxon Amulets and Curing Stones*, BAR British Series 96 (Oxford: BAR, 1981), p. 47.

52 One such remedy is 'ergot', which in medieval times was administered to hasten birth pangs. It is now known that this is the popular name for *Claviceps purpurea*, whose efficacy in the acceleration of labour is recognized by official medicine.

53 Deegan, p. 105.

54 James Joyce, *Ulysses* (Harmondsworth: Penguin Books, 1973) (Paris, 1922), p. 408.

55 Anon., *The Works of Aristotle, the Famous Philosopher, in Four Parts* (New England: Printed for the Publishers, 1827).

56 Ibid., pp. 41–2.

57 See Lucille B. Pinto, 'The folk practice of gynecology and obstetrics in the Middle Ages', *Bulletin of the History of Medicine*, 47 (1973), pp. 513–23, 519.

58 Rogers Forbes, p. 64.

59 John Brand, *Observations on Popular Antiquities. Chiefly Illustrating the Origin of Our Vulgar Customs, Ceremonies and Superstitions* (London: Chatto & Windus, 1900), p. 733.

60 Ibid., p. 331.

61 Ibid., p. 69.

62 Ibid., p. 74.

63 Ibid., p. 77.

64 Gélis, p. 68.

65 Thomas J. Westropp, *Folklore of Clare. A Folklore Survey of County Clare and County Clare Folk-Tales and Myths*, ed. Maureen Comber (Ennis: Clasp Press, 2000), p. 37.

66 Rogers Forbes, p. 79.

67 Meaney, p. 102.

68 Ibid., p. 230.

69 Patrick Logan, *The Holy Wells of Ireland* (Gerrards Cross: Colin Smythe, 1992), pp. 82–4.

70 Information supplied by Conleth Manning (Dúchas).

71 James M. Mackinlay, *Folklore of Scottish Lochs and Springs* (Glasgow: William Hodge, 1893), p. 27.

72 Brand, p. 339.

73 Walter J. Dilling, 'Girdles: their origin and development, particularly with regard to their use as charms in medicine, marriage, and midwifery', *Caledonian Medical Journal*, 9 (1912–14), pp. 337–57, 403–25.

74 Ibid., p. 412.

75 Marija Gimbutas, *The Language of the Goddess* (San Francisco: Harper & Row, 1989), p. 110.

76 Ibid., p. 409.

77 Ibid., pp. 409ff.

78 Dilling, p. 421.

79 Ibid., pp. 417–18.

80 Ibid., p. 418.

81 Rogers Forbes, p. 125.

82 Dilling, p. 419.

83 Ibid., pp. 421–2; Pinto, p. 513; Curt F. Bühler, 'Prayers and charms in certain Middle English scrolls, *Speculum*, 39 (1964), pp. 270–8.

84 According to a Middle Irish text Jesus was taller, measuring 190 cm. There is no reference to a birthgirdle here, but the measurement itself possesses magical qualities because

the day you see it you are assured you will not suffer sudden death and you will be safe from the devil. See Kuno Meyer, 'Die Leibeslänge Christi', *Zeitschrift für Celtische Philologie*, 10 (1915), pp. 401–2.

85 Bühler, p. 275.
86 Brand, p. 333.
87 Dilling, p. 422.
88 Ibid., p. 422.
89 Ibid., p. 424.
90 Meaney, p. 20.
91 Rogers Forbes, p. 80.
92 Ibid., p. 80.
93 Kruse, pp. 67–8.
94 Rogers Forbes, p. 81.
95 Jacobsen, p. 105.
96 Logan, p. 84.
97 Brand, p. 198.
98 L. M. C. Weston, 'Women's medicine, women's magic: the old English metrical child-birth charms', *Modern Philology*, 3 (February 1995), pp. 279–93, 288–9.
99 Ibid., p. 289.
100 Grattan and Singer, p. 191.
101 Kruse, p. 69.
102 Rogers Forbes, pp. 81–2.
103 Ibid., p. 82.
104 Lisa Bitel, 'Conceived in sins, born in delights: stories of procreation from early Ireland', *Journal of the History of Sexuality*, 3(2) (1992), pp. 181–201, 191–2.
105 Davies, p. 52.
106 Ibid.
107 *The Poetic Edda*, trans. Lee M. Hollander (Austin: University of Texas Press, 1962), pp. 235, 279–80.
108 Nils Lid, 'Light-mother and earth-mother', *Studia Norvegica*, 4 (1946), pp. 3–20, 20.
109 *Genesis* (35:17 and 38:28), *Exodus* (1:15–16).
110 Rogers Forbes, p. 112.
111 Séamas O Catháin, *The Festival of Brigit: Celtic Goddess and Holy Woman* (Blackrock: DBA Publications, 1995), p. 149.
112 Lid, pp. 13–14; Brand, pp. 330–1.
113 Brand, p. 331.
114 Wilson, p. 134.
115 Gélis, p. 97.
116 Heinz Kirchhoff, 'Die Gebärhaltung der Frau. Von der Prähistorie bis auf den heutigen Tag', *Gynäkologische Praxis*, 3 (1979), pp. 203–23, 203.
117 *Exodus* (1:15–16).
118 Gélis, pp. 121–33.
119 Ibid., p. 132.
120 Ibid., pp. 114, 136; Kruse, p. 190; Anon., *The Works of Aristotle*, pp. 54–5, 130.
121 Kruse, p. 190, 195; Gélis, p. 136.
122 Kruse, p. 188.
123 Anon., *The Works of Aristotle*, p. 41.
124 Gélis, p. 136.
125 Ibid., pp. 137–8.
126 Brand, p. 333.
127 Quoted in Rogers Forbes, p. 145.
128 Ibid., pp. 147–8.
129 Brand, p. 333.
130 Quoted in Rogers Forbes, p. 146.
131 Anon., *The Works of Aristotle*, p. 43.
132 Gélis, p. 111.

133 Ibid., p. 99.
134 Ulrike Schweikert's historical novel *Die Hexe und die Heilige* (Munich: Droemersche Verlagsanstalt Th. Knaur Nachf., 2001), on the theme of midwives and medieval motherhood, is based on scholarly research. According to this practically all the obstetrical aids referred to in this chapter were very much in use in early seventeenth-century Germany. The novel also dramatically highlights how easily midwives were made the target of witch hunts.
135 Richard L. Brubaker, 'The untamed goddesses of village India', in Carl Olson, ed., *The Book of the Goddess. Past and Present. An Introduction to Her Religion* (New York: The Crossroad Publishing Company, 1983), pp. 145–60, 145–8; John Middleton, *Magic, Witchcraft, and Curing* (Garden City, NY: The Natural History Press, 1967), pp. ix–x; Gustav Ränk, 'Lapp female deities of the Madder-akka group', in Nils Lid, ed., *Studia Septentrionalia*, volume VI (Oslo: H. Aschehoug & Co., 1955), pp. 7–79 (passim); E. Manker, 'Seite-Kult und Trommelmagie der Lappen', in V. Diószegi, ed., *Glaubenswelt und Folklore der sibirischen Völker* (Budapest: Verlag der Ungarischen Akademie der Wissenschaften, 1963), pp. 29–43, 32; Karen Louise Jolly, 'Magic, miracle, and popular practice in the early Medieval West: Anglo-Saxon England', in Jacob Neusner, Ernest S. Frerichs and Paul Virgil McCracken Flesher, eds, *Religion, Science and Magic. In Concert and in Conflict* (Oxford: Oxford University Press, 1989), pp. 166–82.
136 Edith Guest, 'Irish Sheela-na-gigs in 1935', *JRSAI*, 66 (1936), p. 122; Andersen, p. 26; James O'Connor, *Sheela na gig* (Fethard: Historical Society, 1991), p. 21; Eamonn P. Kelly, *Sheela-na-Gigs. Origins and Functions* (Dublin: Country House, 1996), p. 40; Anthony Weir and James Jerman, *Images of Lust. Sexual Carvings on Medieval Churches* (London: Batsford, 1986), p. 116.
137 Ulrike Schweikert refers to this peculiar habit when she writes, 'Als die erste Presswehe kam, ließ sich die Bettlerin instinktiv mit auswärts gedrehten Füßen in eine Hockstellung sinken' (At the onset of the first labour pains the beggar woman instinctively squatted down on her heels turning both feet outwards.). *Die Hexe* . . . , p. 187.
138 Rump on the other hand sees this particular object clearly as representing the placenta. Erling Rump, '"Mater Ecclesia" (Moder Kirke): "Jeg er vejen, sandheden, og livet" (Johs. XIV, 6)', *ICO, Den Iconographiske Post*, 1/2 (1976), pp. 40–8, 48.
139 I owe this information to John Billingsley, editor of *Northern Earth*.
140 J. G. R. Forlong, *Faiths of Man. A Cyclopaedia of Religions* (London: Bernard Quaritch, 1906), 3 vols, volume 3, p. 302.
141 W. F. Wakeman, 'The church on White Island, Lough Erne, Parish of Magheraculmoney, County of Fermanagh', *JRSAI*, 4th series, 5 (1879–82), pp. 276–92, 282.
142 Guest, 'Irish Sheela-na-gigs . . .', p. 111.
143 Andersen, p. 153.
144 Rump, p. 45.
145 Christen Noerrelykke 'En sheela fra Vendsyssel', *ICO, Den Iconographiske Post*, 2 (1977), pp. 34–7, 36–7.
146 Ränk, 'Lapp female . . .'; Gustav Ränk, 'Die Hausgottheiten der Frauen und das Geschlechtstabu bei den nordeurasischen Völkern', *Ethnos*, 3/4 (1948), pp. 153–70; Manker; E. I. Rombandjejewa, 'Einige Sitten und Bräuche der Mansen (Wogulen) bei der Geburt der Kinder', in Diószegi, ed., pp. 85–92; O. Nahodil, 'Mutterkult in Sibirien', in Diószegi, ed., pp. 491–511.
147 O Catháin, pp. x–xi.
148 Ränk, 'Lapp female . . .', p. 75.
149 Ibid., p. 43.
150 Ibid., pp. 51, 54, 56, 58, 60–4, 68, 71; Ränk, 'Die Hausgottheiten . . .', pp. 155–61.
151 Rombandjejewa, p. 87; Nahodil, p. 497; Ränk, 'Die Hausgottheiten . . .', p. 159.
152 Nahodil, p. 495.
153 Ränk, 'Lapp female . . .', p. 65.
154 Ränk, 'Die Hausgottheiten . . .', p. 161.
155 Ränk, 'Lapp female . . .', pp. 21–3.

156 Ibid., pp. 58–9.

157 O Catháin, pp. 189, 170.

158 Andersen, p. 141.

159 Edith Guest, 'Ballyvourney and its Sheela-na-gig', *Folklore*, 48 (1937), pp. 374–84, 383.

160 Douglas Fraser, 'The heraldic woman: a study in diffusion', in Douglas Fraser, ed., *The Many Faces of Primitive Art. A Critical Anthology* (Englewood Cliffs, NJ: Prentice Hall, 1966), pp. 36–99, 40; Ian Hodder, 'Contextual archaeology: an interpretation of Catal Hüyük and a discussion of the origins of agriculture', *London University Institute of Archaeology Bulletin*, 24 (1987), pp. 43–56, 49; Mary Condren, *The Serpent and the Goddess. Women, Religion, and Power in Celtic Ireland* (New York: Harper San Francisco, 1989), passim; Anne L. Barstow, 'The prehistoric goddess', in Carl Olson, ed., *The Book of the Goddess. Past and Present. An Introduction to Her Religion* (New York: The Crossroad Publishing Company, 1983), pp. 7–15, 8; Ronald Hutton, *The Pagan Religions of the Ancient British Isles. Their Nature and Legacy* (Oxford: Blackwell, 1991), pp. 41ff.

161 Green, pp. 113–14; Marija Gimbutas, 'Pre-Indo-European goddesses in Baltic mythology', *The Mankind Quarterly* (1985), pp. 19–25; Carlo Ginzburg, *Ecstasies. Deciphering the Witches' Sabbath* (New York: Pantheon Books, 1991. Originally published in Italy as *Storia Notturna*, Turin, 1989), p. 105.

162 Gélis, pp. 165–8; Philip Rawson, *Primitive Erotic Art* (New York: G. P. Putnam's Sons, 1973), pp. 7, 22; Starhawk, *The Spiral Dance. Rebirth of the Ancient Religion of the Great Goddess* (San Francisco: Harper & Row, 1989), p. 17.

163 Gélis, p. 110.

164 Hutton, p. 328.

165 Joseph Balogh, 'Tänze in Kirchen und auf Kirchhöfen', *Niederdeutsche Zeitschrift für Volkskunde*, 6 (1928), pp. 1–14; Seán O Súilleabháin, *Irish Wake Amusements* (Cork: Mercier Press, 1967), pp. 31, 159ff; Ohler, *Sterben und Tod . . .* , pp. 83–4.

166 T. C. Lethbridge, *Gogmagog. The Buried Gods* (London: Routledge and Kegan Paul, 1957), p. 158; Brand, pp. 437–47.

167 Vivian Mercier, *The Irish Comic Tradition* (Oxford: Oxford University Press, 1962), p. 56.

168 E. Estyn Evans, *Irish Folk Ways* (London: Routledge & Kegan Paul, 1957), p. 283; Green, p. 114.

169 O Súilleabháin, p. 173.

170 Ibid., p. 130.

171 Brand, p. 462.

172 Ibid., p. 469.

173 *The Penguin Book of Irish Verse*, introduced and edited by Brendan Kennelly (Harmondsworth: Penguin Books, 1970), pp. 227–8.

174 O Súilleabheáin, p. 173.

175 Brand, p. 446.

176 Wilhelm Mannhardt, *Letto-Preussische Götterlehre*. Magazin der Lettisch-Litärischen Gesellschaft, 21 (Riga, 1936), pp. 419, 429, 468, 476, 479.

177 Gurevich, p. 87.

178 Crofton Croker, pp. 166–7.

179 Estyn Evans, p. 293.

180 Mannhardt, pp. 257, 304, 602.

181 Estyn Evans, p. 293.

182 Mannhardt, pp. 303, 467, 477.

183 Ibid., p. 415.

184 Ibid., p. 487.

185 Quoted in Kevin Danaher, *The Year in Ireland. Irish Calendar Customs* (Cork and Dublin: Mercier, 1972), p. 228.

186 Ibid., p. 228.

187 Estyn Evans, p. 277.

188 Ibid., pp. 608–9.

189 J. M. McPherson, *Primitive Beliefs in the North-East of Scotland* (London: Longman, Green and Co., 1929), pp. 126–7.

190 Edward MacLysaght, *Irish Life in the Seventeenth Century: After Cromwell* (Dublin: The Talbot Press, 1939), p. 322.
191 O Súilleabháin, pp. 170–2.
192 Mannhardt, p. 487.
193 O Súilleabháin, p. 28.
194 Ränk, 'Lapp female . . .', p. 16.
195 Françoise Loux, 'Frauen, Männer und Tod in den Ritualen um die Geburt', in Jürgen Schlumbohm, Barbara Duden, Jacques Gélis, Patrice Veit, eds, *Rituale der Geburt. Eine Kulturgeschichte* (Munich: C. H. Beck'sche Verlagsbuchhandlung, 1998) pp. 30–65, 55; Gélis, p. 39.
196 Ibid.
197 Ibid.
198 Quoted by Jones, p. 106.
199 Ränk, 'Lapp female . . .', p. 51.
200 Ibid., p. 71.
201 Ibid., pp. 16–18, 61, 63, 67; Ränk, 'Die Hausgottheiten . . .', pp. 156, 161, 163.
202 Ränk, 'Lapp female . . .', pp. 51–2.
203 Nahodil, p. 497.
204 Gimbutas, *The Language* . . . , pp. 210–11.
205 Gélis, p. 73.
206 Ränk, 'Lapp female . . .', p. 52.
207 Jacobsen, p. 104.
208 Margaret Murray, *The Witch-Cult in Western Europe. A Study in Anthropology* (Oxford: Clarendon Press, 1921), p. 169.
209 Gélis, p. 16.
210 McPherson, p. 50.
211 Ibid., p. 53.
212 Gimbutas, 'Pre-Indo-European . . .', p. 24.
213 Wright, pp. 195ff. This idol is also referred to by Robert Craig MacLagan, *Scottish Myths. Notes on Scottish History and Tradition* (Edinburgh: Maclachlan and Stewart, 1882), p. 153, and Estyn Evans, p. 302.
214 Mackinlay, p. 219.
215 I owe this information to George Willoghby, Thurles.
216 A. G. Van Hamel, 'Odinn hanging on the tree', *Acta Philologica Scandinavia*, 7 (1932/3), pp. 260–88.
217 Lotte Motz, 'The winter goddess: Percht, Holda, and related figures', *Folklore*, 95(ii) (1984), pp. 151–66.
218 Jones, p. 104.
219 Quoted in Estyn Evans, p. 275.
220 This would be the correct spelling, rather than Kohl's *Shila na Gigh*.
221 McPherson, pp. 89–92.
222 Ellen Ettlinger, 'Documents of British superstition in Oxford', *Folklore*, 54 (1943), pp. 227–49, 239.
223 MacLagan, p. 80.
224 Gimbutas, 'Pre-Indo-European . . .', p. 23.
225 Danaher, pp. 24–5.
226 William Jolly, 'On cup-marked stones in the neighbourhood of Inverness', *Proceedings of the Society of Antiquaries of Scotland*, n.s., 4 (1882), pp. 300–401, 377–8, 387; Arthur Mitchell, *The Past in the Present: What Is Civilisation?* (Edinburgh: David Douglas, 1880), pp. 263–5; McPherson, pp. 50–1.
227 Estyn Evans, p. 276.
228 Ibid., p. 283.
229 Despite the fact that one regularly finds the oft-repeated notion that Sheelas had an apotropaic function in medieval times, there is no evidence to show that this ever was the case.
230 O Súilleabháin, pp. 166–7.

231 Guest, 'Ballyvourney . . .', pp. 375, 382.

232 Ibid., p. 380.

233 Ibid., p. 376.

234 David Rorie, 'On Scottish folk-medicine', *Caledonian Medical Journal*, 13 (1926), pp. 3, 70–237, 86.

235 O Catháin, p. 149.

236 Jones, p. 106.

237 Katie Donovan, 'Touching faith in a stone Sheela', *Irish Times* (7 July 1994, New Features), p. 11.

238 Guest, 'Ballyvourney . . .', p. 380.

239 Andersen, p. 26.

240 Jim Wallace's handwritten letters are dated 21 January 1991 and 19 February 1991. I sincerely thank Mary Woodworth, widow of the Dean, for her very kind permission to let me go through the correspondence of her late husband.

241 John Hogan, *Kilkenny: The Ancient City of Ossory, the Seat of Its Kings, the See of Its Bishops and the Site of Its Cathedral* (Kilkenny: Egan, 1884), pp. 4–5.

242 John Hargreaves, 'Dallying with sheela in the sanctuary', *Guardian*, 'Weekend' supplement (28 October 1989), p. 8.

243 O'Connor, p. 11.

244 Anthony Weir, 'Three carved figures in County Louth', *Louth Arch. J.*, 18/19 (1973–80), pp. 67–73, 69.

245 I acknowledge with thanks the help of Enda O'Boyle, a local historian and retired school teacher, who directed me to Mrs Johnston and who accompanied me when I interviewed her on 7 June 1999.

246 Jim Higgins is the author of *Irish Mermaids* (Galway: The Crow's Rock Press, 1995).

247 The outcome of the Sheela project was an art exhibition by these three artists called: 'Sheela-na-gig: tracing the walled woman', which was staged in the United States and in Ireland.

248 Robin Lane Fox, *Pagans and Christians* (Harmondsworth: Viking Penguin Books, 1986), p. 276.

249 Hutton, pp. 248, 261.

250 Lane Fox, p. 287.

251 Ibid., pp. 284, 293.

252 Ibid., p. 289; Leyser, pp. 24–5.

253 Quoted by Balogh, p. 11.

254 From Bede's *Ecclesiastical History* I, quoted in Valerie I. J. Flint, *The Rise of Magic in Early Medieval Europe* (Oxford: Clarendon Press, 1991), pp. 76–7.

255 Flint, p. 69.

256 Ibid., pp. 71–3.

257 Gélis, pp. 146–7.

258 Flint, p. 400.

259 William Smith and Samuel Cheetham, eds, *A Dictionary of Christian Antiquities* (London: John Murray, 1875) 2 vols, under heading *Idolatry*; John T. McNeill and Helena M. Gamer, *Medieval Handbooks of Penance. A Translation of the Principal 'libri poenitentiales' and Selections from Related Documents* (New York: Columbia University Press, 1990); Súilleabháin, pp. 138ff, 154, 156, 159; MacLysaght, pp. 288–9; P. Goessler, 'Germanisch–Christliches an Kirchen und Friedhöfen Südwestdeutschlands', *Archiv für Religionswissenschaft*, 35(1/2), pp. 65–92, 67ff.; Georg Troescher, 'Keltisch–Germanische Götterbilder an Romanischen Kirchen?', *Zeitschrift für Kunstgeschichte*, 16 (1953), pp. 1–42, 30–1.

260 It is preserved in Codex Vat. Pal. Lat. 577, where it follows the canons of the council held under Carloman and Boniface, 742. The translated text and comments are taken from McNeill and Gamer, pp. 419–21.

261 The *Canons of St Patrick* (*c*.450) appears to be the earliest compilation, followed by various Welsh penitentials of the sixth century.

262 McNeill and Gamer, pp. 318–19, 333.

263 Ibid., p. 350.

264 Ibid., p. 313.
265 Forlong, *Faiths of Man*, under heading *hair*.
266 McNeill and Gamer, p. 338.
267 Ibid., pp. 41, 227, 275, 305.
268 Ibid., p. 341.
269 Gurevich, pp. 58ff.
270 McPherson, pp. 38–9.
271 Ibid., pp. 42–3.
272 Ibid., p. 44.
273 Gélis, pp. 73–5; Gwenc'hlan Le Scouëzec, *Guide de la Bretagne mystérieuse* (Claude Tchou, 1967), pp. 123–4.
274 Gwenc'hlan Le Scouëzec, p. 129.
275 Gélis, p. 74.
276 Ibid., pp. 146–7.
277 Anne Ross, 'Celtic and northern art', in Philip Rawson, ed., *Primitive Erotic Art* (New York: Putnam's Sons, 1973), pp. 77–106, 79.
278 Jolly, pp. 174–5.
279 Gurevich, p. 79.
280 Troescher, pp. 1–42.
281 Anthony Weir, 'Exhibitionists and related carvings in the Irish Midlands: their origins and functions', in H. Murtagh, ed., *Irish Midland Studies: Essays in Commemoration of N. W. English* (Athlone, 1980), pp. 57–72, 69.
282 P. Goessler, pp. 65–92.
283 Edwin Oliver James, *The Cult of the Mother-Goddess. An Archaeological and Documentary Study* (London: Thames and Hudson, 1959), pp. 11–13; Barstow; Rita M. Gross, 'Hindu female deities as a resource for the contemporary rediscovery of the goddess', in Carl Olson, ed., *The Book of the Goddess. Past and Present* (New York: The Crossroad Publishing Co., 1983), pp. 7–15, 217–30; Gimbutas, *The Language . . .* , passim; Rawson, ed., *Primitive Erotic Art*, pp. 4–18; H. Kirchhoff, 'Muttergottheiten, weibliche Fruchtbarkeitsidole und Mutterschaft', *Geburtshilfe und Frauenheilkunde*, 35 (1975), pp. 429–41; James Mellaart, 'Earliest of neolithic cities: the third season of excavations at Anatolian Chatal Hüyük. Part 1: shrines and images, of 9000 years ago', *The Illustrated London News: Archaeological Section* No. 2169, (February 1964), pp. 158–60; Hodder, pp. 43–56; Fraser, pp. 36–99.
284 James, pp. 13–14.
285 Ibid., pp. 44–6.
286 Franz Hancar, 'Zum Problem der Venusstatuetten im eurasiatischen Jungpaläolithikum', *Prähistorische Zeitschrift*, 40(30/1) (1939/40), pp. 85–156, 144.
287 Ibid., pp. 93–5.
288 Hutton, p. 235.
289 Ross called the relief of three naked goddesses from Alauna, Cumberland, 'unusual', commenting that this was not a typical representation of the divine mothers, 'who are always clothed'. *Pagan Celtic Britain*, p. 214.
290 Ross, 'Celtic . . .', p. 80.
291 Ibid., p. 81.
292 Ibid., p. 103. Ross was now aware of Sheelas outside Ireland. She specifically refers to examples in Britain, and she also mentions 'German Switzerland'. Although no location is specified, it seems clear that she had the figure at Basle in mind, which Boswell had mentioned in his diary.
293 Robert Christison, 'On an ancient wooden image, found in November last at Ballachulish peat-moss', *Proceedings of the Society of Antiquaries of Scotland*, 15 (1880/1), pp. 158–78; Bryony Coles, 'Anthropomorphic wooden figures from Britain and Ireland', *Proceedings of the Prehistoric Society*, 56 (1990), pp. 315–33. The figure is now in the Royal Museum of Scotland, Edinburgh.
294 Coles, pp. 326–8.
295 This figure is now on display in the National Museum of Ireland, Dublin.
296 Coles, p. 322.

297 It is now in the Colchester and Essex Museum.
298 Coles thinks that the figures were perhaps deliberately intended to be ambiguous, female in one context and male in another. Coles, p. 332.
299 Ibid., p. 332.
300 Andersen, p. 83.
301 McMahon and Roberts, *The Sheela-na-gigs* . . . , pp. 82–3.

BIBLIOGRAPHY

SHEELA-RELATED ARTICLES AND BOOKS

Jørgen Andersen, 'Sheela-na-gig at Clenagh Castle, Co. Clare', *NMAJ*, 18 (1976), 75–6, pl. VI.

Jørgen Andersen, 'Fodsel eller Dod?', *ICO, Den Iconographiske Post*, 1/2 (1976), 36–9.

Jørgen Andersen, *The Witch on the Wall. Medieval Erotic Sculpture in the Britsh Isles* (London: Allen & Unwin, 1977).

E. C. R. Armstrong, 'Sheela-na-gig discovered by Major H. Trevelyan', *JRSAI*, 6 (1911/12), 69, 385–7.

Richard N. Bailey, 'Apotropaic figures in Milan and North-West England', *Folklore*, 94(1) (1983), 113–17.

Mary M. Banks, 'Female fertility figures', *MAN*, 35 (1935), 63.

James Byrne, 'The parishes of Templeroan and Wallstown', *JCHAS*, 8 (1902), 83–95.

Frans Carlsson, 'Naked truth still veiled?', *ICO, Den Iconographiske Post*, 3 (1978), 30–7.

William Carrigan, *The History and Antiquities of the Diocese of Ossory*, 4 vols (Dublin: Sealy, Bryers & Walker, 1905).

Stella Cherry, *A Guide to Sheela-na-gigs* (Dublin: National Museum of Ireland, 1992).

Stella Cherry, 'Sheela-na-gigs from County Cork', *JCHAS*, 98 (1993), 107–12.

E. Clibborn, 'On an ancient stone image presented to the Academy by Charles Halpin, MD', *PRIA*, series 1, 2 (1840–4), pp. 565–76.

V. C. C. Collum, 'Female fertility figures', *MAN*, 35 (1935), 62–3.

Thomas B. Costello, 'A County Galway Sheela-na-gig', *JRSAI*, 66 (1936), 312.

K. de B. Codrington, 'Iconography: Classical and Indian', *MAN*, 35(70) (1935), 65–6.

Robert Christison, 'On an ancient wooden image, found in November last at Ballachulish peat moss', *Proceedings of the Society of Antiquaries of Scotland*, 15 (1880/1), 158–78.

Henry S. Crawford, 'Ballynahinch Castle, Co. Tipperary', *JRSAI*, 36 (1906), 424.

C. C. Das Gupta, 'Female fertility figures', *MAN*, 36 (1936), 183–4.

K. M. Dickie, 'Stone figure from Tomregan, Co. Cavan', *JRSAI*, 93 (1963), 198–9.

Dina Portway Dobson, 'Primitive figures on churches', *MAN*, 30 (1930), 10–11.

Dina Portway Dobson, 'Primitive figures on churches', *MAN*, 31 (1931), 3–5.

John Dunlea, 'A new Sheela-na-gig', *JRSAI*, 75 (1945), 114.

George V. Du Noyer, 'Remarks on ancient Irish effigies sculptured on the walls of the ancient church on White Island, Lough Erne, Parish of Magheraculmoney, Co. of Fermanagh', *JRSAI*, n.s., 3(6) (1860/1), 62–9.

Caroline, Countess of Dunraven and Edwin, Earl of Dunraven, *Memorials of Adare Manor* (Oxford: Parker, 1865).

Review of 'Frederick Thomas Elworthy, The Evil Eye; an account of this ancient and widespread superstition. London: John Murray, 1895', *The Reliquary and Illustrated Archaeological Journal* (1895), 247–51.

Ellen Ettlinger, 'Sheila-na-gigs', *Folklore*, 85 (1974), 62–3.

John Feehan and George Cunningham, 'An undescribed exhibitionist figure (Sheela-na-gig) from County Laois', *JRSAI*, 108 (1978), 117–18.

Alfred Fell, *A Furness Manor: Pennington and Its Church* (Ulverston: Kitchin & Co., 1929)

Walter Fitzgerald, 'Sheelah-na-gig', *JKAS*, 2 (1896–8), 33.

Walter Fitzgerald, 'Sheela-na-gig in the Fitzeustace Castle of Blackhall', *JKAS*, 2 (1896–8), 330.

David Freeman, 'Female fertility figures', *MAN*, 34 (1934), 208.

Dermot F. Gleeson, 'Sheela-na-gig, Clenagh Castle, Co. Clare', *JRSAI*, 7 (1937), 127–8.

Dermot F. Gleeson, 'Sheela-na-Gig at Burgesbeg', *JRSAI*, 9 (1939), 47–8.

Dermot F. Gleeson, 'Sheela na Gig at Ballyportry Castle, Co. Clare', *NMAJ*, 11 (1940/1), 174.

Dermot F. Gleeson, 'Sheela ny Gig in Co. Clare', *JRSAI*, 12 (1943), 24.

J. P. Godwin, 'Sheela-na-gigs and Christian saints', *Folklore*, 80 (1969), 222–3.

D. H. Gordon, 'Irish "Sheela-na-gigs"', *MAN*, 34 (1934), 206.

Pierre Bettez Gravel, *The Malevolent Eye. An Essay on the Evil Eye, Fertility and the Concept of Mana*. American University Studies Series XI, Anthropology and Sociology, vol. 64 (New York: Peter Lang, 1995).

James Graves, 'Correspondence', *The Irish Builder*, 12 (1870), 303.

H. J. M. Green, 'St Ives Priory', *Proceedings of the Cambridge Antiquarian Society*, 51 (1958), 35–6.

Edith M. Guest, 'A Sheela-na-gig at Clonmacnoise', *JRSAI*, 9 (1939), 48.

Edith M. Guest, 'Some notes on the dating of Sheela-na-gigs', *JRSAI*, 7 (1937), 176–80.

Edith M. Guest, 'Irish Sheela-na-gigs in 1935', *JRSAI*, 66 (1936), 107–29.

Edith M. Guest, 'Ballyvourney and its Sheela-na-gig', *Folklore*, 48 (1937), 374–84.

John Hargreaves, 'Dallying with Sheela in the sanctuary', *Guardian* 'Weekend' supplement (28 October 1989), 8.

P. J. Hartnett, 'Malahide "Abbey", Co. Dublin. Sheela na gig', *JRSAI*, 84 (1954), 179.

P. J. Hartnett, 'Sculptured figure of Sheela-na-gig, Abbeylara, Co. Longford', *JRSAI*, 84 (1954), 181.

Richard Hayward, *Munster and the City of Cork* (London: Phoenix House, 1964).

W. J. Hemp, 'Some unrecorded "Sheela-na-gigs" in Wales and the Border', *Archaeologica Cambrensis*, 93 (1938), 136–9.

Françoise Henry, 'The decorated stones at Ballyvourney, Co. Cork', *JCHAS*, 57 (1952), 41–2.

Helen Hickey, *Images of Stone. Figure Sculpture of the Lough Erne Basin* (Belfast: Blackstaff, 1976).

R. Hitchcock, 'Notes made in the Archaeological Court of the Great Exhibition of 1853', *JKAS*, 2(2) (1852/3), 282–3.

John Hunt, 'An unrecorded Sheela-na-gig from Co. Limerick', *JRSAI*, 17 (1947), 158–9.

John Hunt, 'Bishop Wellesley's tomb carvings', *JCKAS*, 15 (1975/6), 490–2.

John Hunt, *Irish Medieval Figure Sculpture, 1200–1600. A Study of Irish Tombs with Notes on Costume and Armour, volume 1* (text and catalogue) (Dublin: Irish University Press and London: Sotheby, 1974).

A. L. and G. E. Hutchinson, 'Distribution of Sheela-na-gigs in Great Britain', contained in 'The Idol or Sheela-na-gig at Binstead', *Proceedings of the Isle of Wight Natural History and Archaeological Society*, 6(4) (1970), 237–49.

Sidney Jackson, *Celtic and Other Stone Heads* (Shipley: Jackson, 1973).

James A. Jerman, 'The "Sheela-na-gig" carvings of the British Isles: suggestions for a reclassification, and other notes', *Journal of the Co. Louth Archaeological and Historical Society*, 20(1) (1981), 10–24.

D. Newman Johnson, 'Sheela-na-gig at Rahan, Co. Offaly', *JRSAI*, 101(2) (1972), 169–70.

Marcus Keane, *The Towers and Temples of Ancient Ireland. Their Origin and History Discussed from a New Point of View* (Dublin: Hodges, Smith and Co., 1867).

David Keeling, 'An unrecorded exhibitionist figure (Sheela-na-gig) from Ardcath, County Meath', *Riocht na Midhe*, 7(3) (1984), 102–4.

Eamonn P. Kelly, *Sheela-na-Gigs. Origins and Functions* (Dublin: Country House, 1996).

Eamonn P. Kelly, 'Sheela-na-gigs in the National Museum of Ireland, together with a brief description of their origin and function', in Michael Ryan, ed., *Irish Antiquities. Essays in Memory of Joseph Raftery* (Wicklow: Wordwell 1998), 173–84.

Charles E. Keyser, 'Notes on the churches of Ampney Crucis, Ampney St Mary's and Ampney St Peter's', *Journal of the British Archaeological Association*, 20 (1914), 81–90.

Heather King, 'A "face" in the river – a Sheela-na-gig rescued', *Archaeology Ireland*, 7(1) (1993), 13.

Johann Georg Kohl, *Reisen in Irland*, 2 vols (Dresden and Leipzig: Arnold, 1843).

H. C. Lawlor, 'Two typical Irish "Sheela-na-gigs"', *MAN*, 31(4) (1931), 5–6.

H. C. Lawlor, 'Two more Irish Sheela-na-gigs', *MAN*, 32, (1932), 44–5.

H. G. Leask, 'Sheela-na-gig, Bunratty Castle, Co. Clare', *JRSAI*, 66 (1936), 313.

Dorothy Lowry-Corry, 'The stones carved with human effigies on Boa Island and on Lustymore Island, in Lower Lough Erne', *PRIA*, 142(1) (1932), 200–4.

A. T. Lucas, 'National Museum of Ireland: archaeological acquisitions in 1964', *JRSAI*, 97 (1967), 1–28.

P. J. Lynch, 'Liathmore-Mochoemog', *NMAJ*, 3 (1914), 73–91.

Patrick Lyons, 'Sheela-na-gig at Kilmacomma, Co. Waterford', *JRSAI*, 7 (1937), 127–8.

Robert A. S. Macalister, *The Archeology of Ireland* (London: Methuen, 1928; rev. edn 1996, Bracken Books, London).

James E. Canon M'Kenna and Dorothy Lowry-Corry, 'White Island, Lough Erne: its ancient church and unique sculptures', *JRSAI*, 60 (1930), 23–37.

Joanne McMahon and Jack Roberts, *The Sheela-na-gigs of Ireland and Britain. The Divine Hag of the Christian Celts – An Illustrated Guide* (Cork/Dublin: Mercier Press, 2001).

Conleth Manning, 'A Sheela-na-gig from Glanworth Castle, Co. Cork', in Etienne Rynne, ed., *Figures from the Past: Studies on Figurative Art in Christian Ireland in Honour of Helen M. Roe* (Dublin: Glendale Press and Royal Society of Antiquarians of Ireland, 1987), 278–82.

Conleth Manning, 'A Sheela-na-gig at Ballinaclogh, Co. Tipperary', *Keimella, Studies in Medieval Archaeology* (1989), 71–3.

T. van Marle, 'Sheela-na-gig: Keltische Heks of Christelijk Embleem', in R. H. F. Hofman, B. Smelik and K. Jongeliong, eds, *Kelten van Spanje tot Ierland* (Utrecht: De Keltische Draak, 1996), 93–117.

R. R. Martin, 'The Sheela-na-gig at Oxford', *MAN*, 29 (1929), 134–5.

Vivian Mercier, *The Irish Comic Tradition* (Oxford: Oxford University Press, 1962).

Margaret A. Murray, 'Female fertility figures', *Journal of the Royal Anthropological Institute*, 64 (1934), 93–100.

Margaret A. Murray, 'A "Sheila-na-gig" figure at South Tawton', *MAN*, 36 (1936), 184.

Margaret A. Murray and A. D. Passmore, 'The Sheela-na-gig at Oaksey', *MAN*, no. 86 (September 1923), 140–1.

D. Newman Johnson, 'Sheela-na-gig at Rahan, Co. Offaly', *JRSAI*, 101(2) (1971), 169–70.

J. P. Nolan, 'The castles of Clare Barony', *Journal of the Galway Archaeological and Historical Society*, 1 (1900), 31–4.

R. O'Brien Smyth, 'Sheela-na-gig, Ballyfinboy Castle, near Borrisokane', *JRSAI*, 16 (1906), 88.

James O'Connor, Sheela na Gig (Fethard: Historical Society, 1991).

Sean O'Doherty, 'Sheela-na-Gig at Cooliagh', *Old Kilkenny Review*, n.s., 2(1) (1979), 72–4.

Pádraig O Maidín, 'Pococke's tour of south and south-west Ireland in 1758', *JCHAS*, 64 (1959), 35–56.

Charles A. Parker, 'Early sculptured stones at Gosforth, Ponsonby, St Bridget's, Haile, and Egremont', *Transactions of the Cumberland and Westmorland Antiquarian and Archaeological Society*, 2 (1902), 84–98.

Patrick Power, *Sex and Marriage in Ancient Ireland* (Dublin and Cork: Mercier, 1976).

Jo Pacsoo, 'The heritage of Sheila-na-gig', *Everywoman* (August 1989), 14.

Nikolaus Pevsner, *Yorkshire: York and the East Riding* (Harmondsworth: Penguin, 1972).

Stuart Piggott, 'A primitive carving from Anglesey', *MAN*, 30 (1930), 122–3.

Ellen Prendergast, 'A fertility figure from Tullaroan', *Old Kilkenny Review*, 4(4) (1992), 1027–31.

Bob Quinn, *Atlantean. Ireland's North African and Maritime Heritage* (London: Quartet Books, 1986).

Joseph Raftery, 'A Sheela-na-gig from Burgesbeg, Co. Tipperary', *NMAJ*, 12 (1969), 92–3.

Joseph Raftery et al., 'Archaeological Acquisitions in the Year 1964', *JRSAI*, 97 (1967), 1–28.

Jack Roberts, *The Sheela-na-gigs of Britain and Ireland* (Skibbereen: Key Books, 1995).

Jack Roberts and Joanne McMahon, *The Sheela-na Gigs of Britain and Ireland. An Illustrated Map/Guide* (Bandia Publishing, 1997).

Etienne Rynne, 'A Sheela-na-gig at Clonlara, Co. Clare', *NMAJ*, 10 (1967), 221–2.

H. D. Sankalia, 'The nude goddess or "shameless woman" in Western Asia, India, and South-Eastern Asia', *Artibus Asiae*, 23 (1960), 111–23.

Albert Siggins, 'Heads and tails of stone', *Roscommon Historical and Archaeological Society Journal*, 13 (1990), 45–8.

Denis Staunton, 'Shameless Sheelas still make Irishmen blush', *Observer* (22 December 1996).

FRSAI, Figures known as Hags of the Castle, Sheelas, or Sheela na gigs, *JRSAI*, 24 (1894), 77–81.

W. F. Wakeman, 'The church on White Island, Lough Erne, Parish of Magheraculmoney, County of Fermanagh', *JRSAI*, 5 (1879–82), 276–92.

J. N. A. Wallace, 'Sheela-na-gig at Bunratty Castle', *NMAJ*, 39 (1936–9), 39.

Webber Smith, *An Essay on the Round Towers of Ireland as Compared with Other Monuments* (Dublin: Milliken & Son, 1838).

Anthony Weir, 'Three carved figures in County Louth', *Louth Archaeological Journal*, 18/19 (1973–80), 67–73.

Anthony Weir, 'Exhibitionists and related carvings in the Irish Midlands: their origins and functions', in H. Murtagh, ed., *Irish Midland Studies: Essays in Commemoration of N. W. English* (Athlone, 1980), pp. 57–72.

Anthony Weir and James Jerman, *Images of Lust: Sexual Carvings on Medieval Churches* (London: Batsford, 1986), reprinted 1999 by Routledge.

Anthony Weir and James Jerman, 'Potency and sin: Ireland and the phallic continuum', *Archaeology Ireland*, 4(2) (1990), 52–6.

James Grove White, *Historical and Topographical Notes on Buttevant, Castletownroche, Doneraile, Mallow, and Places in Their Vicinity*, 4 vols (Cork: Guy and Co., 1905).

W. R. Wilde, *A Descriptive Catalogue of the Antiquities in the Museum of the Royal Irish Academy, Volume 1: Articles of Stone, Earthen, Vegetable, and Animal Materials, and of Copper and Bronze* (Dublin: RIA House, 1863).

Josephine Withers, 'Nancy Spero's American-born Sheela-na-gig', *Feminist Studies*, 17 (1991), 51–6.

Thomas Wright, *The Worship of the Generative Powers during the Middle Ages of Western Europe* (1866); reprinted in *Sexual Symbolism. A History of Phallic Worship* (New York: Julian Press, 1957).

THE CELTIC CONNECTION

Frank Battaglia, 'Goddess religion in the early British Isles', in Miriam Robbins Dexter and Edgar C. Polomé, eds, *Varia on the Indo-European Past: Papers in Memory of Marija Gimbutas* (Journal of Indo-European Studies Monograph, vol. 19, Washington, DC, 1997), 48–82.

Diane E. Bessai, 'Who was Cathleen Ni Houlihan?', *The Malahat Review*, 42 (April 1977), 114–29.

R. I. Best and Osborn Bergin, eds, *Lebor na Huidre. Book of the Dun Cow* (Dublin: RIA, 1929).

Maire Bhreathnach, 'The sovereignty goddess as goddess of death?', *Zeitschrift für Celtische Philologie*, 39 (1982), 243–60.

John Billingsley, *A Stony Gaze. Investigating Celtic and Other Stone Heads* (Chieveley: Capall Bann Publishing, 1998).

Lisa Bitel, 'Conceived in sins, born in delights: stories of procreation from early Ireland', *Journal of the History of Sexuality*, 3(2) (1992), 181–201.

Lisa Bitel, *Land of Women. Tales of Sex and Gender from Early Ireland* (New York: Cornell University Press, 1996).

R. A. Breatnach, 'The lady and the king. A theme of Irish literature', *Studies*, 42 (Autumn 1953), 321–36.

Peter Buchholz, 'Odin: Celtic and Siberian affinities of a Germanic deity', *Mankind Quarterly*, 24(4) (1984), 427–37.

James Carney, *Studies in Irish Literature and History* (Dublin: Dublin Institute for Advanced Studies, 1979).

Rosalind Clark, *The Great Queens. Irish Goddesses from the Morrigan to Cathleen ni Houlihan* (Gerrards Cross: Colin Smythe, 1991).

Mary Condren, *The Serpent and the Goddess. Women, Religion, and Power in Celtic Ireland* (New York: HarperSanFrancisco, 1989).

Tom Pete Cross and Clark Harris Slover, eds, *Ancient Irish Tales* (New York: Barnes & Noble, 1996).

Barry Cunliffe, *The Celtic World* (Maidenhead: McGraw-Hill, 1979).

James Doan, 'Five Breton "Cantiques" from "Pardons"', *Folklore* (1980), 27–40.

James Doan, *Women and Goddesses in Early Celtic History, Myth and Legend*. Working Papers in Irish Studies, 87–4/5 (Chicago: Northeastern University, 1987).

Charles Donahue, 'The Valkyries and the Irish war-goddesses', *PMLA*, 56 (March 1941), 1–12.

Maartje Draak, 'Some aspects of kingship in pagan Ireland', in *The Sacral Kingship. Contributions to the Central Theme of the VIIIth International Congress for the History of Religions* (Leiden: Brill, 1959), pp. 651–63.

James H. Dunn, 'Sile-na-Gcioch', *Eire-Ireland. A Journal of Irish Studies*, 12 (1977), 68–85.

Paul-Marie Duval, 'Early Celtic art', in Geroid MacEoin, ed., *Proceedings of the Sixth International Congress of Celtic Studies* (Dublin: Dublin Institute for Advanced Studies, 1983), pp. 55–72.

Patrick K. Ford, 'Celtic women: the opposing sex', *Viator*, 19 (1988), 417–38.

J. F. M. ffrench, *Prehistoric Faith and Worship. Glimpses of Ancient Irish Life* (London: Nutt, 1912).

Miranda Green, *Celtic Goddesses. Warriors, Virgins and Mothers* (London: British Museum Press, 1997).

Monika Gsell, *Die Bedeutung der Baubo. Zur Repräsentation des weiblichen Genitales* (Frankfurt: Stroemfeld Verlag, 2001).

Máire Herbert, 'Goddess and king: the sacred marriage in early Ireland', in Louise Olga Fradenburg, ed., *Women and Sovereignty* (Cosmos. The Yearbook of the Traditional Cosmology Society, 7, Edinburgh: Edinburgh University Press, 1992), pp. 264–75.

August Knoch, 'Die Ehescheidung im alten irischen Recht', in Rudolf Thurneysen et al., eds, *Studies in Early Irish Law* (Dublin: RIA, 1936), pp. 235–68.

Robert A. S. Macalister, *Tara: A Pagan Sanctuary of Ancient Ireland* (London: Charles Scribner's Sons, 1931).

Proinsias MacCana, 'Aspects of the theme of king and goddess in Irish literature', *Etudes Celtiques*, 7 (1955/6), 76–114, 356–413.

Proinsias MacCana, 'Aspects of the theme of king and goddess in Irish literature (*suite et fin*)', *Etudes Celtiques*, 8 (1958/9), 59–65.

Proinsias MacCana, *Celtic Mythology* (Feltham: Newnes Books, 1983).

Proinsias MacCana, 'Women in Irish mythology', in M. P. Hederman and R. Kearney, eds, *The Crane Bag. Book of Irish Studies (1977–1981)* (Dublin: Blackwater Press, 1982), pp. 520–4.

Kim McCone, *Pagan Past and Christian Present in Early Irish Literature* (Maynooth: An Sagart, 1990).

Greg McGarry, *Sheila Na Gig. A Celtic Treasure Hunt* (An Inis, Contae Dhun Na ngall, Preas An Phuca, 1993).

Eoin MacNeill, *Celtic Ireland* (Dublin: The Academy Press, 1921).

Kuno Meyer, 'Die Leibeslänge Christi', *Zeitschrift für Celtische Philologie*, 10 (1915), 401–2.

Kathleen Mulchrone, 'The rights and duties of women with regard to the education of their children', in Rudolf Thurneysen et al., eds, *Studies in Early Irish Law* (Dublin: RIA, 1936), pp. 187–206.

Muireann Ní Bhrolcháin, 'Women in early Irish myths and sagas', in M. P. Hederman and R. Kearney, eds, *The Crane Bag. Book of Irish Studies (1977–1981)* (Dublin: Blackwater Press, 1982), pp. 525–32.

Nicholas O'Kearney, 'Folk-lore', *JRSAI*, 2 (1852/3), 32–9.

Tomas O Maille, 'Medb Chruachna', *Zeitschrift für Celtische Philologie*, 18 (1928), 129–46.

Alwyn Rees and Brinley Rees, *Celtic Heritage. Ancient Tradition in Ireland and Wales* (London: Thames and Hudson, 1978).

Kevin P. Reilly, 'Irish literary autobiography: the goddess that poets dream of', *Eire-Ireland. A Journal of Irish Studies*, 16(3) (1981), 57–80.

Anne Ross, *Pagan Celtic Britain* (London: Routledge and Kegan Paul, 1967).

Anne Ross, 'The divine hag of the pagan Celts', in Venetia Newall, ed., *The Witch Figure. Folklore Essays by a Group of Scholars in England Honouring the 75th Birthday of Katharine M. Briggs* (London: Routledge and Kegan Paul, 1973), pp. 139–64.

Anne Ross, 'Celtic and northern art', in Philip Rawson, ed., *Primitive Erotic Art* (New York: Putnam's Sons, 1973), pp. 77–106.

Etienne Rynne, 'A pagan Celtic background for Sheela-na-gigs?', in Etienne Rynne, ed., *Figures from the Past. Studies on Figurative Art in Christian Ireland. In Honour of Helen M. Roe* (Dublin: Glendale Press and Royal Society of Antiquarians of Ireland, 1987), pp. 189–202.

Helmut Schoppa, 'Zu einem Steinrelief aus Hofheim. Ein Denkmal keltischer Tradition?', in Otto-Herman Frey, ed., *Marburger Beiträge zur Archäologie der Kelten* (Bonn: Habelt, 1969), pp. 202–6.

John Sharkey, *Celtic Mysteries. The Ancient Religion* (London: Thames and Hudson, 1975).

Marie-Louise Sjoestedt, *Gods and Heroes of the Celts* (London: Methuen, 1949).

Rudolf Thurneysen, *Die irische Helden- und Königssage bis zum 17. Jahrhundert* (Hildesheim: Georg Olms Verlag, 1921).

Josef Weisweiler, *Heimat und Herrschaft. Wirkung und Ursprung eines irischen Mythos*. Heft 11. Schriftenreihe der Deutschen Gesellschaft für keltische Studien, hrsg. von L. Mühlhausen (Halle/Saale: Max Niemeyer Verlag, 1943).

Thomas Johnson Westropp, 'The ancient sanctuaries of Knockainey and Clogher, County Limerick, and their goddesses', *PRIA*, 34, sec. C (1917–19), 47–67.

Thomas Johnson Westropp, 'The earthworks, traditions, and the gods of south-eastern Co. Limerick, especially from Knocklong to Temair Erann', *PRIA*, 34, sec. C (1917–19), 129–83.

David M. Wilson, 'An Irish mounting in the National Museum, Copenhagen', *Acta Archaeologica*, 26 (1955),163–72.

THE NORDIC CONNECTION

Brian Branston, *The Lost Gods of England* (London: Thames and Hudson, 1957).

Reidar Th. Christiansen, 'Ecstasy and Arctic religion', in Nils Lid, ed., *Studia Septentrionalia* (Oslo: H. Aschehoug, 1955), part 1, 19–79.

W. G. Collinwood, 'Christian Vikings', *Antiquity*, 1 (1927), 172–80.

Hilda Ellis Davidson, *The Lost Beliefs of Northern Europe* (London and New York: Routledge, 1993).

V. Diószegi, 'Zum Problem der ethnischen Homogenität des tofischen (karagassischen) Schamanismus', in V. Diószegi, ed., *Glaubenswelt und Folklore der sibirischen Völker* (Budapest: Akadémiai Kiadó, 1963), pp. 261–358.

N. P. Dyrenkowa, 'Kinderschutz bei den Schoren', in V. Diószegi, ed., *Glaubenswelt und Folklore der sibirischen Völker* (Budapest: Akadémiai Kiadó, 1963), 257–9.

Phebe Fjellström, 'Nordic and Eurasian elements in Lapp culture', *Anthropos*, 66 (1971), 535–49.

Aron Ya. Gurevich, 'Space and time in the Weltmodell of the old Scandinavian peoples', *Mediaeval Scandinavia*, 2 (1969), 42–53.

Aron Ya. Gurevich, 'Wealth and gift-bestowal among ancient Scandinavians', *Scandinavica*, 7 (1968), 126–38.

A. G. van Hamel, 'Odinn hanging on the tree', *Acta Philologica Scandinavia*, 7 (1932/3), 260–88.

G. W. Jussupow, 'Totemistische Relikte bei den Kasaner Tataren', in V. Diószegi, ed., *Glaubenswelt und Folklore der sibirischen Völker* (Budapest: Akadémiai Kiadó, 1963), pp. 209–22.

C. Krollmann, 'Das Religionswesen der alten Preußen', *Altpreussische Forschungen*, 4(2) (1927), 5–19.

T. C. Lethbridge, *Gogmagog: The Buried Gods* (London: Routledge and Kegan Paul, 1957).

Nils Lid, 'Light-mother and earth-mother', *Studia Norvegica*, 41 (1946), 1–20.

E. Manker, 'Seite-Kult und Trommelmagie der Lappen', in V. Diószegi, ed., *Glaubenswelt und Folklore der sibirischen Völker* (Budapest: Akadémiai Kiadó, 1963), pp. 29–43.

Wilhelm Mannhardt, *Letto-Preussische Götterlehre*. Magazin der Lettisch-Literärischen Gesellschaft, 21 (Riga, 1936).

W. I. Matjustschenko, 'Zur Kunst der alten Stämme an der Mündung des Tom', in V. Diószegi, ed., *Glaubenswelt und Folklore der sibirischen Völker* (Budapest: Akadémiai Kiadó, 1963), pp. 513–18.

Audrey L. Meaney, 'Aethelweard, Aelfric, the Norse gods and Northumbria', *Journal of Religious History*, 6 (1970), 105–32.

G. A. Menowstschikow, 'Wissen, religiöse Vorstellungen und Riten der asiatischen Eskimos', in V. Diószegi, ed., *Glaubenswelt und Folklore der sibirischen Völker* (Budapest: Akadémiai Kiadó, 1963), pp. 463–81.

Edward Moffat Weyer, *The Eskimos: Their Environment and Folkways* (New Haven, CT: Yale University Press, 1932).

Lotte Motz, 'The winter goddess: Percht, Holda and related figures', *Folklore,* vol. 95(2) (1984), 151–66.

Lotte Motz, 'Freyja, Anat, Ishtar and Inanna: some crosscultural comparisons', *Mankind Quarterly*, 23 (1982), 195–212.

Soren Nancke-Krogh, 'De forlosende ord', *ICO, Den Iconographiske Post*, 4 (1975), 29–31.

O. Nahodil, 'Mutterkult in Sibirien', in V. Diószegi, ed., *Glaubenswelt und Folklore der sibirischen Völker* (Budapest: Akadémiai Kiadó, 1963), pp. 491–511.

Christen Noerrelykke, 'En sheela fra Vendsyssel', *ICO, Den Iconographiske Post*, 2 (1977), 34–7.

Gustav Ränk, 'Lapp female deities of the Madder-akka group', in Nils Lid, ed., *Studia Septentrionalia* (Oslo: H. Aschehoug, 1955), part VI, pp. 7–79.

Gustav Ränk, 'Die Hausgottheiten der Frauen und das Geschlechtstabu bei den nordeurasischen Völkern', *Ethnos*, 3/4 (1948), 153–70.

E. I. Rombandjejewa, 'Einige Sitten und Bräuche der Mansen (Wogulen) bei der Geburt der Kinder', in V. Diószegi, ed., *Glaubenswelt und Folklore der sibirischen Völker* (Budapest: Akadémiai Kiadó, 1963), pp. 85–92.

Erling Rump, '"Mater Ecclesia" (Moder Kirke): "Jeg er vejen, sandheden, og livet" (Johs. XIV,6)', *ICO, Den Iconographiske Post*, 1/2 (1976), 40–8.

Erling Rump, 'Sheela-na-gig diagnostik', *ICO, Den Iconographiske Post*, 3 (1978), 38–43.

Ake V. Ström, 'The king god and his connection with sacrifice in old Norse religion', in *The Sacral Kingship. Contributions to the Central Theme of the VIIIth International Congress for the History of Religions* (Leiden: Brill, 1959), pp. 702–15.

Tsch. M. Taksami, 'Zu den alten religiösen Riten und Verboten der Nivchen (Giljaken)', in V. Diószegi, ed., *Glaubenswelt und Folklore der sibirischen Völlker* (Budapest: Akadémiai Kiadó, 1963), pp. 437–52.

E. O. G. Turville-Petre, *Myth and Religion of the North. The Religion of Ancient Scandinavia* (London: Weidenfeld and Nicolson, 1964).

THE SOCIO-CULTURAL BACKGROUND

James Aird, *A Selection of Scotch, English, Irish and Foreign Airs. Adapted to the Fife, Violin, or German Flute* (Glasgow: Aird, 1782–1801).

John Allen, 'Review of "The Evil Eye" by F. T. Elworthy', *The Reliquary and Illustrated Archaeologist*, n.s., 1 (1895), 247–51.

Paul Andrews, 'Pagan mysteries and Christian sacraments', *Studies* (Spring 1958), 55–65.

Klaus Arnold, 'Die Einstellung zum Kind im Mittelalter', in Bernd Herrmann, ed., *Mensch und Umwelt im Mittelalter* (Stuttgart: Deutsche Verlags-Anstalt, 1986), pp. 53–64.

Joseph Balogh, 'Tänze in Kirchen und auf Kirchhöfen', *Niederdeutsche Zeitschrift für Volkskunde*, 6 (1928), 1–14.

Michael Banim, *Crohoore of the Billhook* (New York: Sadlier, 1881).

William Battersby, *The Three Sisters at the Well. A Detection of Roots and Branches* (Navan: William Battersby, 1991).

Judith M. Bennett, *Women in the Medieval English Countryside. Gender and Household in Brigstock before the Plague* (Oxford: Oxford University Press, 1987).

Nachman Ben-Yehuda, 'Witchcraft and the occult as boundary maintenance devices', in Jacob Neusner, Ernest S. Frerichs and Paul Virgil McCracken Flesher, eds, *Religion, Science, and Magic. In Concert and in Conflict* (Oxford: Oxford University Press, 1989), pp. 229–60.

Ludwig Bieler ed., *The Works of St Patrick. St Secundinus Hymn on St Patrick* (London: Longman, Green and Co., 1953).

Lisa M. Bitel, *Land of Women. Tales of Sex and Gender from Early Ireland* (Ithaca, NY: Cornell University Press, 1996).

Lisa M. Bitel, 'Women's monastic enclosures in early Ireland: a study of female spirituality and male monastic mentalities', *Journal of Medieval History*, 12 (1986), 15–36.

William Copeland Borlase, *The Dolmens of Ireland, Their Distribution, Structural Characteristics, and Affinities in Other Countries, together with the Folk-lore Attaching to Them; Supplemented by Considerations on the Anthropology, Ethnology, and Traditions of the Irish People* (London: Chapman & Hall, 1897).

Franck Bourdier, *Préhistoire de France* (Paris: Flammarion, 1967).

John Brand, *Observations on Popular Antiquities. Chiefly Illustrating the Origin of Our Vulgar Customs, Ceremonies and Superstitions*, new edn with the additions of Sir Henry Ellis (London: Chatto & Windus, 1900).

Dorothy Ann Bray, 'The image of St Brigit in the early Irish Church', *Etudes Celtiques*, 24 (1987), 209–15.

Maurice Broens, 'The resurgence of pre-Indoeuropean elements in the Western medieval cult of the dead', *Diogenes*, 30 (1960), 75–103.

George Hardin Brown, 'Solving the "Solve" riddle in BL MS Harley 585', *Viator*, 18 (1987), 45–51.

Charles R. Browne, 'The ethnography of Carna and Mweenish, in the Parish of Moyruss, Connemara', *PRIA*, 6 (1900–2), 503–34.

Richard L. Brubaker, 'The untamed goddesses of village India', in Carl Olsen, ed., *The Book of the Goddess. Past and Present. An Introduction to Her Religion* (New York: The Crossroad Publishing Company, 1983), pp. 145–60.

Curt F. Bühler, 'Prayers and charms in certain Middle English scrolls', *Speculum*, 39 (1964), 270–8.

John Carr, *The Stranger in Ireland, or, A Tour in the Southern and Western Parts of That Country in the Year 1805* (London: printed for Richard Phillips, 1806).

Gordon Childe, *The Dawn of European Civilization* (London: Routledge & Kegan Paul, 1925).

R. Pearse Chope, 'Frithelstock Priory', *Transactions of the Devonshire Association for the Advancement of Science, Literature, and Art*, 61 (1929), pp. 167–91.

David Clarke, 'The head cult: tradition and folklore surrounding the symbol of the severed human head in the British Isles', Thesis submitted for the degree of doctor of philosophy, National Centre for English Cultural Tradition and Language, Division of Adult Continuing Education, University of Sheffield, November 1998.

David Clarke with Andy Roberts, *Twilight of the Celtic Gods. An Exploration of Britain's Hidden Pagan Tradition* (London: Cassell, 1996).

Arthur Clery, 'Early Irish history. Chapter XII. The religion of the Gael before Saint Patrick', *New Ireland Review*, 22/3 (1904/5), 218–32, 276–87.

William Laird Clowes, *The Royal Navy. A History* (Boston: Little, Brown & Co., and London: Sampson, Lowe, Marston & Co., 1899).

Georges Colonna-Ceccaldi, 'Découvertes en Chypre. Les fouilles de Curium', *Revue archéologique*, 33(1) (1877), 177–89.

Patrick J. Corish, *The Catholic Community in the Seventeenth and Eighteenth Centuries* (Dublin: Helicon, 1981).

T. Crofton Croker, *Researches in the South of Ireland. Illustrative of the Scenery, Architectural Remains, and the Manners and Superstitions of the Peasantry* (London: John Murray, 1824).

T. Crofton Croker, *Fairy Legends and Traditions of the South of Ireland*, 2nd edn, 3 vols (London: John Murray, 1826).

Kevin Danaher, *The Year in Ireland. Irish Calendar Customs* (Cork and Dublin: Mercier, 1972).

Wendy Davies, 'The place of healing in early Irish society', in Donnchadh O Corráin, Liam Breatnach and Kim McCone, eds, *Sages, Saints and Storytellers. Celtic Studies in Honour of Professor James Carney* (Maynooth: An Sagart, 1989), pp. 43–55.

Nicholas Flood Davin, *The Irishman in Canada* (Shannon: Irish University Press, 1969; Toronto, 1877).

Thomas Dineley (or Dingley), Gent. in the Year 1681, *Observations in a Voyage through the Kingdom of Ireland: Being a Collection of Several Monuments, Inscriptions, Draughts of Towns, Castles etc.* (Dublin: Printed at the University Press, by M. H. Gill, 1870).

Patrick S. Dinneen, *Foclóir Gaedhilge agus Béarla* (Dublin: The Educational Company of Ireland, 1927).

Elliott van Kirk Dobbie, ed., *The Anglo-Saxon Minor Poems* (London: George Routledge & Sons, 1942).

D. E. Easson, *Medieval Religious Houses: Scotland* (London: Longman, Green & Co., 1957).

Edith Ennen, *Frauen im Mittelalter* (Munich: Beck, 1984).

Edith Ennen, 'Die Frau in der mittelalterlichen Stadt', in Bernd Herrmann, ed., *Mensch und Umwelt im Mittelalter* (Stuttgart: Deutsche Verlags-Anstalt, 1986), pp. 35–52.

Ellen Ettlinger, 'Documents of British superstition in Oxford', *Folklore*, 54 (1943), 227–49.

E. Estyn Evans, *Irish Folk Ways* (London: Routledge and Kegan Paul, 1957).

Valerie I. J. Flint, *The Rise of Magic in Early Medieval Europe* (Oxford: Clarendon Press, 1991).

J. G. R. Forlong, *Faiths of Man. A Cyclopaedia of Religions*, 3 vols (London: Bernard Quaritch, 1906).

Robin Lane Fox, *Pagans and Christians* (Harmondsworth: Viking Penguin, 1986).

W. H. C. Frend, 'Religion in Roman Britain in the fourth century AD', *Journal of the British Archaeological Association*, 18 (1955), 1–18.

Carlo Ginzburg, *Ecstasies. Deciphering the Witches' Sabbath* (New York: Pantheon Books, 1991). Originally published in Italy as *Storia Notturna* (Turin, 1989).

P. Goessler, 'Germanisch-Christliches an Kirchen und Friedhöfen Südwestdeutschlands', *Archiv für Religionswissenschaft*, 35(1/2), 65–92.

George Gomme, 'The President's Address', *Folk-Lore*, 3(1) (1892), 9–10.

Roger Goodland, *A Bibliography of Sex Rites and Customs. An Annotated Record of Books, Articles and Illustrations in All Languages* (London: George Routledge & Sons, 1931).

L. Gougaud, 'La danse les eglises', in *Revue D'Histoire Ecclesiastique, Volume 15* (Louvain: Université Catholique de Louvain, 1914), 5–22; 229–45.

J. H. G. Grattan and Charles Singer, *Anglo-Saxon Magic and Medicine. Illustrated Specially from the Semi-pagan Text 'Lacnunga'* (Oxford: Oxford University Press, 1952).

Jacob Grimm, *Deutsche Mythologie*, 3 vols (Graz: Akademische Druck- und Verlagsanstalt, 1968).

Gisela Grupe, 'Umwelt und Bevölkerungsentwicklung im Mittelalter', in Bernd Herrmann, ed., *Mensch und Umwelt im Mittelalter* (Stuttgart: Deutsche Verlags-Anstalt, 1986), pp. 24–34.

Aron Gurevich, *Medieval Popular Culture: Problems of Belief and Perception* (Cambridge: Cambridge University Press, 1988).

Arthur West Haddan and William Stubbs, *Councils and Ecclesiastical Documents Relating to Great Britain and Ireland* (Oxford: Clarendon Press, 1871).

Herbert Halpert, 'Ireland, Sheila and Newfoundland', in Alison Feder and Bernice Schrank, eds, *Literature and Folk Culture: Ireland and Newfoundland* (St John's: Memorial University of Newfoundland, 1977), 147–71.

John Hargreaves, 'Dallying with Sheela in the sanctuary', *Guardian* 'Weekend' supplement (28 October 1989), 8.

Richard Hayes, 'Ireland's links with Compostella', *Studies*, 37 (1948), 326–32.

David Hepper, *British Warship Losses in the Age of the Sail* (Rotherfield: Jean Boudriot Publications, 1994).

John Hogan, *Kilkenny: The Ancient City of Ossory, the Seat of Its Kings, the See of Its Bishops and the Site of Its Cathedral* (Kilkenny: Egan, 1884).

William Hone, *The Everlasting Calendar of Popular Amusements, . . . in Two Volumes* (London: Hunt and Clarke, Volume I, 1826; Volume II, 1827).

Kathleen Hughes, *The Church in Early Irish Society* (London: Methuen 1980).

Kathleen Hughes and Ann Hamlin, *The Modern Traveller to the Early Irish Church* (Dublin: Four Courts Press, 1997).

Robert Hunt, ed., *Popular Romances of the West of England. Or The Drolls, Traditions, and Superstitions of Old Cornwall* (London: Chatto and Windus, 1881).

Ronald Hutton, *The Pagan Religions of the Ancient British Isles. Their Nature and Legacy* (Oxford: Blackwell, 1991).

Tom Inglis, *Moral Monopoly. The Catholic Church in Modern Irish Society* (Dublin: Gill and Macmillan, 1987).

E. M. Johnston, 'Problems common to both Protestant and Catholic churches in eigtheenth-century Ireland', in Oliver MacDonagh, W. F. Mandle and Pauric Travers, eds, *Irish Culture and Nationalism 1750–1950* (London: Macmillan Press, 1983), pp. 14–39.

Karen Louise Jolly, 'Anglo-Saxon charms in a context of a Christian world view', *Journal of Medieval History*, 11 (1985), 279–93.

Karen Louise Jolly, 'Magic, miracle, and popular practice in the early medieval West: Anglo-Saxon England', in Jacob Neusner, Ernest S. Frerichs and Paul Virgil McCracken, eds, *Religion, Science, and Magic. In Concert and in Conflict* (Oxford: Oxford University Press, 1989), 166–82.

Noragh Jones, *Power of Raven. Wisdom of Serpent* (Edinburgh: Floris Books, 1995).

Andrea Kammeier-Nebel, 'Wenn eine Frau Kräutertränke zu sich genommen hat, um nicht zu empfangen . . . Geburtenbeschränkung im frühen Mittelalter', in Bernd Herrmann, ed., *Mensch und Umwelt im frühen Mittelalter* (Stuttgart: Deutsche Verlags-Anstalt, 1986), 65–73.

Gundolf Keil, 'Seuchenzüge des Mittelalters', in Bernd Herrmann, ed., *Mensch und Umwelt im frühen Mittelalter* (Stuttgart: Deutsche Verlags-Anstalt, 1986), 109–28.

John V. Kelleher, 'Early Irish history and pseudo-history', *Studia Hibernica* (1963), 3, 113–27.

David Knowles and R. Neville Hadcock, *Medieval Religious Houses: England and Wales* (London: Longman, Green & Co., 1953).

Ida and Johann Georg Kohl, *Englische Skizzen* (Dresden and Leipzig: Arnoldsche Buchhandlung, 1845).

Carlo Levin, *Christ Stopped at Eboli* (New York, 1947).

Henrietta Leyser, *Medieval Women. A Social History of Women in England, 450–1500* (London: Weidenfeld and Nicolson, 1995).

Nils Lid, ed., *Studia Septentrionalia, Volume 6* (Oslo: H. Aschehoug & Co., 1955).

Patrick Logan, *The Holy Wells of Ireland* (Gerrards Cross: Colin Smythe, 1992).

David Lyon, *The Sailing Navy List. All ships of the Royal Navy – Built, Purchased and Captured – 1688–1860* (Conway: Maritime Press, 1993).

Sean Mac Airt, ed., *The Annals of Inisfallen* (Dublin: Dublin Institute for Advanced Studies, 1951).

James M. Mackinlay, *Folklore of Scottish Lochs and Springs* (Glasgow: William Hodge & Co., 1893).

Robert Craig MacLagan, *Our Ancestors: Scots, Picts, & Cymry and What Their Tradition Tells Us* (London and Edinburgh: T. N. Foulis, 1913).

Robert Craig MacLagan, *Scottish Myths. Notes on Scottish History and Tradition* (Edinburgh: Maclachlan and Stewart, 1882).

Edward MacLysaght, *Irish Life in the Seventeenth Century: After Cromwell* (Dublin and Cork: Talbot Press, 1939).

John T. McNeill and Helena M. Gamer, *Medieval Handbooks of Penance. A Translation of the Principal 'libri poenitentiales' and Selections from Related Documents* (New York: Columbia University Press, 1990).

Joseph M. McPherson, *Primitive Beliefs in the North-east of Scotland* (London: Longman, Green and Co., 1929).

Elizabeth Malcolm, 'Popular recreation in nineteenth-century Ireland', in Oliver MacDonagh, W. F. Mandle and Pauric Travers, eds, *Irish Culture and Nationalism, 1750–1950* (London: Macmillan Press, 1983), 40–55.

Martin Martin, *A Description of the Western Islands of Scotland* (London, printed for Andrew Bell, at the Cross-Keys and Bible, in Cornhill, near Stocks-Market, 1703).

Martin Martin, *A Late Voyage to St Kilda, the Remotest of all the Hebridies, or Western Isles of Scotland* (London: printed for D. Brown and T. Godwin: At the Black Swan and Bible, 1698).

Audrey L. Meaney, *Anglo-Saxon Amulets and Curing Stones*. BAR British Series 96 (Oxford: BAR, 1981).

John Middleton, ed., *Magic, Witchcraft, and Curing* (New York: The Natural History Press, 1967).

Kerby A. Miller, *Emigrants and Exiles. Ireland and the Irish Exodus to North America* (Oxford: Oxford University Press, 1985).

Arthur Mitchell, *The Past in the Present: What Is Civilisation?* Rhind Lectures on Archaeology delivered in 1876 and 1878 (Edinburgh: David Douglas, 1880).

Vilhelm Möller-Christensen, 'Umwelt im Spiegel der Skelettreste vom Kloster Aebelholt', in Bernd Herrmann, ed., *Mensch und Umwelt im Mittelalter* (Stuttgart: Deutsche Verlags-Anstalt, 1986), 129–39.

Margaret Murray, *The Witch-Cult in Western Europe. A Study in Anthropology* (Oxford: Clarendon Press, 1921).

Jacob Neusner, Ernest S. Frerichs and Paul Virgil McCracken Flesher, eds, *Religion, Science, and Magic. In Concert and in Conflict* (Oxford: Oxford University Press, 1989).

Séamus O Catháin, *The Festival of Brigit. Celtic Goddess and Holy Woman* (Blackrock: DBA Publications, 1995).

Eugene O'Curry, *Manuscript Materials of Ancient Irish History* (Dublin: James Duffy, 1861).

Mary O'Dowd, 'Property, work and home: women and the economy, *c.*1170–1850', in Angela Bourke et al., eds, *The Field Day Anthology of Irish Writing V: Irish Women's Writing and Traditions* (Cork: Cork University Press, 2002), 464–71.

Dáithi O Hógáin, *Irish Superstitions* (Dublin: Gill & Macmillan, 1995).

J. C. O'Keeffe and Art O'Brien, *A Handbook of Irish Dances, with an Essay on Their Origin and History* (Dublin: O'Donoghue and Co., 1902).

Colman O Mahony, 'Shipbuilding and repairing in nineteenth century Cork', *JCHAS* (1989), 74–86.

Seán O Súilleabháin, *Irish Wake Amusements* (Cork: Mercier Press, 1967).

Norbert Ohler, *Sterben und Tod im Mittelalter* (Düsseldorf: Patmos Verlag, 2003).

Carl Olson, *The Book of the Goddess. Past and Present* (New York: The Crossroad Publishing Co., 1983).

Hugh Popham, *A Damned Cunning Fellow* (Par: Old Ferry Press, 1991).

Frederick A. Pottle, ed., *Boswell on the Grand Tour: Germany and Switzerland (1764)*. (London: William Heinemann, 1953).

Patrick C. Power, *Sex and Marriage in Ancient Ireland* (Cork: Mercier, 1976).

John G. A. Prim, 'Olden popular pastimes in Kilkenny', *JRSAI*, 2 (1853), 319–35.

Charles Rogers, *Social Life in Scotland. From Early to Recent Times* (Edinburgh: William Paterson, 1886).

David Rorie, 'On Scottish folk-medicine', *Caledonian Medical Journal*, 13 (1926), 3, 70–6, 85–102, 153–63, 231–7.

William Smith and Samuel Cheetham, eds, *A Dictionary of Christian Antiquities*, 2 vols (London: John Murray, 1875).

Edmund Spencer, *A View of the State of Ireland, Written Dialogue-wise, between Eudoxus and Irenaeus, in the Yeare 1596* (Dublin, 1633; reprinted at the Hibernia Press, Temple-Lane by John Morrisson, 1809).

Whitley Stokes, ed., *Felire Oengusso Celi De. The Martyrology of Oengus the Culdee* (London, 1905. Reprinted and published by the Dublin Institute for Advanced Studies, Dublin, 1984).

R. Thurneysen, Nancy Power, Myles Dillon, Kathleen Mulchrone, D. A. Binchy, August Knoch and John Ryan, *Studies in Early Irish Law* (Dublin: Hodges Figgis & Co.; London: Williams & Norgate, 1936).

J. M. C. Toynbee, 'Christianity in Roman Britain', *Journal of the British Archaeological Association*, 3rd series, 16 (1953), 1–24.

Georg Troescher, 'Keltisch-Germanische Götterbilder an Romanischen Kirchen?' *Zeitschrift für Kunstgeschichte*, vol. 16 (1953), 1–42.

Herman J. Viola, 'Seeds of change', in Herman J. Viola and Carolyn Margolis, eds, *Seeds of Change. Five Hundred Years since Columbus* (Washington, DC: Smithsonian Institute Press, 1991).

Barbara G. Walker, *The Woman's Encyclopedia of Myths and Secrets* (San Francisco: Harper, 1983).

F. W. H. Wasserschleben, ed., *Die Bussordnungen der abendländischen Kirche nebst einer rechtsgeschichtlichen Einleitung* (Halle: Graeger, 1851).

Thomas J. Westropp, 'A study of the folklore on the coasts of Connacht, Ireland', *Folklore*, 34(4) (1923), 333–49.

Thomas J. Westropp, *Folklore of Clare. A Folklore Survey of County Clare and County Clare Folk-tales and Myths*, ed. Maureen Comber (Ennis: Clasp Press, 2000).

Thomas Willis, *Facts Connected with the Social and Sanitary Condition of the Working Classes in the City of Dublin* (1845), newly edited under the title *The Hidden Dublin* (Dublin: Trinity History Workshop, 2002).

ART AND ARCHAEOLOGICAL STUDIES

Anne L. Barstow, 'The prehistoric goddess', in Carl Olson, ed., *The Book of the Goddess. Past and Present. An Introduction to Her Religion* (New York: The Crossroad Publishing Company, 1983), pp. 7–15.

John Billingsley, *Stony Gaze. Investigating Celtic and Other Stone Heads* (Chieveley: Capall Bann, 1998).

Richard Bradley, *The Social Foundations of Prehistoric Britain. Themes and Variations in the Archaeology of Power* (Harlow: Longman, 1984).

Richard Rolt Brash, *The Ecclesiastical Architecture of Ireland, To the Close of the Twelfth Century; Accompanied by Interesting Historical and Antiquarian Notices of Numerous Ancient Remains of That Period* (Dublin: Kelly; London: Simpkin, Marshall, 1875).

C. J. P. Cave, *Roof Bosses in Medieval Churches. An Aspect of Gothic sculpture* (Cambridge: Cambridge University Press, 1948).

Robert Christison, 'On an ancient wooden image, found in November last at Ballachulish peat-moss', *Proceedings of the Society of Antiquaries of Scotland*, 15 (1880/1), 158–78.

Bryony Coles, 'Anthropomorphic wooden figures from Britain and Ireland', *Proceedings of the Prehistoric Society*, 56 (1990), 315–33.

Georges Colonna-Ceccaldi, 'Découvertes en Chypre. Les fouilles de Curium', *Revue archéologique*, n.s., 33(1) (1877), 177–89.

Henri Frankfort, *The Art and Architecture of the Ancient Orient. The Pelican History of Art*, ed. Nikolaus Pevsner (Harmondsworth: Penguin Books, 1954).

Douglas Fraser, ed., *The Many Faces of Primitive Art. A Critical Anthology* (Englewood Cliffs, NJ: Prentice Hall, 1966).

Sigfried Giedion, *The Eternal Present: The Beginnings of Art* (London: Oxford University Press, 1962).

Marija Gimbutas, *The Language of the Goddess* (San Francisco: Harper & Row, 1989).

Marija Gimbutas, *The Gods and Goddesses of Old Europe 7000 to 3500 BC. Myths, Legends and Cult Images* (London: Thames and Hudson, 1974).

Marija Gimbutas, 'Pre-Indo-European goddesses in Baltic mythology', *Mankind Quarterly* (1985), 19–25.

Aubrey Gwynn and Neville Hadcock, *Medieval Religious Houses. Ireland. With an Appendix to Early Sites* (London: Longman, 1970).

Franz Hancar, 'Zum Problem der Venusstatuetten im eurasiatischen Jungpaläolithikum', *Prähistorische Zeitschrift*, 30/1 (1939/40), 85–156.

Françoise Henry, 'L'Art Irlandais de 8.e siècle et ses origins', *Gazette des Beaux Arts* (1937), 131–44.

Françoise Henry, *Irish Art in the Early Christian Period* (London: Methuen, 1940).

Françoise Henry and George Zarnecki, 'Romanesque arches decorated with human and animal heads', *Journal of the British Archaeological Association*, 3rd series, 20/1 (1958), 1–34.

Ian Hodder, 'Contextual archaeology: an interpretation of Catal Hüyük and a discussion of the origins of agriculture', *London University Institute of Archaeology Bulletin*, 24 (1987), 43–56.

Moritz Hoernes, *Urgeschichte der Bildenden Kunst in Europa. Von den Anfängen bis um 500 vor Christi* (Vienna: Kunstverlag Schroll, 1925).

John Hunt, *Irish Medieval Figure Sculpture, 1200–1600. A Study of Irish Tombs with Notes on Costume and Armour*, 2 vols (Dublin: Irish University Press and Sotheby Parke Bernet, 1974).

Edwin Oliver James, *The Cult of the Mother-Goddess. An Archaeological and Documentary Study* (London: Thames and Hudson, 1959).

Edwin Oliver James, *Seasonal Feasts and Festivals* (London: Thames and Hudson, 1961).

William Jolly, 'On cup-marked stones in the neighbourhood of Inverness. With an appendix on cup-marked stones in the Western Islands', *Proceedings of the Society of Antiquarians of Scotland*, 16 (1882), 300–401.

H. Kirchhoff, 'Muttergottheiten, weibliche Fruchtbarkeitsidole und Mutterschaft', *Geburtshilfe und Frauenheilkunde*, 6 (1975), 429–41.

Raymond Lantier, 'Le dieu Celtique de Bouray', *Monuments et Memoires Academie des insciptions et belles lettres foundation Eugene Piot* (1934), pp. 35–58.

John Marshall, *Mohenjo-Daro and the Indus Civilization: Being an Official Account of Archaeological Excavations at Mohenjo-daro Carried out by the Government of India between the Years 1922 and 1927*, 3 vols (London: Arthur Probsthain, 1931).

Audrey L. Meaney, *Anglo-Saxon Amulets and Curing Stones* (Oxford: BAR, 1981).

James Mellaart, 'Earliest of Neolithic cities: the third season of excavations at Anatolian Chatal Hüyük. Part 1, shrines and images, of 9000 years ago', *Illustrated London News*, 244 (February 1964), 158–60.

James Mellaart, *Earliest Civilizations of the Near East* (London: Thames and Hudson, 1965).

Friedrich Moebius, *Die Dorfkirche im Zeitalter der Kathedrale (13. Jh.): Plaedoyer für eine strukturgeschichtliche Vertiefung des Stilbegriffs* (Berlin: Akadamie-Verlag, 1988).

Maria Ines Ruiz Montejo, 'La tematica obscena en la iconografia del Romanico rural', *Goya*, 147 (1978), 36–46.

Stuart Piggott, *Neolithic Cultures of the British Isles. A Study of the Stone-using Agricultural Communities of Britain in the Second Millennium BC* (Cambridge: Cambridge University Press, 1954).

Edwin C. Rae, 'The tomb of Bishop Walter Wellesley at Great Connell Priory, County Kildare', *JCKAS*, 14(5) (1970), 544–63.

Philip Rawson, ed., *Primitive Erotic Art* (New York: G. P. Putnam's Sons, 1973).

Dragoslav Srejovic, *Europe's First Monumental Sculpture: New Discoveries at Lepenski Vir*, trans. Lovett F. Edwards (Aylesbury: Hazell Watson and Viney, 1972).

Starhawk, *The Spiral Dance. Rebirth of the Ancient Religion of the Great Goddess* (San Francisco: Harper & Row Publishers, 1989).

Madho Sarup Vats, *Excavations at Harappa: Being an Account of Archaeological Excavations at Harappa Carried out between the Years 1920–21 and 1933–34*, 2 vols (Delhi: Manager of Publications, 1940).

Gordon Williams, *A Dictionary of Sexual Language and Imagery in Shakespearean and Stuart Literature*, 3 vols (London: The Athlone Press, 1994).

MEDIEVAL CHILDBEARING

Anon., *The Works of Aristotle, the Famous Philosopher, in Four Parts* (New England: Printed for the Publishers, 1827).

A. Aymar, 'Le sachet accoucheur et ses mystères', *Annales du Midi*, 38 (1926), 273–347.

P. P. A. Biller, 'Birth-control in the West in the thirteenth and early fourteenth centuries', *Past and Present*, 94 (1982), 3–26.

Vern Bullough and Cameron Campbell, 'Female longevity and diet in the Middle Ages', *Speculum*, 55 (1980), 317–25.

Kedarnath Das, *Obstetric Forceps. Its History and Evolution* (Calcutta: The Art Press, 1929; reprinted Leeds: Medical Museum Publications, 1993).

Marilyn Deegan, 'Pregnancy and childbirth in the Anglo-Saxon medical texts: a preliminary survey', in Marilyn Deegan and D. G. Scragg, eds, *Medicine in Early Medieval England* (Manchester: Centre for Anglo-Saxon Studies, University of Manchester, 1987), 17–26.

Dem Hebammenwissen auf der Spur. Zur Geschichte der Geburtshilfe. Katalog zur Ausstellung der Arbeitsgruppe Gesundheitswissenschaften (AGW) – Gesundheits – und Krankenlehre, Psychosomatik an der Universität Osnabrück in Zusammenarbeit mit der Universitätsbibliothek Osnabrück (Schriften der Universität Osnabrück, 1997).

Paul Diepgen, *Die Frauenheilkunde der alten Welt* (Munich: Bergmann, 1937).

Walter J. Dilling, 'Girdles: their origin and development, particularly with regard to their use as charms in medicine, marriage, and midwifery', *Caledonian Medical Journal*, 9 (1912–14), 337–57, 403–25.

Heinrich Fasbender, *Geschichte der Geburtshilfe* (Hildesheim: Olms 1964).

Thomas Rogers Forbes, *The Midwife and the Witch* (New Haven, CT: Yale University Press, 1966).

Jacques Gélis, *History of Childbirth. Fertility, Pregnancy and Birth in Early Modern Europe* (Cambridge: Polity Press, 1991).

Monica H. Green, 'Obstetrical and gynecological texts in Middle English', *Studies in the Age of Chaucer*, 14 (1992), 53–88.

Grethe Jacobsen, 'Pregnancy and childbirth in medieval north: a topology of sources and a preliminary study', *Scandinavian Journal of History*, 9 (1984), 91–111.

Heinz Kirchhoff, 'Die Gebärhaltung der Frau. Von der Prähistorie bis auf den heutigen Tag', *Gynäkologische Praxis*, 3 (1979), 203–23.

Peter Köpp, ed., *Vademecum eines frühmittelalterlichen Arztes* (Arau: Verlag Sauerländer, 1980).

Britta-Juliane Kruse, *Verborgene Heilkünste. Geschichte der Frauenmedizin im Spätmittelalter* (Berlin: de Gruyter, 1996).

Françoise Loux, 'Frauen, Männer und Tod in den Ritualen um die Geburt', in Jürgen Schlumbohm, Barbara Duden, Jacques Gélis and Patrice Veit, eds, *Rituale der Geburt. Eine Kulturgeschichte* (Munich: C. H. Beck'sche Verlagsbuchhandlung, 1998), 30–65.

William F. MacLehose, 'Nurturing danger: high medieval medicine and the problem(s) of the child', in John Carmi Parsons and Bonnie Wheeler, eds, *Medieval Mothering*. New York: Garland Publishing, 1996), 3–24.

Michael J. O'Dowd and Elliot E. Philipp, *The History of Obstetrics and Gynaecology* (New York: Parthenon, 1994).

Lucille B. Pinto, 'The folk practice of gynecology and obstetrics in the Middle Ages', *Bulletin of the History of Medicine*, 47 (1973), 513–23.

Heinrich Ploß, *Das Kind in Brauch und Sitte der Völker. Völkerkundliche Studien*, 2 vols (Leipzig: Th. Grieben's Verlag, 1911).

Beryl Rowland, *Medieval Woman's Guide to Health. The First English Gynecological Handbook* (Kent, OH: Kent State University Press, 1981).

Stanley Rubin, 'The Anglo-Saxon physician', in Marilyn Deegan and D. G. Scragg, eds, *Medicine in Early Medieval England* (Manchester: Centre for Anglo-Saxon Studies, University of Manchester, 1987), 7–15.

Manuel Simon, *Heilige. Hexe. Mutter. Der Wandel des Frauenbildes durch die Medizin im 16. Jahrhundert* (Berlin: Dietrich Reimer, 1993).

Harold Speert, *Histoire illustrée de la gynécologie et de l'obstétrique* (Paris: Les Éditions Roger Dacosta, 1976).

Fiona Harris Stoertz, 'Suffering and survival in medieval English childbirth', in Cathy Jorgensen Intyre, ed., *Medieval Family Roles. A Book of Essays* (London: Garland Publishing, 1996), 101–20.

Fritz Weindler, *Geschichte der Gynäkologisch-Anatomischen Abbildung* (Dresden: Zahn & Jaensch, 1908).

L. M. C. Weston, 'Women's medicine, women's magic: the old English metrical childbirth charms', *Modern Philology*, 3 (February 1995), 279–93.

INDEX